Totally Awesome 80s

Also by Matthew Rettenmund

Encyclopedia Madonnica

Boy Culture

Queer Baby Names

Totally Awesome 80s

Matthew Rettenmund

St. Martin's Griffin
New York

All stills courtesy of Photofest.

All photos of objects and all collages by Lori DeVito, Mahwah, New Jersey.

Most of the objects in this book are from the personal collection of Matthew Rettenmund.

Special thanks to Kate Hachadourian for the loan of her dolls, to Marc Hachadourian for the loan of his sister, and to Charles Criscuolo of Flashback for the loan of a truckload of indispensable 80s objects.

Spin magazine covers: Courtesy of *Spin*.

Interview magazine covers: Originally published in **INTERVIEW**, Brant Publications, Inc., February 1989, February 1988, and October 1983, respectively.

Benetton ad: United Colors of Benetton ad campaign. Concept and photo by O. Toscani.

Hush Puppies ad: Courtesy Wolverine Worldwide, Inc.

L'Oreal ad: Courtesy of L'Oreal.

Michael Jackson, Boy George, Prince, and Divine illustrations: Robert W. Richards.

Playboy magazine cover: Courtesy *Playboy*.

Tons of collectibles from the 60s, 70s, 80s, and beyond (lunchboxes, posters, dolls, toys, records, books, and other memorabilia)—including some of the objects found in this book—are available from Flashback. To inquire, send $3 U.S. for a catalog to Flashback, 3450 N. Clark St., Chicago, IL 60657, U.S.A.

Copyedited by Sona Vogel

Library of Congress Cataloging-in-Publication Data

Rettenmund, Matthew.
    Totally awesome 80s : a lexicon of the music, videos, movies, TV shows, stars, and trends of that decadent decade / by Matthew Rettenmund. — 1st ed.
        p. cm.
    ISBN 0-312-14436-9
    1. Motion pictures—United States. 2. Television programs—United States. 3. Rock music—United States—1981–1990—History and criticism. 4. Rock videos—United States. 5. Popular culture—United States.
PN1993.5.U6R46 1996
306'.0973'09048—dc20
                                       96-6989
                                         CIP

First St. Martin's Griffin Edition: November 1996
10 9 8 7 6 5 4 3 2 1

Books are available in quantity for promotional or premium use. Write to Director of Special Sales, St. Martin's Press, 175 Fifth Avenue, New York, NY 10010, for information on discounts and terms, or call toll-free (800) 221-7945. In New York, call (212) 674-5151 (ext. 645).

This book is dedicated to José Vélez, without whose attention, love, friendship, and support I might never have made it from the 90s to the 80s and *back*.

This book is also dedicated to . . .

my mother, Linda Rettenmund, who is one of those "cool moms." When I was in high school in the 80s, she let me stick Cyndi Lauper posters on the ceiling;

my sister, Melissa Rettenmund, who always supports everything I do and who will never know how many of her priceless 80s toys I have in my possession.

Contents

Acknowledgments

I would like to thank the following people for their help in the making of this book and/or for their support:

Dana Albarella, David Bloom, Mauro Bramati, Jane Jordan Browne, Charles Criscuolo/Flashback, Lori DeVito, Ensley Eikenburg, Sandra Engle, J. J. Fenza, Kate and Marc Hachadourian, Cyndi Lauper, Howard Mandelbaum/Photofest, Zafar Mawani, Doug McClemont, Danielle Egan-Miller, So What? Media, Frank Tantillo, Carol X. Vinzant, Gordon Wallace (who contributed his classic "Old Master" joke), and Timothy Wright.

If you have any comments about this book, please address them to Matthew Rettenmund, P.O. Box 149, New York, NY 10113-0149, U.S.A. Only those queries that include a self-addressed, stamped envelope (or two IRCs) will be answered. You may reach the author on America Online at MATTRETT@AOL.COM (please use "80s" as your subject line).

Totally Awesome 80s

Introduction

Remember the 80s?

How could you forget them? They just happened ten minutes ago, right?

Read Friday's
WHAT DID REAGAN SAY?
Chicago Sun-Times

Read Sunday's
NANCY REAGAN SOUNDS OFF
Chicago Sun-Times

Wrong. The era that brought us Valley Girls and Eurofags, power suits and parachute pants, Rick Springfield and Samantha Fox, and the personal computer revolution started happening over fifteen years ago already. Max Headroom is practically a teenager.

The baby boomers put off nostalgia until they were well into middle age, but we 80s Gen Xers (aw, c'mon, it sure beats being called whippersnappers or punk brats, eh?) can't wait that long. When you raise a child on a steady diet of sitcoms and MTV, is it any surprise that he or she will live at an accelerated pace?

Popular theory has us wasting our lives away in McJobs. In truth, we wanted to skip college or finish it ahead of schedule, step into our dream careers, and/or start our own businesses all by age twenty-one, and all to a killer soundtrack. We are not underachievers, we are simply impatient. If we happen to be working a McJob at any given time, it is because they McPay McNow. They are a means to an end, the end being fantastic goals of becoming self-supporting filmmakers, writers, actors, or Wall Street whiz kids.

Still miles away from achieving all we want in life, we found that the single best way to communicate with others in our age bracket was by comparing notes on Duran Duran or by debating who was better, Shelley Long or Kirstie Alley. Terms like "the Brat Pack" find their way into every conversation, along with references to "Krystle," and "Alexis," and what the best Cyndi Lauper song was (it's gotta be "Girls Just Want to Have Fun," right? Or is it "Money Changes Everything"?), and just how ridiculous

George Michael looked in white shorts with feathered blond hair. "Choose Life?" Choose a *stylist*.

All of this does not mean that we are shallow or that we are even all the same. We are the most diverse generation in recent history, with a fully integrated pantheon of gods and goddesses and with so much trivial knowledge that it puts to shame our forebears with their simplistic reminiscences of poodle skirts and Elvis's pelvis.

During the 80s, Trivial Pursuit inspired us to seek out information that we didn't need to know to survive. We found ourselves mesmerized by *Billboard*'s charts, by the colorful, carefully designed packaging in which our favorite music and home videos arrived, and by—for the first time ever—every single detail of our icons' lives. Gone were the days of discretion and the glamour machine; if it was happening, we wanted the lowdown. Enquiring minds wanted to know. Just ask Vanessa Williams.

In short, the children and teens of the 80s have a thirst for information, for lists, for the details.

And that, more than anything, is what *Totally Awesome 80s* is about. Our critics are wrong when they brand the 80s as shallow and empty, and *Totally Awesome 80s* proves it. This is a book that gathers so many bits of information about a decade that the big picture will prove that ours was the most information-dense, visually stimulating, multiculturally charged, fast-paced, aggressively hip decade of all time.

The 50s were only "cute." The 60s were embarrassingly pretentious. The 70s? *Getting* there, but kinda lame. The 80s were, simply, radical. *Rad*.

So, you can use this book as a document to prove to nonbelievers that the 80s were a smart decade with a great sense of humor, or you can just use this book for loads of laughs over names you thought you'd never see in print again and reminiscences of things you thought were cool a million, er, *several* years ago.

Either way, Atari beats Hula Hoops by a mile.

The 80s: What a Concept!

Before plunging (back) into the music, music videos, TV, and movies of the 80s, you need a general survey of all things 80s to get you in the mood.

Master and Servant: Ten Major Forces That Shaped the Pop Culture of the 80s

I.   President Ronald Reagan. The Teflon Republican president won his two terms in landslides against incumbent Jimmy Carter (1980) and challenger Walter Mondale (1984). One of the most popular presidents of all time, Reagan benefited from his youthful, photogenic appearance (in spite of his advanced age), his history as a Hollywood movie actor (not very good, since his claim to fame was *Bedtime for Bonzo*, but he knew where all the cameras were and how to work them), and his no-nonsense attitude. He was so Hollywood that his pet project, a multibillion-dollar space station dubbed "Star Wars," took its name from the biggest movie of the 70s .

You can take the girl out of Hollywood, but . . . Nancy "Mommy" Reagan sounds off with Marvin Hamlisch.

Though he helplessly avoided saying the word "AIDS" until his second term in office, Reagan had the swagger of John Wayne, a man who always seemed very much in control. He survived an assassin's bullet (1981), having James Watt in his cabinet (1981–1983), and a much publicized bout with colon cancer (1985); and when the nation's air traffic controllers went on strike (1981), he had no qualms about firing them lock, stock, and barrel.

He effectively villainized the Soviet Union as an "evil empire" and convinced the vast majority of Americans that rumors of his incompetence were unfounded. Some wags charged that bossy, shrewish Nancy Reagan—she of the large head and lavish dinnerware—was *really* running the country. Who knows? Maybe she was.

Having such a diehard conservative in power during the 80s—one who had even participated in the McCarthy hearings of the 50s—only made the artists of the 80s more rebellious. Androgyny, drag, and sexually provocative lyrics and performances were the rule of the day, if only to tweak Grandpa Reagan's nose.

> "You may have questions, but I don't have any answers."
> —Ronald Reagan, 1987

Reagan's popularity was so immense that it guaranteed the election of his unpopular vice president, George "Read My Lips" Bush, as his successor in 1988, though the Republican honeymoon was over by 1992.

2. AIDS (acquired immune deficiency syndrome). The sudden rise of the incurable disease with a 100 percent mortality rate shaped how we lived and what we thought in the 80s.

The disease first struck the gay male community in 1981 but was generally understood to be a nondiscriminatory plague by decade's end. This initial association with homosexuality (it was first named "gay cancer") led to the opening of the floodgates for gay material and issues in the media. Whenever AIDS was discussed, so was homosexuality, and the effect was that gay and antigay activists had an issue to rally around. Without AIDS, gay issues would not have been as commonly and openly discussed as they are today.

AIDS also led to candid discussions of sex—the word "condom" was banned from TV until their function in preventing the spread of AIDS could no longer be ignored and educational pamphlets were distrib-

BE A LIFEGUARD...

PLAY SAFE!

As new AIDS infections among gay men increased, this safer sex pamphlet ironically took a cue from 80s commercial advertising and used the one thing guaranteed to catch every gay guy's attention: a lusty lifeguard. Nothing will come between me and my lifeguard, but if anything does, it'll be into a rubber.

uted far and wide. Still, though sex was being frankly discussed, the sexual liberation of the 60s and sexual smorgasbord of the 70s suffered serious setbacks. Some religious zealots saw AIDS as a sign from God, or at the very least a rightful comeuppance for the promiscuous. People still had sex, but attitudes about it were changing to the negative.

Since having sex with someone could win you a death sentence, sex in movies, on TV, in music, and in music videos became a voyeuristic substitute. Though due partially to the availability of videos for home (and therefore private) consumption, the adult movie (that's porno to you, buddy) boom certainly owed a great deal to the threat of real-life sex. In the 80s, the sale of porn videos ballooned into a multibillion-dollar business.

There is not one facet of life that was unaffected by the unexpected impact of AIDS, and the entertainment industry gradually reflected that impact through telefilms, benefits, and the occasional hit record.

3. MTV. The music revolution *will* be televised.

MTV, a cable station to air music videos twenty-four hours a day every day, was launched August 1, 1981, with very little fanfare and five unassuming "video jockeys" (VJs). Within a year it had become an absolute must for every teenager fascinated by the novelty of four-minute performance pieces or conceptual clips by their favorite bands, set to the tune of their latest singles.

MTV attracted millions of households to cable television, providing the perfect next step for adolescents bored with *Brady Bunch* reruns and too old for *Sesame Street*.

The advent of the music video influenced music itself. Stars of the 70s could get away with looking boring or dowdy or even downright ugly, but in order to appease MTV's unblinking eye, the artists of the 80s found that looking good, showing some skin, having an outlandish outfit or two, and/or wearing more makeup than a circus clown helped to make a lasting impression on impressionable record buyers.

Consequently, music stars became TV stars as well, increasing their album sales exponentially. Michael Jackson's pioneering videos from *Thriller* (1982) certainly helped make it the best-selling album of all time, and for the first time in rock history, acts were having five and more hits from single albums (Huey Lewis and the News, Cyndi Lauper, Tina Turner, Bruce Springsteen, and others).

As it became a hotter and hotter commodity, MTV invented highly creative ad campaigns featuring unforgettable slogans ("I want my MTV!") and experimental film shorts ("Now do you understand?"). The station presented itself as revolutionary from day one, using as its first logo the 1969 moon landing, jazzed up with neon and a rock hook.

Music videos influenced other forms, from TV (*Miami Vice*, with its rapid-fire editing and pop soundtrack) to movies (pop music–driven films like *Footloose* and *Flashdance*). By the 90s, music videos were considered by many to be a full-fledged art form in their own right.

> "I'd rather my son watch MTV than watch the evening news."
> —Bob Pittman, president of MTV, 1986

4. The Cold War. President Reagan referred to the Soviet Union as an "evil empire," setting the tone for American attitudes toward Russia in the 80s. Communism was the ultimate enemy of capitalism. So great was the riff that schoolchildren lived in constant fear of a nuclear confrontation between the United States and the Soviets, and Sting had a hit record ("Russians") in which he wondered whether the Russians loved their children enough to rule out a nuclear war.

By the end of the decade, the Berlin Wall had fallen (1989) and Russia's leader, Gorbachev, had ushered in a new era of peace, or glasnost, a possibility that had seemed inconceivably remote just eight years earlier.

5. VCRs. Introduced in the late 70s and popularized in the mid-80s, VCRs provided heaps of fertile soil for couch potatoes. Home videocassette recorders allowed us to record favorite material from TV or to record things that we were not around to watch. They also allowed us to rent movies to watch in private, at home, whenever we felt like it. This convenience distracted millions of us who might otherwise actually go out to the cinema yet created a whole new outlet for films that would ultimately allow many box office bombs to recoup their investment. Some people took to renting everything in sight, just to have seen it all.

After 1984, when home recording of programs from TV was ruled perfectly legal in a landmark supreme court case, there was no stopping the mighty VCR: in 1982 only 4.3 percent of American homes had VCRs, but by 1989 the percentage had risen to 65.8 percent.

What had started as a luxury had quickly become near necessity, giving people the power they'd craved since the advent of TV—the ability to control what was on the tube at any given time.

6. Yuppies. Baby boomers who had been hippies and anti-Establishment activists in the 60s became super-Established in the 80s, developing quite a taste for expensive clothes, homes, and toys. The yuppies made enormous salaries as computer technicians, entrepreneurs, doctors, and lawyers, and in other cutthroat positions, inspiring the kids of the 80s to aspire to the same.

This quest for the material was reflected in pop culture. There was a return to glitz and glamour, both in our icons (Madonna, Prince, Michael Jackson) and in our favorite TV stars (the entire cast of *Dynasty*), and everyone's number one goal seemed to be to make a million bucks.

Is that so wrong?

7. Jane Fonda. No, not because of her stunning work in *9 to 5* (1980) or *Old Gringo* (1989), but because she single-handedly launched the fitness craze with her aggressively marketed series of aerobics books and videos. Starting with *The Jane Fonda Workout Book* (1981), the leggy Vietnam-protester-turned-body-guru inspired millions of couch potatoes to make it burn while she raked in millions of dollars.

The workout (or the guilt over its absence) became a part of our daily lives, creating a demand for dozens of national gym chains and home fitness products like Soloflex and also providing work for the peripatetic Richard Simmons.

8. The War on Drugs. First Lady Nancy Reagan tried to popularize the concept of "Just Say No," and though she was much derided for her rather unimpassioned, unrealistic antidrug message, the country was swept into an antidrug frenzy. Use of even the most common illegal drug—pot—decreased significantly among teens, even as crack, a highly addictive form of that old standby, cocaine, ravaged the inner city (1985). Self-righteous adolescents formed antidrug groups (along the lines of the antialcohol group Students Against Drunk Driving, or SADD), signing "contracts" promising not to partake.

Though it became extremely unhip to show drug use on TV or even in R-rated movies, drugs were never conquered and would return with a vengeance by the 90s. Good news for the guys on *Miami Vice*.

9. Political Correctness. Though the concept has been around since the 60s, the late 80s saw a resurgence of a codified system of speech and behavior that was intended to offend absolutely no one. Retarded children were called "special," handicapped people were to be referred to as "physically challenged." You were supposed to call yourself "African-American," not black, and games of cowboys and Indians were deemed offensive to "Native Americans." The news of the movement became extremely widespread, though the majority of Americans resisted the idea of making an effort to keep from annoying various groups.

Still, PC (which also stands for "personal computers") popped up everywhere, from the immediate phasing out of the term "chick" to the unspoken outlawing of the phrase "you people." PC was not limited to speech; certain beliefs, such as antifur and pro–Nelson Mandela sympathies, also fell into the realm of the politically correct.

PC survives in the 90s, with increasing resistance from the "politically challenged."

10. Madonna. The first real female rock superstar (even if the bulk of her *oeuvre* consisted of pop, disco, and ballads) and the one who ushered in a

Madonna in one of her many visitations to the cover of *Spin*.

wave of other female stars. She set the standard in the field of music videos, and her unswerving ambition mirrored one of the most desired characteristics of the 80s.

Madonna's uncompromisingly sexual image opened the floodgates for sex in music, videos, and even film. She embodied the "rags to riches" American dream, but she also represented the new concepts of the pop star as businessperson, the continual image make-over for freshness, and multiple references to classic Hollywood and other sources within a pop catalog. Though the song was a parody, her "Material Girl" (1985) reflected the quest for dollars so popular among yuppies and gave a nasty nickname to the decade: the Material 80s.

> "People have this idea that if you're sexual and beautiful and provocative, then there's nothing else you could offer."
> —Madonna, 1987

The Twenty Greatest Events of the 80s

1. The fall of the Berlin Wall (1989). A symbol of hope that was almost marred by Pink Floyd's ridiculous concert.

2. The release of the American hostages in Iran (1981). Even if Ronald Reagan *did* take all the credit.

3. Glasnost (1988). The thawing of our chilly relationship with Mother Russia.

4. Post-it notes are invented (1980). How did we survive without them?

5. Satellite dishes are ruled legal (1981). Now there's no need to leave the house. *Ever.*

6. The first space shuttle launch (1983). Renewed our fascination with the universe at large and showed that with a little hard work and billions upon billions of dollars, man can conquer space.

7. Wendy O. Williams nominated for a Grammy (1985). What took them so long?

8. Cash machines go nationwide (1985). So you could have access to that last $10 in your account *right now*.

9. Live Aid (1985). Even if there were logistic and political problems in seeing to it that the money raised by the world's greatest pop singers actually got to Ethiopia, their tonsils were in the right place.

10. "Dave" and "Maddie" finally get horizontal on *Moonlighting* (1986). After years of flirting, TV's most talkative couple gets down and dirty. Of course, everything that came after was boring as hell.

11. The word "condom" makes its network television debut on *The Hogan Family* (1987). Six years into the AIDS epidemic, its single greatest preventive (aside from abstinence) is allowed onto the airwaves, and it has to come from a sitcom that killed off its star in a car accident?

12. Macaulay Culkin is born (1980). An especially major event if you're John Hughes.

13. The Statue of Liberty gets a major face lift (1986). A nice gift on her hundredth birthday, though we probably could have done without the Elvis impersonators.

14. CNN is born (1980). *All* the news. Period.

15. The first mini-TV is mass-marketed (1982). Now you can watch TV while doing that Jane Fonda workout.

16. Raquel Welch stops making movies (1979). After *L'Animal*, the great beauty wouldn't make another movie until the 90s. Absence makes the heart forget just how bad she was in the first place.

17. *USA Today* **is born (1982).** Because you just don't know *enough* about Hollywood.

18. NutraSweet (1981). Guilt-free soda.

19. The first issue of *Sassy* **hits the streets (1988).** The kids are all right.

20. CDs win the war against vinyl (1988). Gone is the warmth of vinyl and that great big jacket art, but face it: CDs sound better, and owning one thousand of them doesn't hinder moving.

The Twenty Biggest Disasters of the 80s

"Federal officials consider it an epidemic, but you rarely hear a thing about it."
—Dan Rather on AIDS, *CBS Evening News*, 1983

1. AIDS. A plague that nobody knew existed in 1979 had decimated Africa and the gay population of America by 1990, and was picking up speed in other places and communities. There were over eighty thousand confirmed deaths due to the disease during the 80s. No one-liners spring to mind.

2. Herpes. Remember when this mild annoyance was considered the worst, most shameful thing in the world? In 1981 *Life* magazine ran a photo of a herpes support group, and all but two of the members posed with bags over their heads. For its habit of breaking out on your mouth and/or genitalia at regular intervals for the rest of your life, herpes became known as "the gift that keeps on giving."

3. Anorexia/bulimia. Privileged white girls were the main sufferers of these eating disorders. Fat urban chicks and their admirers weren't particularly saddened. Poster child: Karen Carpenter, who died chug-a-lugging ipecac in 1983 after the disease had ravaged her body.

4. "Greed is good." Ivan Boesky sucks for saying this, since these are the three words that 60s and 70s fans say when you pine for the 80s. Greed isn't good, *work* is. And money isn't half bad, either.

By the time *Fast Times at Ridgemont High* was released (1982), antidisco sentiment was rampant. Disco's enemies were the teens whose older siblings had enjoyed boogie nights in the 70s. These surly sibs didn't care that the phrase "disco sucks" was charged with antiblack and antigay sentiments, they just preferred A Flock of Seagulls, okay? They slapped "disco sucks" stickers everywhere in sight, as captured in this ha-ha angst scene from *Fast Times*, whose characters epitomized antidisco 80s babies.

5. Mount St. Helens makes an ash of itself (1980).

6. Changing of Coca-Cola formula (1985). How many cases did you store in your cellar? How relieved were you when New Coke bit the dust?

7. Chernobyl (1986). God, this was like a worldwide nuclear event. Maybe this should've been higher on the list?

8. "Disco sucks." In a bad way?

9. Bryan Adams. Musically. But while we're on the subject, it's called a skin peel.

"I mean, how many 'Run to You's can you write, you know?"
—Bryan Adams, 1987

10. Studio 54 closes (1980). Will we ever find Elizabeth Taylor, Brooke Shields, Rip Taylor, Calvin Klein, and Divine under the same roof again?

11. Explosion of space shuttle *Challenger* **(1986).** Reagan's big plans for "Star Wars," schoolteacher Christa McAuliffe, and America's affection for the space program evaporate in midair.

12. Cancellation of *Bosom Buddies* (1982). Now Tom Hanks has time to make movies.

13. ABBA breaks up (1983). Mamma mia! It'll be another ten years or so before we can admit to liking them again.

14. Oral Roberts claims God says he'll die if he doesn't collect enough money . . . then he *lives*.

15. The ERA (Equal Rights Amendment) fails (1982). Perhaps they needed someone a little more persuasive to represent the issue . . . like Grace Jones.

16. Plane disasters. DC-10s are dropping like flies, 103 hostages are held on the runway in Damascus (1981), the Russians shoot Korean Air flight 007 out of the sky "accidentally" (1983), and a plane full of students is bombed over Lockerbie, Scotland, killing everyone aboard (1988). Take the train.

17. Suicide bomber drives into and demolishes U.S. marine barracks in Beirut (1983), helping to move Americans toward a noninterventionist mood.

18. 60s revival. Some of the cutest girls now have long, scraggly hair . . . no, wait—those are the guys! Preppies shudder around the globe.

19. *Hard to Hold* (1984). Yeah, your guffaws. Say it ain't so, Rick!

20. Medflies invade California (1981). I needed twenty.

Hart Breakers: The Ten Biggest Scandals of the 80s

1. Gary Hart (1987). Democratic presidential hopeful Gary Hart was exposed as a philanderer, as illustrated by a photo of him posing with blonde nymphet Donna Rice on his knee.

2. The P.T.L. Club (1987). Jim Bakker skimmed money from his ministry, the P.T.L. Club. When he was thrown in jail, faithful wifey Tammy Faye—who had earlier released a single called "If It Had Not

Been"— may have promised to wait for him, but she must've had her fingers crossed: she divorced him and remarried while he entertained the inmates.

Future ex–talk show hostess Tammy Faye marketed several holy roller singles while she and future ex-hubby Jim Bakker were riding high in the P.T.L. Club. On her "If It Had Not Been" 45, she posed in a way carefully orchestrated to convey a sweet, angelic friendliness, but her makeup looked like it'd been applied with rollers and her sour expression and long, catty nails made her look less like an angel than the "Wicker" Witch of the West.

"That girl knew exactly why she was going down there. Besides, it only lasted fifteen minutes." —Tammy Faye Bakker, of homewrecker Jessica Hahn, 1987

3. Iran-contra (1986). When it was revealed that the U.S. had actually supplied its own archenemy—Iran—with arms covertly, the shit hit the fan. President Ronald Reagan and Vice President (and future President) George Bush denied they knew anything about the affair, and a career military man—Colonel Oliver North—became the fall guy. He also became an unlikely hero for his insistence that his part in the illegal exchange had been solely the result of "following orders." His paper-shredding secretary, Fawn Hall, even became a celebrity, dating Rob Lowe for a while.

4. The Miss America nude photo scandal (1984). After being heavily favored to win, Vanessa Williams became the first black Miss America. As an illustration of just how beloved she became, recall that she landed that most prized of TV roles: a guest spot on *The Love Boat*. Ten months into fulfilling her obligations (and being the most in-demand title holder in pageant history), nude photos of her—including poses with another woman—were published in *Penthouse* magazine. A teary Williams was forced to resign July 23 by pageant officials. However, she resurfaced at the end of the 80s as a highly successful pop singer.

5. Jimmy Swaggart (1988). The Goody Two-shoes televangelist was caught with a prostitute, sobbed for forgiveness, and went right back to preaching.

6. The Rob Lowe video (1989). After thoroughly embarrassing himself with the hands-down cheesiest opening number in Oscar history (1988's duet with "Snow White" singing "Proud Mary"), pretty boy Brat Packer Lowe got caught with his pants down in a video he'd made of himself with a young lady and a gentleman friend. He wound up doing community service and bootlegged copies of his X-capade became hot collectors' items.

7. The Milli Vanilli lip-synching scandal (1989–1990). Girl, you know it's false. The heavily choreographed, braid-covered duo was proven to be a marketing hoax. Rob and Fab were just mouthing the words sung by three other singers. A court ruling favored offering refunds to fans who wanted to return their Milli music, and the straw canaries had to give back their Best New Artist Grammy. You heard me, they won a Grammy.

> "They were two of the dumbest motherfuckers I've ever laid eyes on."
> —publicist Wayne Rosso on Milli Vanilli

8. Rock Hudson (1985). The beefcake movie star of the 50s and TV star of the 70s was Hollywood's most famous closet case. When he finally issued a statement that he had AIDS, he was at death's door. His criminally cavalier behavior—carrying on a sexual relationship with Marc Christian without telling *him*—exposed Rock as a wimp and cost his estate millions when Christian sued.

9. Vicki Morgan (1983). The model sued Alfred Bloomingdale's estate, claiming a right to a chunk of his money as his longtime lover. Alfred had been a close friend of President Reagan's, and his widow, Betsy, was *thisclose* with Nancy Reagan. Luckily for Betsy, Vicki ran with the wrong crowd and wound up bludgeoned to death with her son's baseball bat. Morgan's killer died of AIDS in prison.

10. The Mayflower Madam (1984). Sidney Biddle Barrows, who could trace her family lineage back to the *Mayflower,* was arrested for running a "high-class call girl ring" (whatever that means). After her arrest, all she could hope for was an offer to star in a John Waters movie . . . or a major book contract somewhere down the road.

Hit Me with Your Best Shot: Five Major Assassination Attempts (Successes and Failures) of the Early 80s

1. President Reagan (1981). John Hinckley made an effective argument for gun control, a proposal the Republicans (ironically) opposed—✚ *Failed*

2. The Pope (1981). Attack the Pope? Go to Hell. Go directly to Hell. Do not pass "Go"— ✚ *Failed*

3. John Lennon (1980). Mark David Chapman snuffs out pop's poetic genius right in front of wife Yoko Ono at a time when he was making a major comeback—⊕ *Succeeded*

> "If Mark David Chapman had aimed a little to the right, he'd have been a hero."
> —Judy Tenuta, on the loss of Lennon vs. the loss of Ono, 1986

4. Anwar al-Sadat (1981). The Egyptian president never had a chance—slain by his own men— ⊕ *Succeeded*

5. Indira Gandhi (1984). The first female prime minister of India offed by her own bodyguards. It's a Sikh world out there—⊕ *Succeeded*

Communist Leader for a Day: The Rapid-Fire Progression of Russian Presidents in the 80s

1. Leonid Brezhnev (d. 1982)

2. Yuri Andropov (d. 1984)

3. Konstantin Chernenko (d. 1985)

4. Mikhail Gorbachev (survived the decade, but he probably should've kept a closer eye on that Yeltsin dude)

Greatest American Hero: The Heroes of the 80s

1. The American hockey team (1980). Beating seemingly insurmountable odds, the U.S. team defeated the Russian team in the Winter Olympics at Lake Placid. The Cold War subtext was sizzling.

2. Sandra Day O'Connor (1981). As the first woman elected to the supreme court, her greatest feat was making everyone forget that distinction as we guessed how she'd vote on key issues.

> "Loosen up, baby." —football player John Riggins to Supreme Court Justice Sandra Day O'Connor, at a formal dinner

3. Bob Geldof. The scruffy rocker organized "Do They Know It's Christmas?" (1984) *and* Live Aid (1985), and he *still* couldn't get a hit record for his band, the Boomtown Rats?

4. Geraldine Ferraro (1984). The first woman on a presidential ticket, and the first to fail miserably, but she will go down in history for tartly telling George Bush not to patronize her.

5. Astronaut Sally Ride (1983). One small step for woman . . .

6. Greg Louganis (1984). Diver who came back from a humiliating misstep at the 1984 Olympics to win the gold. A hero of a different sort in the 90s, when he announced he had AIDS.

7. Samantha Smith (1983). The little girl who wrote a letter to Russian leader Yuri Andropov, urging world peace. She died in a plane crash before her request was fulfilled.

8. Robert Jarvik (1982). He created the world's first artificial heart, even if it *did* only work for about four months.

9. Jaron Lanier (1989). The inventor of virtual reality. Thank God, because the regular kind sucks.

10. Mike Tyson (1987). This beloved heavyweight champion of the world converted into an antihero after he rubbed wife, Robin Givens, the wrong way (1988). He was also later convicted of raping a beauty contestant, which for many meant that this hero had taken a fall.

Enemy Mine: The Villains of the 80s

1. Muammar al-Qaddafi. However you chose to spell it, the radical Libyan dictator spelled trouble, daring cowboy Ronnie Reagan to cross his "line of death." Reagan crossed it.

> "I'll make music *despite* Qaddafi." —Robert Palmer, 1986

2. The Ayatollah Khomeini (1980). The man behind the Iranian hostage crisis of 1979–1980, and a candidate for Mr. Blackwell's worst-dressed list. Caftans were *so* 70s.

3. The Russians. According to Reagan, they were even more despicable than the Democrats (who found themselves vilified for being "the L-word"—liberal).

4. John Wayne Gacy (1980). The boy killer of Chicago whose dramatic habit of burying corpses in his basement forever tainted the word "crawlspace" and ignited a durable serial killer fad.

5. Freddy Krueger. More than any of his filmic predecessors or imitators, this walking *Nightmare on Elm Street* (1984) haunted our dreams.

6. Stalkers. Mark David Chapman mowed down John Lennon (1980) after getting his autograph, and obsessed fan Robert John Bardo paid a private dick $250 to obtain *My Sister Sam* (1986–1988) star Rebecca Schaeffer's home address before shooting her in the chest with a hollow-point bullet (1989). Even John Hinckley Jr.—who shot President Reagan in a 1981 assassination attempt—falls in this category, if not for his attack on the most famous actor in America, then for his crush on Jodie Foster, whom he was trying to impress when he attacked Reagan.

> "I was a fan of hers. I may have carried it too far." —Robert John Bardo of his victim Rebecca Schaeffer, 1989

7. Patient Zero (1981). As identified by the late writer Randy Shilts, an irresponsible male flight attendant who—upon learning he had a mysterious disease (eventually identified as AIDS)—willfully infected a series of gay men, leading to the rapid spread of AIDS in America.

8. "J. R. Ewing" (1979–1991). This is what happens when you deprive a man of his "Jeannie."

9. Leona Helmsley (1989). The "queen of mean," thrown in jail for tax evasion, was said to have uttered the infamous line, "Only the little people pay taxes."

10. "Alexis Carrington" (1981–1989). This Joan Collins character was no Qaddafi but then she never had an army at her fingertips, either. Count yourself lucky, "Krystle."

You and I: Couples of the 80s

1. Sylvester Stallone and Brigitte Nielsen. Beast and the Beast.

2. Sean Penn and Madonna. The "Poison Penns"—thank God she *didn't* keep her baby.

3. Casey and Jean Kasem. The small fry, his (good?) witch, and her wardrobe.

4. Donald and Ivana Trump. Here today, gone to Marla.

5. Grace Jones and Dolph Lundgren. The Bob and Rod Jackson-Paris of the 80s.

6. Michael Jackson and Bubbles. *M.J. and the Bear.*

"We don't even *fight* anymore. Actually, it's getting happier by the minute."
—Eddie Van Halen, on his marriage to Valerie Bertinelli, 1985

7. Cher and Rob Camiletti. Proving that bagel boys are strictly dime a dozen.

8. Eddie Van Halen and Valerie Bertinelli. Yes, they *are* two different people.

9. Tatum O'Neal and John McEnroe. The *enfant terrible* of tennis must have been a father figure to O'Neal, considering her father is renowned brute Ryan O'Neal.

10. Janet Jackson and James DeBarge. Janet lost *Control* when she said "I do" in her teens, but the curvy baby diva (and her wise, powerful family) *did* have the sense to have this impulsive elopement annulled.

Imaginary Couples of the 80s

1. "Heathcliff and Clair Huxtable" (Bill Cosby and Phylicia Rashad), *The Cosby Show*. Family values.

2. "Luke and Laura" (Tony Geary and Genie Francis), *General Hospital*. The young and the breathless.

3. "Sam Malone and Diane Chambers" (Ted Danson and Shelley Long), *Cheers*. "Sam": "Are you as turned on as I am?" "Diane": "More!"

4. "David Addison and Maddie Hayes" (Bruce Willis and Cybill Shepherd), *Moonlighting*. So much foreplay, there was almost no need to do the deed.

5. "Jonathan and Jennifer Hart" (Robert Wagner and Stefanie Powers), *Hart to Hart*. The couple that sleuths together, stays together.

6. "The Roses" (Michael Douglas and Kathleen Turner), *The War of the Roses*. The ideal 80s couple: wealthy, successful, and plotting to kill each other.

7. "Steven and Elyse Keaton" (Michael Gross and Meredith Baxter-Birney), *Family Ties*. Hippies that became their parents.

8. "Remington Steele and Laura Holt" (Pierce Brosnan and Stephanie Zimbalist), *Remington Steele*. Brosnan and his retroactive Bond girl.

No love was lost between "J.R. and Sue Ellen Ewing."

9. "J.R. and Sue Ellen Ewing" (Larry Hagman and Linda Gray), *Dallas.* In name only.

10. "Blake and Krystle Carrington" (John Forsythe and Linda Evans), *Dynasty.* Even though he was on the verge of retirement before she was even born.

Thinking About You: Twenty Major Celebrity Deaths of the 80s

1. Princess Grace (Kelly) of Monaco (1982). The fairy-tale princess died after having a massive stroke while driving with her rebellious daughter, singer/model/androgyne, Princess Stephanie.

2. Natalie Wood (1981). The third cast member of the classic *Rebel Without a Cause* to die young, she drowned after slipping drunkenly into the sea. She became a punch line to the dead celebrity joke: What kind of wood doesn't float?

3. Bette Davis (1989). The biggest goddamned star of all lived for years with cancer before finally succumbing, but not before shriveling away to an eighty-pound, still-brassy shell. Kim Carnes made a song about her, "Bette Davis Eyes" (1980), into one of the biggest hits of the decade.

4. Lucille Ball (1989). The most popular TV personality of all time died after a heart attack, still in possession of the greatest pair of gams in Hollywood.

5. Andy Warhol (1987). The walking sandwich board for pop art in the 60s, experimental filmmaker, and posthumous diarist died after a gallbladder operation. His estate became the subject of the most talked about celebrity auction in history until the Jackie O. debacle earlier this year.

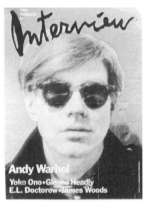 

Andy Warhol Is Dead

Interview **featured its deceased founder on its cover when his estate auction was kicking into high gear, and talked to Divine just a few months before s/he joined Andy at that increasingly huge 70s reunion party in the sky.**

6. Mae West (1980). She's probably putting the moves on St. Peter as we speak, if he's got any kind of a decent body.

7. Alfred Hitchcock (1980). One of the greatest directors of all time, with one of the creepiest countenances on TV.

8. Henry Fonda (1982). One of Tinseltown's most durable actors and father to mother-of-fitness Jane.

9. John Belushi (1982). When he died after being injected with a speedball, it did more for the "Just Say No" movement than anything Nancy Reagan could ever say.

10. Cary Grant (1986). Mr. Suave and Debonair, and one of the only corpses about whom that old cliché "He looks so good" was actually true.

11. Divine (1988). Camp movie star of John Waters movies who had just hit it big in the movie *Hairspray* before his own obesity caused him to asphyxiate in his sleep.

12. Sir Laurence Olivier (1989). The most respected actor on stage and in film.

13. Rita Hayworth (1987). Alzheimer's killed the World War II pinup and glamorous star of *Gilda*.

14. Orson Welles (1985). The enormous talent behind what's considered the greatest American movie ever made, *Citizen Kane*.

15. Rock Hudson (1985). The classic hunk was forced out of the closet when AIDS had ravaged him. The scandal that was hyped was how Rock had failed to tell Linda Evans he was dying of AIDS when the two swapped spit on *Dynasty*.

16. Fred Astaire (1987). The most famous hoofer on film survived *The Towering Inferno* but died of natural causes thirteen years later.

17. Liberace (1987). The flamboyant, self-deluded pianist claimed to have lost weight on a watermelon diet, but when he died his bluff was called: it was AIDS.

18. James Cagney (1986). He shoved a grapefruit in Mae Clarke's face in *The Public Enemy* but was one of the most beloved stars of Hollywood's Golden Age.

19. Gilda Radner (1989). She once joked that she'd rather have cancer than be fat since guys prefer skinny girls with cancer to fat, healthy girls, but her real-life death after a battle with ovarian cancer was a tragedy that stunned fans of *Saturday Night Live*.

20. Gloria Swanson (1983). The former silent movie queen who lampooned deluded stars in her *Sunset Boulevard*, eerily announcing that she was "ready for my close-up, Mr. DeMille."

Ten Reasons Why the 80s Were More Totally *Awesome* Than the 70s

1. Shorter gas lines.

2. Guys get to wear eyeliner.

3. The Gap. Fall into it.

4. Condoms. They're actually kind of fun, if you open your mind to mint-flavored rubbers, French ticklers, and the kind that refuse to break.

5. You get to say the word "bitch" on TV (*Designing Women*, 1986).

6. Teen exploitation slasher movies. What a great way to blow off steam after that popular cheerleader turns you down for a date—watching a movie in which every popular cheerleader in the tristate area gets offed.

7. Trapper Keeper notebooks. I'd like to see the dog try to eat homework trapped in *these*.

8. New Kids on the Block vs. Bay City Rollers.

9. Atari 2600 vs. Pong.

10. Cher is respected.

I Wanna Be a Toy: The Twenty Coolest Toys, Games, Hobbies, and Fads of the 80s

1. Trivial Pursuit. An ACT exam disguised as a board game. How did we ever let our parents con us into enjoying such brain food? The only problem was that after about three major TP parties, even your dumbest friends knew enough answers to get a

Whether you called them "pies" or "wedges," your pursuit of those colorful little triangles drove you crazy.

brown wedge and your little sister had to pretend to be thinking before successfully "guessing" that Charles Laughton won the 1933 Oscar for *The Private Life of Henry VIII.*

2. Rubik's Cube. Who says the 80s were full of air-headed Vals? Have you ever tried to solve one of these three-dimensional puzzles from hell?

3. Atari. If you didn't have one, what was the point of having a TV?

4. Break dancing. There was no stoppin' us—getting down on the floor to spin your legs around, stomping and shuffling in a complex series of movements, often to music containing lots of scratching and rapping. Went from the streets of Harlem to the gymnasiums of Boise in no time flat and ruined many a school dance for those unwilling to trash their rental tuxedoes.

5. Personal computers (PCs). It may seem surprising to see computers so low, but face it: They weren't very fun until the early 90s. They were just a lot of *work.*

6. Lip-synching. TV's *Puttin' on the Hits* (1985) helped make this a major fad. No high school worth its salt neglected to have a "mock rock" lip-synching contest, giving preps a chance to perform "I Love Rock and Roll" as Joan Jett and the Blackhearts.

7. Cabbage Patch Dolls (1983). Little girls wanted these dolls so badly that parents engaged in near riots at Christmastime trying to secure one from "Santa." The gimmick was that you adopted these dolls. Considering how ugly they were, was it any won-

Hard to believe, but this freckle-faced tot caused riots at Christmas.

der these things were given up by their doll parents? As for the official-looking adoption papers that came with the deal, what's next? Foreign dolls with phony papers to buy and forge?

8. Mud wrestling. Two babes in bikinis duke it out in a tub of mud while bar patrons cheer them on. One job for which women could be certain men weren't getting paid more.

Gregory Harrison, playing a male stripper, was just following ancient history. Gratuitous Adam Ant references aside, Harrison's TV movie *For Ladies Only* was the first of many exploitation pics cashing in on the craze for crotch created by the popularity of male stripping in the 80s. Harrison's character's use of this Zorro outfit inspired thousands of sexy lunkheads, making a mask and fencing sword standard issue for any decent male stripper.

9. Male strippers. Revenge of the housewives.

10. Dungeons and Dragons/role-playing games ("RPGs"). Every nerd on earth became obsessed with "D&D," a medieval fantasy game so elaborate that it could take weeks to complete a single session, or "adventure." The idea was to create an entirely new identity (choosing from such exotic races as elves, halflings, and dwarves, and professions like magic user or thief) and fight your way through carefully constructed settings, all on the whim of the person controlling the game, the "dungeon master." Everyone got freaked out when a Michigan State University student and many others took to enacting the game for real, sometimes resulting in accidental death. But anyone inclined to run around in the sewers pretending to slay dragons was bound to die anyway, right? Classic TV movie on the subject was Rona Jaffe's *Mazes and Monsters* (1982), in which Tom Hanks played a D&D psycho.

11. Tag. We're not talking about "You're it!" here. Tag was a game where players chose pieces of paper from a hat. On the slip was the name of the player you were assigned to "kill." You accomplished this either using a squirt gun, paint pellet gun, or back-pocket comb (simulating a knife). Once you killed your prey, you then had to kill whomever he was assigned to kill, and so on, until only one person was left alive. Like D&D, this one got out of hand sometimes, but nothing beats the sensation of sinking a plastic comb into the back of the class show-off and shouting, "Tag!"

12. Care Bears. Fuzzy little critters that came in all the colors of a faded rainbow. Or, if you were raising a monster, had him/her tackle a Transformer, an insidious technobot capable of transforming into a killing machine. For loads of fun, pit a Care Bear against a Transformer. Who do *you* think would win?

13. Arcade games. Pac-Man (from the Japanese *paku*, "to eat") caused a sensation in the arcades, munching millions of dollars in quarters from enthusiastic youngsters who later grew up to be slot machine junkies. Pac-Man begat Ms. Pac-Man, another monstrous success. Donkey Kong, Mario Bros., Joust, and Berzerk were other major arcade attractions before the fad died in the late 80s as PCs and home systems became more popular.

14. Strawberry Shortcake. The Holly Hobbie of the 80s, and besides being cute, this toy character

"Johnny Slash" (Merritt Butrick) tries to liberate "Marshall Blechtman" (John Femia) from the influence of Pac-Man (1982).

made an excellent dessert as well. *My*, she's looking *sweet. . . .*

15. Graffiti and other forms of pop art. The late Keith Haring (one of many from the art world to succumb to AIDS) popularized graffiti as an art form, decorating as he did the subway stations of New York with his spacy doggies and radiant babies. Before long, his works were selling for over ten thousand dollars, he had his own merchandise shop in the Village, and galleries were displaying his art even as they paid to have graffiti sandblasted off the outside of their buildings. He was a close pal of Andy Warhol's, pop art's pop icon, who enjoyed a resurgence in the 80s (but probably didn't enjoy dying, which he also did in the 80s).

16. Garfield. Garfield the zaftig cat debuted in 1978 and by the early 80s was one of the hottest licenses in the toy industry. The sarcastic, orange feline was *everywhere* in the 80s: on lunch pails, pencils, T-shirts, notepads, in prime-time specials (voiced to perfection by Lorenzo Music), even as a plush toy, though his personality was anything *but* warm and fuzzy.

17. My Little Pony. Ferociously popular toys for girls that plugged into two things no little girl can resist: horses and hair. These pastel-colored ponies sported long, flowing tresses—er, manes—that just begged to be brushed and braided. Top Christmas toy for years.

18. Gummi Bears. Clear, chewy candy bears with the consistency of pencil erasers. They also came in the shape of worms, but real worms are so much easier to *eat.*

19. The wedding of Charles and Di. Lady Diana Spencer had no idea what she was in for when she said "Mmm-hmmm" to Prince Charles, thus virtually guaranteeing that she'd become the next queen of England.

Well . . . *virtually.*

When Charles and Di exchanged vows on July 29, 1981, the entire planet watched, lace hankies at the ready (the couple received six thousand gifts from around the globe). Charles and Di mania swept the world, even places like America, where royalty was a uniquely foreign affair. Charles and Di dolls were manufactured, commemorative plates were cast, and women began imitating Di's Dorothy Hamill 'do.

Charles and Di made it out of the 80s with two sons but without the bliss of their early days. The royal couple separated romantically, though they stubbornly stayed married until 1996.

Charles later confessed that he'd never really loved Di, but that's okay—everyone else did.

20. Baby on Board. Those infernal signs stuck on the inside windows of cars to alert other drivers to be especially careful. They went from being a cautionary tool to a national joke (and the subject of countless permutations, from "Republican on Board" to "Embryo on Board") and found their way into millions of cars. There's no way to measure their effectiveness in keeping baby passengers safe, but as the fad got stale, some motorists were reported to view the signs as dares . . . or targets.

Read 'em and Weep: The Ten Quintessentially 80s Books

1. *Hollywood Wives,* Jackie Collins (1983). Pulp friction.

2. *Less Than Zero,* Bret Easton Ellis (1984). The ultimate Los Angeles tragedy, like *The Grapes of Wrath* except with parties.

3. *Vanna Speaks!,* Vanna White (1987). Now if only we could get her to *think.*

4. *The Beverly Hills Diet,* Judy Mazel (1981). Of course, the *real* "Beverly Hills Diet" is, Eat all you want, worry about liposuction later.

5. The works of Stephen King. The man averaged out to more than one book a year throughout the 80s. Now *that's* scary.

6. *When Bad Things Happen To Good People,* Harold S. Kushner (1982). . . . *Bad People Can't Help but Snicker.*

7. *Princess Daisy,* by Judith Krantz (1980). The best beach read of all time, responsible for an epidemic of sunstroke in avid readers too spellbound to sunblock.

8. The works of Danielle Steel. Passionate adventures from a writer with an actual past more interesting than her imagination.

9. *Fatherhood,* Bill Cosby (1986). If anyone knows how to capitalize on fatherhood, Cosby does.

10. *Miss Piggy's Guide to Life,* Miss Piggy, as told to Henry Beard (1981). Pork on the hoof gives her views on living well. Not to be confused with Elizabeth Taylor's *Elizabeth Takes Off* (1987).

Advertising Age: Ten Quintessentially 80s Print Ads

1. Soloflex (1983). If that guy pulling his shirt over his head wasn't enough to turn you off Twinkies forever, you're hopeless.

2. Benetton (1985). The multiculti United Colors of Benetton ads made having Egyptian friends supercool.

3. Maxell (1986). A fabulously airbrushed Marilyn Monroe representing "the tape that lasts as long as the legend." One major sign of the renewed interest in the icon twenty-five years after her death.

4. Honda (1985). Grace Jones or the scooter—which is more polished?

Match the faces to the Hush Puppies.
No one in America matches more faces to more shoes with more comfort, style and affordability than Hush Puppies' shoes. America's best-loved shoes. To find out where to buy these and over 130 other Hush Puppies shoes, call 1-800-283-0100.

In this still from his most popular movie, the old folks romp *Cocoon*, Steve Guttenberg looks like he himself is searching for the reason he was so popular in the 80s. This moment marked a rare use of Guttenberg as a sex object—he more typically played a (supposedly) charming boob. Perhaps all that chest hair was behind *Cocoon*'s supersuccess. And you thought it was Jessica Tandy.

5. Christian Brothers Brandy (1986). A sailor gets a faceful of seltzer. Gee, do you think there's anything subliminal going on here?

6. Amaretto di Saronno (1988). Amaretto di *YOUR FAVORITE STAR HERE.*

7. Lucky Strike cigarettes (1982). You should be so Lucky.

8. Obsession (1987). Pushing the boundaries of acceptable advertising, a gaggle of nude models resembling statuary.

9. Raintree (1981). Natalie Wood for Raintree—as if her skin needed any more moisture.

10. Hush Puppies shoes (1987). Tip O'Neill in sensible pumps.

Twenty Big Stars of the 80s Who Are Big Jokes in the 90s

1. Lionel Richie. *Can't Slow Down . . .* Wanna *bet?*

2. Paul Hogan. Down Under and out.

3. Bobby Brown. Score one for feminism: it used to be that the *women* were the ones who gave up their careers when they got married.

4. Michael Keaton. Has-bat.

5. Steve Guttenberg. What were we *thinking?*

6. Billy Idol. He tried so hard to be a cyber-punker, but why not just get a new hairdo or something? His spiky 'do was in evidence on all his record sleeves.

7. Ronald Reagan. How soon they forget.

8. David Lee Roth. He ain't got nobody. No hair, either, and not one iota of the talent of Mr. Sammy Hagar.

9. Dr. Ruth. She fucked off. Let's hope she used a condom.

10. Bill Cosby. The only mystery is how the star of the movies *The Devil and Max Devlin* (1981) and *Leonard Part 6* (1987) managed to create the most popular TV series of all time.

11. Xavier Roberts. When his Cabbage Patch Kids lost their popularity, he was steamed.

12. Soleil Moon Frye. "Punky Brewster" milked one last spurt of publicity from her boob reduction. What does she have to do to get a new series? Hack off a *leg?*

13. Scott Baio. Joanie never did have very good taste in men.

Maxwell Caulfield (on the left)—last decade's blond. Just as he was always confused with Christopher Atkins, he displays in this frame of *Grease 2* his ability to resemble just about anyone: He looks like both John Schneider and *Risky Business*–era Tom Cruise.

14. Christopher Atkins and Maxwell Caulfield. The only person who can tell these blond bimboys apart is Juliet Mills.

15. Loverboy. Remember when headbands were cool on guys? Oh . . . they never were?

16. Huey Lewis. His band is yesterday's News.

17. Joan Collins. Stooping under all those wigs and more makeup than a cosmetics clerk at Macy's, she now writes books on personal appearance.

18. Patrick Duffy. Was the entire *decade* a dream?

19. Jennifer Grey. I've never kissed a man before . . . where do the noses go? Or, at least, where did *hers* go?

20. Don Johnson and Melanie Griffith. A boy and his ex-dog. Poor Melanie of the mellifluous voice. Since the 80s you haven't been working, girl. And "having work done" doesn't count.

Ten 80s Survivors, or Just When You Thought They Were All Washed Up

1. Heather Locklear. She only got her *Melrose Place* gig because she can really, really act.

2. Brooke Shields. Thanks to a little *Grease*-y kid stuff, one less stage mother, and a fling with André Agassi, 1995 was her biggest year in, well, years.

3. Richard Gere. All it took was bagging pretty woman Cindy Crawford and the most persistent (and persistently denied) urban legend of the 80s and 90s.

Richard Gere: Survival of the fittest. Gere was a star in the early 80s, mostly due to his good looks and willingness to moon audiences in his movies. His sex appeal was arguably at its peak in 1980, when he appeared on the magazine *Wet*. Naked. Again. This photo is a hilarious send-up of his penchant for taking it all off, since he's hugging an anatomical model that's not only nude, it's transparent! As Gere aged and his acting got stronger, his box-office appeal curdled, but he made a huge comeback with *Pretty Woman* in 1990. Of course, it helped that after several unglamorous roles, he'd returned to a salt-and-pepper version of his 1980 look. With more clothes.

4. Cybill Shepherd. This woman has more comebacks than Bruce Willis has children.

5. Sarah Jessica Parker. After *Square Pegs* (1982–1983) closed up shop, it seemed safe to bet that the gawkier of its two nerdette stars was bound for a long, rewarding career as a waitress. Who'd have guessed she'd reemerge as a bombshell actress *and* Matthew Broderick's girlfriend?

6. Daphne Zuniga. Another *Melrose Place* charity case. She was soaring with her first splash in Rob Reiner's *The Sure Thing* (1985), but everyone kissed her off after she did *Spaceballs* (1987).

7. David Hasselhoff. *Knight Rider* (1982–1986) was a fairly inauspicious "peak" in itself, but with *Baywatch* (1989–) and a successful European recording career (perhaps Germans never saw *Knight Rider*?), this walking piece of cheese is a major star of the 90s.

8. Linda Fiorentino. A good actress who slaved through thankless fluff like *Vision Quest* and *Gotcha!* (both 1985) and then disappeared off the face of the earth. Until her star turn in 1994's *The Last Seduction*.

9. Jennifer Jason Leigh. Touted throughout the 80s as the next big thing (*Fast Times at Ridgemont High*, 1982; *The Hitcher*, 1986), she failed to live up to hyped expectations until the early 90s (*Single White*

Twenty Names That Have Not Been Said Aloud Since the 80s

1. Tess Harper
2. Stephanie Zimbalist
3. Steven Bauer
4. Margaret Avery
5. Rae Dawn Chong
6. Catherine Bach
7. Allyce Beasley
8. Limahl
9. David Hartman
10. Jeff Conaway
11. John James
12. Frank Stallone
13. Donna Pescow
14. Julie Hagerty
15. Morton Downey, Jr.
16. Michael Sembello
17. Charlie Sexton
18. JoBeth Williams
19. Clara Peller
20. Andrew Ridgeley

"Shug" (Margaret Avery, right) must be singing the blues over ten years after her big splash.

"Daisy Duke" (Catherine Bach) was left in the dust when "Bo" and "Luke" got the hell out of Hazzard.

The name "John James" is even more obscure than the name "Pamela Sue Martin."

Female, 1992) when she made her mark as the neurotic man's Jodie Foster.

Looking innocent ... or was she looking to score some coke? Drew Barrymore grew up fast after becoming a kiddie star in *E.T.* (1982).

10. Drew Barrymore. She was using coke at twelve after stealing the hearts of moviegoers around the globe in *E.T. The Extra-Terrestrial* (1982), and she seemed thoroughly washed up in her teens. But after a steady stream of interesting roles (*Guncrazy*, *Poison Ivy*, and *The Amy Fisher Story* [TV], all 1992), a breast reduction, a pre-twentysomething autobiography, and hanging with a photogenic crowd, she's shaped up as one of the only major "stars" of Generation X.

She's a Beauty: Ten Major 80s Babes

1. Paulina Porizkova. *Anna* (1987) schmanna, did you see her in that Cars video?!? Keep in mind that she married Ric Ocasek, so it's not like she's unattainable.

2. Belinda Carlisle. *After.*

3. Teri Copley. Comely star of TV's *We Got It Made* (1983–1984, and 1987–1988).

4. Lisa Bonet. Before *Angel Heart* (1987).

5. Samantha Fox. So it makes you a cretin, but did you see her chest? No, of course not, not with those *boobs* in the way!

6. Emma Samms. Refer to 5.

7. Patty Smyth. With or without Scandal—you two could make your own.

8. Angelyne. The coolest poster girl ever, not to mention the best part of the *Moonlighting* opening credits.

9. Debbie Gibson. Those lips, those eyes, that voice, that . . . nose. Okay, even with the nose. Without the nose, she'd be number three with a bullet.

10. Alyssa Milano. Even if she *was* barely out of her teens by the time *Who's the Boss?*—and the 80s—came to an end.

Gay Okay: Twenty Gay Icons of the 80s

1. Madonna. As usual, a straight woman leads the pack.

2. Jimmy Somerville of Bronski Beat and the Communards. The original small-town boy with a Donna Summer fetish.

3. "Steven" on *Dynasty* (1981–1989). Even during his troubled bisexual phase.

"Steven Carrington," gay icon, exercises with the former "Nancy Drew."

4. Catherine Deneuve and Susan Sarandon in *The Hunger* (1983). You know how seeing someone eat makes you hungry, too?

5. Andy Bell of Erasure. The king of screaming queens.

6. Holly Johnson of Frankie Goes to Hollywood. The man whose song taught a generation how to give good head.

7. Mary Stuart Masterson in *Some Kind of Wonderful* (1987). Such a tomboy. Forget about Eric Stoltz, go for Lea Thompson.

8. Boy George. What a drag!

9. Indigo Girls. What? You were expecting lesbians to *not* like their folky rock just because it was the 80s?

10. "Sidney" on *Love, Sidney* (1981–1983). "Yayyy!"

11. Martina Navratilova. A tennis goddess with balls.

12. Sharon Gless on *Cagney & Lacey* (1982–1988). The ideal gal in uniform.

13. The Pet Shop Boys. *Very.*

14. Kristy McNichol on *Empty Nest* (1988–1995). "Buddy" buddy.

15. Marc Almond of Soft Cell. Tainted lust.

16. Pete Burns of Dead or Alive. Even though he was married to a woman. Even after he had his nose fixed. And then again, when he had *that* nose fixed. And also after he had *that* nose fixed. . . .

17. Marilyn, who was Boy George's galpal. What exactly did he/she do for a living?

18. Baltimora. He Tarzan, you Jane.

19. Michelangelo Signorile. For his great big, beautiful mouth.

20. Prince's Wendy and Lisa. Fun Girl Two.

Dress Me in the Fashions of the 1980s: Outfits of the 80s from Head to Toe

Hair Today: Hairstyles and Accessories of the 80s

1. Banana clips. Those bear trap–like contraptions that caught a girl's hair up in a wild, yet carefully constructed 'do. Very Susanna Hoffs.

> "I like looking like a raging queen."
> —John Taylor of Duran Duran, 1986

Mike Reno of Loverboy was the most conspicuous of all headband enthusiasts—he almost never appeared without one. He probably regrets it now as much as TLC's "Left Eye" will regret spending the 90s with a streak of warpaint under one eye.

Deena Freeman, *Too Close for Comfort*

Stephanie Zimbalist, *Remington Steele*

John Travolta, *Staying Alive*

"In the 80s, the music smiled and the clothes smiled."
—David Lee Roth, 1995.

2. Mesh hair ties. Thanks, Madonna, for convincing every teenage girl on the planet that tying a piece of black or white mesh in her hair made her look "hot."

3. Temporary hair dye. So you could look like Cyndi Lauper one day of the week and Siouxsie Sioux the next. In the 80s colorful hair was a must, and this harmless dye sure beat frying your hair on a regular basis.

4. The headband. Whether wide and butch for guys or slim and corded for girls. Too chic for words.

5. The ponytail for men. A sure sign that a guy is hip, sensitive, and financially secure. Yuppies with yippie pasts favored this look.

6. Crimping. Basically, placing your hair in a miniature waffle iron so it could wind up looking like it had been braided for a week.

7. The Corey Hart look. Short, spiky hair on boys. Also known as the hedgehog.

If this boy ever did get stuck in a box, he could always use his hair to saw his way out. The Corey Hart look was absolutely key to the marketing of his singles and albums. His spiked hair and sullen pout were not only reproduced to great advantage on all his products, he was almost always pictured in the same position, with his face tilted to his left and his lips slightly parted. The repetition helped cement his look in the minds of mimicking teens, but it also got old fast—his albums have bombed in the 90s.

8. Mousse. Like rubbing marshmallow in your hair, this 80s invention gave your hair body. Too much body sometimes resulted in hair so full and textured, it might as well have been soufflé.

This L'Oreal ad's a classic, but good luck getting your hair to do this with mousse alone. Maybe if you try a little rubber cement.

9. Helmet-haired bangs. Loni Anderson had them on *WKRP in Cincinnati* (1978–1982), but Linda Evans/"Krystle Carrington" softened that hard look by feathering her steely bangs.

10. The "neat look" for guys. Vitalis dreamed up this concept, which is like saying that Columbus *discovered* America. But in the mousse- and dye-happy 80s, the dapper simplicity of the "neat look" seemed rebellious indeed.

Tie One On: The Neck-cessories of the 80s

1. Skinny ties. The ultimate New Wave statement for men, especially if the skinny tie happened to be black and leather.

2. Knit ties. Woven ties as squared as the prepsters who wore them.

3. Bolos. Leather cords with a badge holding them together at the neck. An essential accoutrement for those indulging in the country and western revival of the early 80s.

4. Power ties. Boldly classical ties to command attention in the boardroom.

Top Fun

Molly Ringwald (in 1984's *Sixteen Candles*) succumbs to the Beals appeal

1. Artistically torn workout top, allowing for Jennifer Beals–ian bare shoulder. Because you're a maniac, *maniac*.

2. Izod shirts in every color of the rainbow (also some with horizontal stripes). Ownership of even one of these defined preppiedom. The collars were to be worn turned *up*, as if you didn't know. For maximum preppie impact, artfully hang a sweater over your shoulders.

3. Slogan T-shirts. Your favorite sports team, your favorite college (like Ted Knight/"Henry Rush" of TV's *Too Close for Comfort* [1980–1983, 1984–1986]), your favorite New Wave band, or even the mysterious "Frankie Say" (introduced by Frankie Goes to Hollywood in 1984). No need for conversation; just read my chest.

4. The *Miami Vice* look. Essential. A simple, pastel jacket with narrow (or no) lapels worn over a solid-colored T-shirt. If you really wanted to be George Michael about it, you could further augment the look with "designer stubble"—a meticulously cultivated five o'clock shadow that was neither too long nor too short.

Mark Harmon prances in argyle during an episode of the short-lived *Flamingo Road*.

5. Argyle vests. For the preppie in you.

6. Eight million buttons on your jean jacket. Tacky, and it destroyed millions of innocent jackets with serial pinholes. This look was often used by people who wanted to communicate their self-perceived "quirkiness."

7. The Michael Jackson "Thriller" jacket. A garish, candy-apple–red leather jacket just like the one Mike wore in his video. Got old faster than milk.

8. Underwear as outerwear. Another Madonna legacy, though Cyndi Lauper first made bustiers hip and Annie Lennox did the entire Eurythmics *Revenge* tour (1986) in a black bra.

9. Navy blue down-filled vest, sleeveless. Which sucked in the summer. Or, if you had the bucks, fur. Fur was in in the 80s, just before People for the Ethical Treatment of Animals (PETA) came up with the idea of spraying fur wearers with red paint to symbolize the bloody murders of all those hapless mink.

10. Blouse or gown with buttons, feathers, and/or rhinestones tracing a path up one side and down one sleeve. Every suburban mom had a closetful of these. The effect was supposed to be artistic and elegant, but looked more like twenty-carat bird droppings.

We've Got Legs, We Know How to Dress Them

1. Parachute pants. The loudest piece of clothing in your closet and the most flammable, but at least you had a fighting chance if you accidentally fell out of a plane.

2. Sweatpants tucked into tube socks, mushrooming at the ankle. Whether or not you played any sports at all, and definitely a good look for the fashion impaired.

3. Jeans with zippers all over them, some of which did not even lead to pockets. Matched in futility by the mid-90s fad of wearing teeny, tiny, empty backpacks.

4. New Wave black leather miniskirts. The miniskirt made its return in the age of AIDS, when it was okay to look as long as you didn't touch.

5. Spandex pants. Great for working out, and there's no denying their flattering habit of pulling in the flab, but kind of gross to see semi-interesting men strutting down the street in them, eh?

6. Jams. Wildly colorful shorts like all the surfer dudes were wearing. Like, *cool.*

7. Floods. Not just for nerds anymore, pants that ended before your ankles did.

8. Designer jeans more expensive than the family car.

9. Leg warmers. What, to avoid getting shin colds?

10. Busy, busy, busy. The most clashing, eye-popping, and just plain outrageous pinstripes, polka dots, and other patterns on your skirt, pants, shirt, or all of the above.

Foot for Thought: What We Wore on Our Feet

1. Dr. Dexter or "Dex"/decks. One pair in dark brown, option to own such colors as tan, white, navy blue, or even maroon. With or (preferably) without socks.

2. Pricey sneakers (Reeboks, hopefully). Only if worn with a business suit/power skirt.

3. Nobody wore anything else on their feet during the 80s.

The Five Hottest Designer Jeans of the 80s

1. Bonjour. The action jean.

2. Sasson. That hair guy makes jeans?

3. Chic. Even if nobody pronounced it right.

4. Calvin Klein. Nothing came between you and your Calvins.

5. Gloria Vanderbilt. Hippy at last.

Ten Labels An 80s Closet Wouldn't Be Caught *Dead* Without

1. Benetton. Because you support an end to apartheid and violence, but not an end to looking your best.

2. Laura Ashley. Very Connie Selleca (as "Christine Francis" on TV's *Hotel,* 1983–1988).

3. Ocean Pacific. Affectionately known as "O.P." Pastels that would make even Don Johnson cringe.

4. Bugle Boy. For a "pardon me" butt.

5. Guess? Because all their stuff was so expensive, it just *had* to be good.

6. Ralph Lauren. Now everybody can be chic, chic, chic.

7. Banana Republic. For thrifty "Indiana Jones" clones.

8. Armani. Miami spice.

9. Goodies. Clothes by Goodwill. Yeah, *right*.

10. Members Only. How exclusive can a club get when their official jackets are marketed in *malls*?

Anything but the Face! What We Decorated Our Heads With

1. Lots of makeup. For girls, blue eye shadow. For women, the Joan Collins look—so much makeup that an Old Master could be concealed several layers beneath the surface. For both sexes, heavily kohled eyes and blood-red lipstick. For musicians, swaths of eye shadow running from lid to forehead.

2. Ray•Bans. Sleek sunglasses like the ones worn by Tom Cruise in *Risky Business* (1983), with the option of wearing them at night like Corey Hart.

The Future's So Bright, I Gotta Wear Shades

Tom Cruise ignited a fad with his *Risky Business* Ray•Bans in 1983.

Vanna White

3. Pierced ears. Multiple pierces for girls and double pierces for guys. Guys could also opt for a single dangling earring from the left (straight or trying to be) or right (gay) ear.

"I've always known that the right earring is as important as the right lyric."
—Michael Des Barres of The Power Station, 1985

First son Ron Reagan, Jr.

Cyndi Lauper

Anthony Michael Hall

4. Boy London baseball caps. "BOY" in huge block letters, which made a confusingly provocative statement if worn by boys *or* girls.

Chris Lowe, Pet Shop "BOY." The Boy cap was a favorite for the Pets. The word communicated a veiled queer identity when worn by one member of a fey pop duo. The fact that their third U.S. single, "Love Comes Quickly," bombed might be due in part to the sexually charged—and sexually confusing?—image they chose for the sleeve. Of course, this sleeve also served to send up a smoke signal to young gay fans: We are, too!

5. Designer glasses. So you can see in high style what everyone else is flaunting.

Eat It: Ten Hottest Foods of the 80s

1. Sushi. Raw fish, just like the Japanese eat. Yuppies helped popularize this food, which they discovered while power lunching with Japanese businessmen.

2. Granola. Supposedly the perfect health treat for Fonda-maniacs, and yet, have you ever checked out the fat content in that gravel?

3. Jelly beans. Thank you, Ronald Reagan.

4. Lean Cuisine. Gourmet diet entrées.

5. Häagen-Dazs. Even if it isn't really made in Denmark, and even if the name translates into absolutely nothing.

6. Mrs. Fields cookies. Scrumptious, but for the money you might as well snack on gold bullion.

7. Lite Beer. Less great.

8. Microwaveable popcorn. For lazy couch potatoes.

9. Domino's Pizza. Back when they gave it to you free if it wasn't delivered in thirty minutes.

10. Nothing. Fad diets were all the rage.

80SPEAK: The Idioms and Idiocies of 80s Speech

Just like every decade, the 80s were filled with their own jargon, some of which lives on today, some of which was inspired by the surfer dialect of the 60s (Valley Girls learned this from their parents), and some of which arose and died in the ten years between 1980 and 1989.

Please do not attempt to use any of these terms unless you are sure they are still in use. Otherwise, just like sending mail to a vacated P.O. box, your effort to communicate will be rejected.

acid house: LSD-inspired house music (1988). See also *house music.*

adult child: The grown-up children from dysfunctional families, as in "Adult children of alcoholics confront their parents, next on *Oprah.*"

airhead: Popularized by Valley Girls. No, they didn't invent it, it was invented to describe them.

art fag: An artist. Not necessarily a gay one, just an artist (mid- to late-80s).

awesome: Not particularly, just "cool," for which this word is a synonym.

bad: In the 1980 Gene Wilder/Richard Pryor film *Stir Crazy,* the former was forced to don blackface and behave like a black guy (yes, it was the 1980s and not the 1880s) in order to escape the villains. His overenthusiastic ad-lib was, "We bad, we bad," meaning "We're cool, we're cool." Bad had already come to mean "good" during the late 70s, but that weirdly memorable scene made it a fashionable phrase until at *least* 1987. See also *bad to the bone.*

bad to the bone: George Thorogood & the Destroyers had a minor hit with the wicked "Bad To the Bone" in the early 80s, cementing the popularity of the term "bad" with this expressive improvement. See also *bad.*

barf bag: The kind of prissy yet precocious insult you might expect to hear "Jennifer" (Tina Yothers) call "Alex" (Michael J. Fox) on *Family Ties* (mid-80s).

barf me out: Valley Girls had weak constitutions. If you said something offensive, like "Let's go make friends with someone outside our race," a Val might have responded with this (early 80s).

bimbette: Bimbo sounded too dated, too moralistic. It meant, after all, a "slut." Bimbette, however, referred to a girl's stupidity, only coincidentally compounded by her slutty attire, manner, or history (mid-80s).

bodacious: Valley Boy–type assessment of a shapely woman. This phrase surfaced around 1983, and five'll get ya ten that the phrase following it was "ta-tas," meaning a shapely woman's large breasts.

---

bogus/bogue: If something is bogus, it is unfair or unfortunate. if someone is bogue, they are backstabbers or just plain inconsiderate (early 80s).

---

boinking: Bruce Willis's *Moonlighting* (1985–1989) character "David Addison" invented this term for fucking (1985).

boho: A bohemian, or artist. This term was influenced by the artsy SoHo district in Manhattan. It sprang up in the late 80s.

bomb: (1) Exclamation that connotes general awesomeness, as in "Bomb out!" or adjective to describe something favorably, as in "My new Gary Numan album is completely bomb." (2) As a verb, to sign your name to your graffiti (mid-80s).

boy toy: Invented by Madonna, who sported a "Boy Toy" belt on her 1984 *Like a Virgin* album, the term originally meant a girl who is a toy for boys, but by the end of the decade it meant a cute guy who was the toy of an older woman or man. Variation in the latter sense: toy boy.

butt ugly: Not just homely, not just ugly, but as ugly as—nay, uglier—than my butt (late 80s).

cheesy/cheezy: Mawkish, overly sentimental, or insincere (late 80s). Also, cheeseball, meaning someone who reflects the above qualities.

chill: Black term that gained popularity through its incessant use in rap music. "Chill out" doubled as a command to calm down and a description of one's own relaxed, thumb-twiddling state. Also chillin'. Opposite: illin' (mid-80s).

chocoholic: Playful variation on alcoholic. This and other overindulgence terms sprang up in response to the popularity of 12 Step alcohol/drug treatment programs, which become all the vogue during the Nancy "Just Say No" Reagan years.

Clydesdale: Big, strapping, all-American WASP boy. Meant as a term of praise, often muttered in the mid-80s by preppie girls.

cocooning: The art of dressing up your home, investing in it for the long run. Poor people make house payments; yuppies cocoon.

couch potato: With the rise of cable and home video, more and more of us camped out on the couch, watching TV. We had eyes, but never spoke. We seemed to be rooted to the smelly sofa. We were the couch potatoes.

crack: The most addictive and purest form of cocaine, which existed for at least fifteen years prior to its popularization in America in 1985. Prince helped spread the word with his politically charged 1987 song "Sign 'O' the Times," in which he sang of someone high on crack, toting a machine gun.

deep house: Gospel-tinged house music (1988). See also *house music*.

deep shit: "You are in deep shit" meant that you were in trouble, though the term "shallow shit" for relatively minor problems never really caught on (late 80s).

dick/dickhead/dickbrain: Major comeback for the antiquated term "dick." "Cock" was way too harsh for the post-Val teens of the early 80s, so these expressions for unpleasant and/or stupid persons proliferated.

DINK: "Dual income, no kids." Childless couples with lots of money to burn.

dipstick: Dumb person, as popularized by "Boss Hogg" on TV's *The Dukes of Hazzard* (1979–1985),

who used the term for the bumbling "Enos" (whose name was certainly chosen for its similarity to the word "penis," another meaning for "dipstick").

ditz: Teri Copley's character on TV's *We Got It Made* (1983–1984) was the personification of a classic ditz. To soften the term, make it into an adjective, as in, "You are so ditzy sometimes, Heather." See also *airhead*.

do lunch: "Let's do lunch" was one of the most omnipresent catchphrases of the decade, and though it has since taken on a broadly humorous meaning, it is one of very few 80s survivors. It means either literally to get together for a lunch meeting or, more commonly, is a nice way of saying "We'd like to get together sometime, but we probably never will, will we?"

do the nasty: To have sex. Popular in the mid-80s, and used to great comedic effect by Robert Townsend in his 1987 film *Hollywood Shuffle* in an imagined film noir-meets-hip-hop scenario.

do the wild thing: To have sex. In vogue up until—and during the chart run of—Tone Loc's 1989 hit "Wild Thing." It became passé immediately thereafter, as did Mr. Loc.

dweeb: Spineless, sometimes completely oblivious nerd. Dweebs of the 80s would include the Anthony Michael Hall character in *The Breakfast Club* (1985) and ousted Secretary of the Interior James Watt.

eat my shorts: Bart Simpson on TV's *The Simpsons* made this one of his signature phrases in 1990, but it was already in heavy use by the late 80s: communicates to the recipient that his or her opinions are valueless. First major exposure: Judd Nelson in *The Breakfast Club* (1985).

eat shit and die: Extreme invective that recommends scat and death, neither of which is endorsed by this book (mid-80s).

ecstasy/X/XTC: Club "designer drug" to enhance sensations while dancing. Gained popularity in the early 80s and showed no signs of slowing down—despite illegality and questionable safety—over fifteen years later.

Eurotrash: Rich, pretentious Europeans who infiltrated the American club scene in the early to mid-80s.

fag: As in "You fag!" The throwaway pejorative of choice by the mid-80s, replacing the "You queer!" of the early 80s. The term did not mean to seriously imply homosexuality. Lost its appeal when political correctness loomed. See also *art fag, Eurofag, fag bashing, fag tag.*

fag bashing: Beating up gay people for kicks, a pastime that was identified and became a major issue in the early 80s with the swelling gay pride movement.

fag tag: As identified in *The Official Preppy Handbook* by Lisa Birnbach (1980), that little loop on the back of your polo shirt. The joke was that the tag was meant to be grabbed while fag bashing or perhaps was just a sign that the wearer was wimpy, nerdy, or faggy, regardless of actual homosexuality.

fer shur/for sure: Must be said with San Fernando Valley accent. An enthusiastic agreement, as in "He is a total Clydesdale," "Fer shur, fer shur!" Also, a way to stress what you are saying: "You are going to flunk ge-omet-ry, fer shur." Part of the refrain of Frank and Moon Unit Zappa's 1982 hit "Valley Girl."

flamer: An openly or obviously gay guy, as opposed to a fag. See also *fag.*

fresh: Hip-hop term for cool, sometimes also used to connote originality, as in "This tune is fresh." Kool and the Gang's 1985 "Fresh" used the term in that sense to describe an appealing woman.

fuckin' A: Exclamation signifying general displeasure over an event and also to connote special wonderment, even pleasure. "Fuckin' A!" could be shouted by an angry pedestrian almost struck by a car, or by someone admiring a really cool, red leather "Thriller" jacket.

gag me with a spoon!: Archetypal Valley Girl response to seeing or hearing something disagreeable. Not meant to be taken literally (early 80s).

galpal: A play on boy toy, this term can mean either a man's girlfriend or a woman's friend or can be used as a euphemism for a woman's female lover, if that woman is not "out."

gang banging: Belonging to an urban street gang, a term that arose in the mid-80s as gang violence (especially in Los Angeles) escalated. Formerly meant a group of guys having sex with one girl.

get horizontal: Have sex. Probably started by Bruce Willis's "David Addison" character on the TV show *Moonlighting.* See also *boinking.*

gnarly: Especially good, as exclaimed by Valley Boys in the early 80s and never again by anyone else, anywhere else on earth.

gross (out)/grotesque: To gross someone out was to make them sick, though not literally. Something that accomplishes this state is referred to as a "gross-out." Being gross is being undesirable, but being grotesque is being so undesirable as to warrant an entire extra syllable (early to mid-80s).

hacker: Computer wiz, particularly one who is dishonest and clever. Matthew Broderick played a charming hacker in the film *WarGames* (1983).

have a cow/give birth to a bouncing baby cow: To get overexcited or to make a big deal out of something.

hellacious: Bad, or more commonly, difficult, as in "That calc final was hellacious!" (late 80s).

homeboy: Though used from the early 80s to mean a gang banger, this term gradually became synonymous with a guy—usually black—who was okay, or acceptable, usually to other urban blacks. Like the original sense of the term from the early part of the century, it referred to someone in a neighborly way, someone you know and like. For example, the affectionate introduction in the 1988 house song by British band M/A/R/R/S, "Pump up the Volume," when a woman alerts all the homeboys in the Bronx that the song is especially for them.

hoser: Loser, jerk, rube. Popularized by Rick Moranis and Dave Thomas as "Bob and Doug McKenzie" in 1982, hoser is Canadian in origin, as are most genuine hosers. See also *take off/take off to the Great White North.*

house music: Heavily repetitive disco-type dance music. House music and rap music started the sampling craze (1985). See also *acid house, deep house.*

ill: Bad, uncool, unhip, sick even. More popularly, illin'. "You be illin'" (which was the title of a 1986 Run-D.M.C. hit) was an observation that someone looks under the weather, unhappy, or that he/she has just suffered a great blow, such as being sentenced to prison or getting that first B after a lifelong 4.0 average in school. Opposite: chill. Never say "Ill out" (mid-80s).

JAP: Jewish American princess, or a Jewish deb who is spoiled, clothes conscious, haughty, and a sexual tease. The term supposedly started out with no anti-Semitic overtones but quickly became invective. Some Jewish people will use it freely, however, just as every other group claims slurs as badges of honor (1983).

joanie: Valley Girl term meaning a boring, square girl, originating from the 70s/80s TV series *Happy Days.* The Erin Moran character, "Joanie Cunningham," typified the sort of unhip girl the Vals loathed (early 80s).

joystick: Synonym for dick, arising from the instrument that came with your Atari 2600 and which seemed to have been designed as a three-dimensional blueprint to teach teenaged boys how to masturbate successfully (early 80s).

"Just Say No": Surreal slogan for First Lady Nancy Reagan's anti-drug "thing" of the early 80s. The slogan's ridiculously oversimplified implications made it a national joke throughout the decade. The slogan's

utility echoed in Chicago mayor Richard Dailey's 1988 anti-AIDS campaign, which at first featured the abortive slogan "I Won't Get AIDS."

lame: Somehow managing to escape the notice of PCers, this adjective was used from the mid-80s to describe uninspiring objects, pieces of art, or events: "This Lionel Richie video is lame."

like: A garnish for every sentence, frequently used automatically and as many as twenty times in one sentence. One famous usage was by Tracy Nelson as "Jennifer DeNuccio" on TV's *Square Pegs* (1982–1983): "I really, like, *like* him."

major: Term from the mid-80s meaning to stress, as in, "He's a major dweeb. *Major.*"

mall chick: Girl who spent hours every day at the mall, the great meeting place of the 80s. They found mastodon bones in tar pits, but when the malls are excavated in the future, what will scientists make of all that Taco Bell refuse and skeletons of teenagers with odd metallic contraptions hooked to their teeth?

---

networking: Yuppies gathered at parties not to meet new people and chat with old friends, but to network, to meet well-connected people whom it would be advantageous to know (late 80s).

New Wave: The kind of pop music performed by acts like Duran Duran, the Waitresses, Gary Numan, A Flock of Seagulls, The Busboys, and Blondie, meaning a heavily synthesized, detached form of disco that seemed spiked with futurism. A New Waver was usually a guy wearing mousse in his hair and makeup on his face or a girl wearing a partially shaved, partially bleached hairdo and warpaint-like streaks of makeup.

-o-rama: Suffix meant to express an entire universe of the term you attach to it. If he said, "Gross-o-rama," he was saying, "I feel as if I am submerged in grossness; grossness is all that's visible as far as the eye can see."

out: Referring to "out of the closet." Openly gay (early 80s).

outing: Revealing publicly that someone is gay, against his or her wishes. Invented by Michelangelo Signorile, who wrote a naming-names column for Manhattan-based gay news magazine *Outweek* in 1989. The practice became a major moral issue on the basis of privacy versus the presumed greater good of gay awareness. Stars who were outed by *Outweek*, radical AIDS group ACT-UP, or tabloids, even though many deny or do not admit to being gay: Whitney Houston, Tom Cruise, Greg Louganis (now out), Kristy McNichol, Calvin Klein, moguls David Geffen and Barry Diller (both now out), Olivia Newton-John and ex-husband Matt Lattanzi, John Travolta, Jodie Foster, and Chastity Bono (now out).

out the door: Attached to the end of statements by Vals, as in "Gross me out the door," meaning "That's so gross I may have to leave," or even "That's so gross that its sheer power threatens to blow me physically out of the room."

paninaro: Italian term referring to clothes-mad and style-conscious Italian teens of the early 80s. Immortalized by the Pet Shop Boys on their 1987 album *Disco*, with the pop-synth song "Paninaro."

party hearty/party hardy: From the early 80s, term meaning to party excessively and with a singular concentration. The "hardy" refers to severity, with a "y" added to make it rhyme.

PC: (1) Personal computer (early 80s). (2) Political correctness, or views and words that are measured so as not to offend any groups, a concept that became politically controversial by the early 80s. To be PC was to conform to unwritten rules of social etiquette, such as refraining from slurs and even from passé words. For example, "African-American" became the PC word for black people living in America with African roots. Saying "Some of my best friends are colored," would be called majorly un-PC (downright racist, actually). Also, the opposite of PC was un-PC.

pencil you in: To tentatively schedule a rendezvous, whether literally or figuratively writing the appointment on a desk calendar in erasable pencil rather than pen. One would pencil something in in the white space, which led to the birth of that term, as in "Do you have any white space in August?" Late 80s yuppiespeak that refuses to die.

penis-breath: Derogatory term invented for use by kiddie Drew Barrymore to insult her brother Henry Thomas in *E.T.* (1982). The term, which implies that the recipient enjoys giving oral sex to men, was another toned-down nasty for the conservative 80s. Think about how clinical this insult is, then think of a million other more graphic ways to say it (many of which were popular pre-80s and which have resurged post-80s).

phat: Don't worry, ladies—if a rapper in 1987 told you you were "phat to death," it didn't mean you had large hips (though you might). Phat is to the 80s what foxy was to the 70s.

POSSLQ: "Persons of opposite sexes sharing living quarters." The message of *Three's Company* coming home to roost.

preppie/preppy: After spending the 70s as a developing cultural phenomenon, preppies came into national consciousness with Lisa Birnbach's 1980 book *The Official Preppy Handbook*, a bestselling opus that spawned *The Official Valley Girl Handbook*, *The Official JAP Handbook*, and many others. A preppie was a collegiate type, someone who could be counted on to show up wearing a polo shirt with an Izod alligator at the breast, a pair of deck shoes, and a cloth belt. Preppies grew up to be yuppies. God save us from what yuppies will probably turn into—snobby, demanding, opinionated old geezers with more money than God. British kids called preppies (who can also be called preps or prepsters) "Sloane Rangers," after a fashionable district in London where they proliferated, and the French called them "BCBGs" (*bon chic, bon genre*). I called them "wieners."

psych!: Exclamation popular in the mid-80s, used just after you'd convinced someone that the Tubes had just broken up or that C. Thomas Howell was on the phone, meaning "Gotcha!"

queer: Throwaway pejorative of the early 80s, as in "You are so queer!" or "How queer!" Did not connote homosexuality—at least not overtly. Coincidentally (?) gave way to yet another throwaway pejorative that doubled as a homosexual slur, fag.

quiche: Quiche came to symbolize all that was weak and effeminate, as in the catchphrase/book title *Real Men Don't Eat Quiche* (1982).

rad/radical: Skateboarding was big in the mid-70s, then became completely uncool, experiencing a major comeback by the mid-80s, when skateboarders invented this approving term. If something is rad, it's not only attractive, it's attractive in an almost uncontrollable way.

---

rap: Speak-singing rhythmically over a backbeat. One who raps is a rapper (not a rap-ist).

---

road pizza: Animal corpses on the road (mid-80s).

rush/head rush: From the early 80s, meaning big thrill, akin to the thrill of taking drugs. "That Rush concert was a total head rush!"

schmooze: A yuppie term meaning to meet and mingle and kiss up to someone for the betterment of one's own career. Schmoozing describes what you do while networking (late 80s). See also *networking*.

scumbag: Though hard-core sex pervs refer to condoms as scumbags, the term more commonly meant an undesirable person in the 80s. Frequent retort: "Die, scumbag." Also popular: scuzzbucket.

shitting bricks: A precursor to having a cow, this term meant that one was extremely nervous.

skank: Filth. If you were skanky, you were presumably physically dirty and/or immoral. In college, the boys were known to use this as a one-word pronouncement of disapproval, saying it with a weird, almost southern accent: "Ska(y)nk!"

slamdance: Punkers threw themselves at each other while "dancing," hoping for maximum bodily impact and risking life and limb. This form of dancing was so in vogue in the early 80s (though never for the masses) that Men Without Hats had a hit with "The Safety Dance" (1983), a comically antislam-dancing tune. By the time the 1987 Tom Hulce film *Slamdance* was released, the term had become passé, though the same sort of dancing occurs in the 90s in mosh pits.

space cadet: Yet another term for a dumb-dumb (early 80s).

spazzing: Overexcited, making a mountain out of a molehill (early 80s).

stoked: Probably marijuana-related, this meant that you were geared up and ready (late 80s).

stud: Guys (especially teenage guys) took to affectionately calling each other by this ancient term, which meant a sexually prodigious macho man. Stud was often used sarcastically or as a challenge. "Studbucket" (probably inspired by the undesirable "sleazebucket") was one variation, "studpuppet" another.

sucks: The early 80s antidisco movement adapted the slogan "Disco sucks," rife with antigay sentiment since disco was seen as a predominantly gay (and/or black) institution. After that there was no stopping every schoolkid from saying that "this sucks" or "that sucks." Sucks even made it onto prime-time TV by the late 80s, after which it lost its shock appeal. It became a throwaway derogatory term, as in "*Poltergeist II* sucks!"

take off/take off to the Great White North: Canadian expression made indelible in 1983 by Rick Moranis and Dave Thomas, whose characters "Bob and Doug McKenzie" were the hilarious, beer-swilling dullard stars of the film *Strange Brew*. The term is roughly equivalent to "fuck off." The "Great White North" would be the frozen Canadian hinterlands. Frequently followed by "eh," a meaningless Canadian vocal tic that can follow almost any word with no rhyme or reason. See also *hoser*.

to the max: The ultimate level of whatever you're expressing, as in "Her hair is grody to the max." The be-all and end-all (early 80s).

totally: Way to stress what you are saying, as in "He is totally awesome." Synonyms: to the max, completely. Often used in conjunction with tubular.

tubular: Why something that is tubular is more cool than something that is, say, spherical, is beyond me, but this term was the early 80s equivalent of saying that something was so fucking great it defied description. Perhaps it refers to being so overwhelmed that you're tongue-tied and just keep babbling the same thing in cycles. Documented on TV's *Square Pegs* (1982) by John "Johnny Slash" Ulasewicz (played by Merrit Butrick), who would lower his New Waver glasses and deadpan, "Tubular. Totally tubular."

UV: You didn't get a tan, you caught some UVs as in ultraviolet rays. Of course, by the end of the 80s you didn't even get a tan—skin cancer awareness had driven former leatherskins to sunblock 30+.

Valley Girl/Val: Originally referred to airheaded, shopping-obsessed, spoiled girls living in California's San Fernando Valley, but spread until it was a virtual plague in the early 80s. The lingo of the Valley Girls—Valspeak—saturated the language of the 80s. It was characterized by quaint expressions of disgust and severity, and also a strangely nerdy tendency to soft-pedal vulgarity. Valley Girls didn't say, "Oh, fuck!" They said, "Like, ohmigod!" By the mid-80s, Vals seemed like relics of another era. Now they are almost unimaginably naive and cutesy in comparison with post-80s urban trends.

veg: To take it easy. The term derives from the concept that those who are paralyzed are "vegetables" and may have contributed to the idea of couch potatoes. "What are you doing this weekend?" "Prob'ly just gonna veg out."

wannabe: Another Madonna-inspired word, derived in 1985 from the *Time* cover story that chronicled her obsessive fans, little girls who attempted to mirror her style. These were the Madonna wannabes, and the term has since become generic, meaning anyone who aspires—in vain—to accomplish just about anything. Synonym: loser.

WASP: White Anglo-Saxon Protestant. This term was around for at least two decades prior to the 80s, but it enjoyed a major resurgence in the category-mad decade that gave us Valley Girls, preppies, and yuppies. To be WASPy is to be extremely white, reserved, and well-to-do.

wicked: Sister term to radical, meaning so good it must be bad.

yuppie: Even more so than the more colorful Valley Girls, yuppies represented the 80s. The term was supposedly derived from an acronym for "young urban professionals" or "young upwardly mobile professionals," but it's likely that definition was added after the fact and that it was coined originally as the antithesis to the radical yippies of the 60s, a yuppie being the yes-man version. A yuppie is well educated, career oriented, invariably white, and driven by money. He or she is also likely to be simultaneously socially well connected and totally pop-culturally clueless and/or bland, if perfectly groomed.

Do not turn to the yuppie for wit, wisdom, or probing insights. Do turn to the yuppie for fashion advice, investment tips, and loans.

Specific forms of yuppies included buppies (black yuppies) and guppies (gay yuppies).

By the end of the 80s yuppie had become a term of great contempt, as in "Die, yuppie scum!"

National day of mourning for yuppies: October 12, 1987: the biggest stock market crash in decades.

Music, or We Got the Beat

The music of the 80s is hard to pin down. After all, the most remarkable thing about the songs that defined the decade is their diversity. Nearly every pre-existing musical form—and a few new ones—enjoyed tremendous popularity in the 80s. Rock 'n' roll and heavy metal returned in full force after spending the 70s in the shadow of disco; country music made a strong return to the mainstream, and the appeal and scope of R&B continued to broaden with the most explosive "new" musical form to gain widespread popularity in the 80s: rap. Full-fledged disco became uncool by the early part of the decade, but its influence was heard in the form of HiNRG, house music, and other forms of "dance music."

If any one innovation most characterizes the music of the 80s, though, it has to be the synthesizer. By the late 70s synthesizers were being marketed so cheaply that even the poorest struggling musician could afford one. The chilly, mechanical sound of synth didn't invade music slowly, it became *de rigueur* immediately, with oddball hits like "Pop Muzik" by M (1979) and "Cars" by Gary Numan (1980), songs that seemed almost artsy and esoteric, but which shared a lot with their direct musical inspiration: disco.

The predominance of synthesizers in popular music only helped to reinvigorate rock 'n' roll: there was a major outcry against synth pop as shallow and artificial, whereas rock 'n' roll was seen by its proponents as "real music" created by "real instruments."

But as the 80s progressed, it became clear that classical definitions of music were wearing thin. Rap eliminated the need for an artist to be able to sing, yet rap is undeniably the most potent sociopolitical music of the century. Sampling eliminated the need for a band to perform large portions of their own songs and created major copyright controversies, yet the ability to capture portions of familiar songs and use them as complex sounds could add layers of familiarity to otherwise innocuous tunes. New musical concepts like world music (including African beats, reggae, and ska) converged to create a pleasingly disparate popular music scene.

And, of course, the 80s had their share of cheesy songs that we all hold dear to our hearts, regardless of how masterfully they *aren't* sung, written, or produced and regardless of where they fit in the grand scheme of things.

The advent of the music video and of MTV, the twenty-four-hour music video channel, affected the music scene profoundly. Small groups and first-timers could become superstars overnight if they could muster an eye-catching video. Cute, photogenic, sexy, and/or outrageously garbed singers and bands were able to win the sort of immediate attention that their music may or may not have won on the radio. One-hit wonders abounded, but so did acts whose musical creativity was only enhanced by their striking look and video artistry.

Another important technical innovation whose popularity had snowballed since its appearance in 1978 was the Sony Walkman, small, portable cassette players for mobile listening of your favorite tapes while running errands or working out. They were cheap enough to guarantee the viability of the cassette tape format.

Not so lucky, vinyl. Vinyl records—albums and 45 singles—were completely phased out in America in the 80s to make way for the new format: CDs. CDs carried higher sound quality (without the warmth and

> "Synthesizer—it's a very hard word to pronounce, isn't it?"
> —Annie Lennox, 1983

charm of scratchy vinyl) and soon became the preferred format around the world.

So, music sounded better, was easy to transport, was accompanied by visuals, and was simplified by a reliance on synthesizers. What more could you ask for?

In compiling the following lists, I've taken care to include songs that are irredeemably 80s, songs that set trends, and/or songs that everyone and their mother owned sometime between 1980 and 1989. Since so many 80s songs are memorable first for their videos, the list of quintessentially 80s videos comes first. In the interest of variety, there are no repeats between the video and song lists.

All sidebars include the 80s *oeuvres* of the acts profiled—no 70s stuff and no 90s stuff. Also, in the case of the major stars of the 80s, each song is followed by a "#," indicating peak position on *Billboard*'s Hot 100 chart.

The Ultimate Music Video of the 80s

"**Take on Me,**" a-ha (1985). If ever a song benefited from having a slick video, this is it. This unknown band from Norway had a number-one hit with their first release in America, an energetic pop song with a grammatically incorrect title. The video features a young girl who is sucked into the pages of a comic book, finds love with a cartoon hero (Morten Harkett), and then escapes with her life after they fend off wrench-wielding thugs. The hero eventually makes it into the real world, and at video's end we are left with an image of the two lovers staring at each other, reunited. The blending of animation and live action is still impressive and wasn't copied by other music videos, making a-ha's minimasterpiece both unique and vividly memorable.

Eighty Quintessentially 80s Music Videos

1. "Sweet Dreams (Are Made of This)," Eurythmics (1983). Annie Lennox with screaming orange hair, a riding crop, and an oblivious cow. Vaguely sadomasochistic, explicitly androgynous, and totally cool.

In a move that would become common, Eurythmics employed a striking image linked to their powerful first hit video ("Sweet Dreams [Are Made of This]") on their album sleeve (*Touch*). Annie Lennox probably wasn't influenced by Gregory Harrison's Zorro outfit (see page 14), but who knows?

How to Make a Great 80s Video

1. "Crank up the whites."—Russell Mulcahy, video director extraordinaire, 1995. He was referring to the process of overlighting: "Words," Missing Persons (1982).

2. Mirror images: "You Can't Hurry Love," Phil Collins (1982).

3. Drums full of milk: "Centerfold," J. Geils Band (1981).

4. Barely restrained lust: "Goody Two Shoes," Adam Ant (1982).

5. Futuristic setting: "Synchronicity II," the Police (1983).

6. Nonsensical events: "Obsession," Animotion (1985).

7. Black and white for class: "The Boys of Summer," Don Henley (1984).

8. Jerky camera movements that approximate dancing, for stars with absolutely no rhythm: "I Wanna Dance with Somebody (Who Loves Me)," Whitney Houston (1987).

9. Cameo by Marilyn Monroe: "Photograph," Def Leppard (1983).

10. References to classic Hollywood movies: every video Madonna ever made.

1. The cow in "Sweet Dreams (Are Made of This)," Eurythmics (1983).

2. Andy Warhol in "Hello Again," The Cars (1984).

3. Arsenio Hall in "Straight Up," Paula Abdul (1988).

3. Paula Abdul in "Nasty," Janet Jackson (1986).

5. Rob Lowe in "Turn to You," The Go-Go's (1984).

6. Marlene Dietrich (fragment of her classic film *Garden of Allah*) in "Time After Time," Cyndi Lauper (1984).

7. Marilyn in "Who's That Girl?" Eurythmics (1984).

8. Milton Berle in "Round and Round," Ratt (1985).

9. Martha Quinn look-alike in "Centerfold," J. Geils Band (1981).

10. Anita Morris in "She Was Hot," the Rolling Stones (1984).

2. "Video Killed the Radio Star," Buggles (1980). The first video ever aired on MTV (August 1, 1980), for a song performed by an Elton John look-alike. The careers of gorgeous silent film stars were once destroyed by their nails-to-the-chalkboard voices with the advent of talkies. In the 80s singing stars with beautiful voices were threatened by video if they happened to be butt ugly. That irony isn't lost on this song or on its garish video whose glaringly white backdrops would set the standard for early 80s videos.

3. "Voices Carry," 'til Tuesday (1985). A great "story video," in which a woman with aspirations (lead singer Aimee Mann) and her goodfella lover skirmish over her musical career and punker haircut. In the end she makes a scene at the opera, singing this subtly feminist song to her boyfriend's eternal embarrassment.

4. "Hungry Like the Wolf," Duran Duran (1983). Undoubtedly based on 1981's *Raiders of the Lost Ark*, a video in which sultry Simon LeBon is on safari in search of an equally sultry native woman, with whom he rolls on the ground. The hunter gets captured by the game.

5. "Material Girl," Madonna (1985). With several top-notch videos already under her garter belt, Madonna announced to the world that she was the Marilyn Monroe of the 80s with this extravagant retooling of the "Diamonds Are a Girl's Best Friend" number from Marilyn's *Gentlemen Prefer Blondes*. Look for Robert Carradine as her suitor. When a yes-man tells him that the Madonna character (Madonna herself?) could be a star, Carradine wisely proclaims that she already is.

6. "Lucky Star," Madonna (1984). An artfully minimalistic video in which Madonna performs her characteristically arch dance moves, models her "boy toy" fashions, and flaunts her navel. This video indoctrinated millions of wannabes.

7. "Whip It," Devo (1980). Devo, one of the most visually stylized bands ever formed, appear with their quirky red helmets and black, body-hugging costumes, cracking a whip at all in sight. Will be a cold day in hell when another video shows a markedly cross-eyed Asian woman having a cigarette whipped out of her mouth.

Small-fry Toni Basil wasn't statuesque, but the severe styling and posturing used in her landmark video and on the cover of her platinum single made her look like a statue.

8. "Mickey," Toni Basil (1982). Choreographer Basil leads a squad of cheerleaders on an all-white backdrop, cheering mechanically to the beat of her infectious song. Pop-eyed Basil's jerky movements make her seem like a department store mannequin come (partly) to life.

Cyndi Lauper's quirkiness was illustrated for potential fans on the outrageous album sleeve of her first solo album, *She's So Unusual*. Her clothes and her artistically shaved scalp, not to mention all the vivid colors (take my word for it), tied into the striking word "unusual" on the sleeve, and a startling star was born.

9. "Girls Just Want to Have Fun," Cyndi Lauper (1984).

Cyndi Lauper introduced her quirky, ragtag, street-urchin chic in this lively video, in which she cavorts with a throng of other fun-loving girls. Her real mother, "Catrine," plays her mom. Her protégé, rock and wrestler Captain Lou Albano, plays her disapproving dad. The video perfectly communicates the song's anthemlike quality, and it made the orange-haired belter a megastar overnight.

10. "Billie Jean," Michael Jackson (1983).

Michael Jackson became the first black artist to receive wide airplay on MTV with this surreal interpretation of his massive hit song about a guy denying that he knocked up the woman of the title. Jackson's neo-dandy wardrobe (check out those floods!) and his incredible dance moves were a sensation. One of the most indelible images in music video history is Jackson strutting across panels that automatically illuminate at his touch.

11. "Do You Really Want to Hurt Me?" Culture Club (1983).

Boy George and Annie Lennox seemed to appear at the same time, ushering in a wave of androgynous pop stars. But George's drag was ten times more scandalous than Annie's crewcut, since he was obviously a flaming queen and she was more likely just stylish. (The now openly gay George was only admitting bisexuality at that point, which must've referred to men and guys.) His brazenly queer performance in "Do You Really Want to Hurt

Cyndi Lauper

PEAK YEARS: 1984–1986

CLAIM TO FAME: Wild orange hair, wrestling, accent to make Archie Bunker say, "Heh?"

The weirdest star of the 80s was also one of the biggest, and one of its most stunning overnight success stories.

Oh, sure, Cyndi Lauper *had* paid her dues hollering Janis Joplin covers at dive bars in and around New York City, to the point where she lost her voice for an entire year. It's also true that she spent time in an unsuccessful—though critically lauded—band, Blue Angel, whose one eponymous album bombed.

Still, when Cyndi hit in 1984, she hit it big, ascending immediately to the (short-lived) rank of "legend." Her debut solo album, *She's So Unusual,* sold over four and a half million copies in the United States alone, and her first single, "Girls Just Want to Have Fun," became an instant anthem. "Time After Time," her follow-up, was an even bigger hit, her first of two number-one songs.

Cyndi Lauper tapped into a niche that had never been explored by a pop artist in quite the same way before: quirkiness. Cyndi played up her uniqueness as a tiny woman with a great big, Queens-accented voice, a shock of orange-red hair with a tic-tac-toe pattern shaved into it, and a seemingly endless wardrobe of completely clashing, retro clothes. She was cute, but glamour was not the selling point here. Cyndi was our funky best galpal, the creative one who got bad grades but always aced art and who always, always understood our innermost turmoil.

This cover shows the delicate image-tinkering going on when Cyndi Lauper released her second solo effort, *True Colors.* Cyndi's oddball image had worked before, so her record company was glad to see that her hair was still unusual, but once that first wave of fans hits junior high, you're in trouble. In order to capture older audiences and give her image legs, the new Cyndi was considerably more glamorous, photographed in a Hollywood pose that managed to seem offbeat due to her oddly positioned arm and fingers.

An MTV artifact—the official T-shirt of the rock and wrestling connection (1985). This T-shirt shows off the cartoonish aspect of pro wrestling and of Cyndi Lauper's image by representing both as loony illustrations. It was a hot seller, available through an MTV 800 number.

As if to prove her sincerity and kindness, she included her family and friends in her videos, especially her mom (who took to calling herself Catrine Dominique) and her longtime lover/manager, David Wolff.

Lauper became the first woman to score five Top 40 hits from the same album, all the more impressive since it was her first. She seemed capable of handling any style: pop, dance, ballads, rock, even Caribbean-influenced tunes. Her misfit status seemed the perfect visual complement to a woman whose musical style was refreshingly schizophrenic.

When she became involved in pro wrestling, the end was near. Lauper managed the career of female wrestler Wendi Richter, made appearances at wrestling matches on TV, and featured wrestler Captain Lou Albano in her music videos. This association prompted the concept "the rock and wrestling connection," though Cyndi Lauper was the entire connection herself.

As Lauper learned the hard way, hanging out with a guy wearing a rubber band in his cheek (Albano) gets you nowhere fast.

More damaging, by 1986, when her sophomore album *True Colors* was released, she had overplayed the quirky card. The first two singles sold like hotcakes, the rest faltered. She closed the 80s with a successful cover of Roy Orbison's "I Drove All Night," her last Top 40 single so far. By that point Lauper had confounded the critics who had always placed her head and shoulders above Madonna—she appeared to be aping her rival, going platinum blonde and posing as a glamour goddess.

Like Madonna, she, too, failed miserably in a silver screen starring role, in the film *Vibes* (1988), in which her unlikely love interest was prebuff Jeff Goldblum. It was a flop, though Cyndi gave a sweet and funny performance, foreshadowing her Emmy-winning recurring role on TV's *Mad About You* in the mid-90s.

She continues to record and perform even if her albums no longer sell platinum in the United States. Nobody has ever remade any of her songs—with that voice, who'd *dare?* Cyndi, that's who. She made a significant comeback abroad in 1995 with her greatest hits CD, *Twelve Deadly Cyns . . . and Then Some,* and a reggae reworking of her own most famous hit, "Hey Now (Girls Just Want to Have Fun)." It tanked in the United States, further proof that America has no taste.

But don't you worry, and don't you fret, Cyndi Lauper ain't over yet. She said in 1995, "What if I sing till I'm eighty?"

ALBUMS:

She's So Unusual (#4) 1983; *The Goonies* **soundtrack (two songs, supervised soundtrack) 1985;** *True Colors* **(#4)1986;** *A Night to Remember* **(#37) 1989.**

SINGLES:

"Girls Just Want to Have Fun" (#2) 1983; "Time After Time" (#1), "She-Bop" (#3), "All Through the Night" (#5) 1984; "Money Changes Everything" (#27), "We Are the World" (major ad-lib, #1), "The Goonies 'R Good Enough" (#10) 1985; "True Colors" (#1), "Change of Heart" (#3) 1986; "What's Going On" (#12), "Boy Blue" 1987; "Hole in My Heart All the Way to China" 1988; "I Drove All Night" (#6), "My First Night Without You" 1989.

FILMS:

The Goonies **(cameo on TV screen) 1985;** *Vibes* **1988.**

See also music appendix, page 145.

Cyndi Lauper was everywhere in the 80s.

Michael Jackson

PEAK YEARS: 1980; 1983–1984; 1987–1988

CLAIM TO FAME: Best-selling album of all time, self-proclaimed king of pop, moonwalk/dancing, falsetto voice, increasingly pale skin and effeminate mannerisms, shyness.

Diana Ross discovered this child prodigy and his brothers in the early 70s and brought him to the attention of Motown prez Berry Gordy, Jr., who made millions of dollars with the Jackson 5.

Ten years and over a dozen big hits later, Michael asserted his independence—and kicked off the 80s—by scoring with a solo album, *Off the Wall* (1979), his first mature effort after such early 70s hits as "Got to Be There," "Rockin' Robin," and the smash hit "Ben."

Though all of his siblings have performed either as part of the Jackson 5/Jacksons or in solo careers (Janet, La Toya, Jermaine, and Rebbie the only ones of note), Michael is easily the most talented, a gifted dancer and pop maestro along the lines of Paul McCartney.

Despite his talents, the title *Off the Wall* best describes how most of the public at large and even his legions of fans have always seen Michael. His girlish demeanor led to widespread speculation that he was gay, a rumor he never bothered to deny until the 90s, when he implied that he was a virgin. It didn't help his cause that he wrote and produced Miss Ross's 1982 hit "Muscles," a frank ode to muscular guys that he tried to pass off as a reference to his pet boa constrictor, Muscles.

After the monster success of songs like "Don't Stop 'Til You Get Enough"—which is the perfect segue between 70s disco and early 80s dance—"Rock with You," "Off the Wall," and "She's Out of My Life," Michael followed up with the best-selling album of all time, *Thriller* (1982).

Thriller could not have happened at a more fortuitous moment. MTV had just been called on its infrequent airing of videos by black artists, the medium was new, and Michael was nothing if not a flashy performer. Propelled by his unique R&B/pop grooves on "Billie Jean" and "Beat It" (boasting guitar by Eddie Van Halen), and by their

Michael Jackson was at least as popular as baseball at his peak (and even now) that it felt like a natural for him to appear on trading cards. The image chosen to sell the cards is a classic *Thriller*esque silkscreen, chosen to identify the cards with that monstrously successful album.

accompanying story-driven, elaborately choreographed videos, the album spent thirty-seven weeks at number one and went on to sell over forty million copies.

Unfortunately Jackson transformed from a mild- mannered genius into an eccentric zillionaire the likes of which the world hadn't seen since Howard Hughes. When accepting the dozens of awards he was given for *Thriller*, he appeared in explicitly militaristic clothing and reflective sunglasses, murmuring a faint, "Thank you." He built himself a fantastic castle complete with a full-scale amusement park, called Neverland. He became obsessed with movie actresses Elizabeth Taylor (who returned the favor), Katharine Hepburn, and silent vamp Vilma Banky, documenting his Liz lust and his preoccupation with the Elephant Man's bones (which he reportedly wanted to buy in the 80s) in his stunning 1989 video "Leave Me Alone." He was photographed in an oxygen chamber, was known for wearing surgical masks, and grew whiter and whiter by the day. In 1984, while filming a fireworks-laden TV commercial for Pepsi, the

Pepsi sponsored the problematic Victory Tour in 1984, sure that Michael Jackson's enormous fan-base would reach for a Pepsi rather than for a Coke. His autograph's appearance—along with those of his brothers—on these highly collectible cans was a testament to the increasingly lucrative aspects of being a superstar in the 80s. No wonder the tour was a bust— their hands must've been sore after signing all those cans.

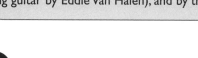

tonic in his hair ignited and burned his scalp, for which he underwent painful skin grafting. In short, he was a wreck. But brilliant.

"Jacko" followed *Thriller* with the overwrought and derivative *Bad* (1987), which nonetheless spewed forth five consecutive number one hits. It didn't come close to matching the sales of his previous LP, but what album could?

The mysterious Michael Jackson would not come out of his shell until the 90s were well under way, and as soon as he did he was socked with a child molestation allegation, though he was not charged or convicted. After a much derided quickie marriage to Lisa Marie Presley, years of abuse from the press, and a greatest hits package that (unlike his hair) failed to ignite, Jackson—more than any of us—must be pining for good ole 1982.

ALBUMS:

Off the Wall (#3) 1979; *Thriller* (#1) 1982; *Bad* (#1) 1987.

SINGLES:

"Don't Stop 'Til You Get Enough" (#1), "Rock with You" (#1) 1979; "Off the Wall" (#10), "She's Out of My Life" (#10) 1980; "The Girl Is Mine" (duet with Paul McCartney) (#2) 1982; "Billie Jean" (#1), "Beat It" (#1), "Wanna Be Startin' Something" (#5), "Human Nature" (#7), "Say Say Say" (duet with Paul McCartney) (#1), "P.Y.T. (Pretty Young Thing)" (#10) 1983; "Thriller" (#4), "Farewell My Summer Love" (rerelease of a 1973 song) (#38) 1984; "We Are the World" (#1) 1985; "I Just Can't Stop Loving You" (duet with Siedah Garrett) (#1), "Bad" (#1), "The Way You Make Me Feel" (#1) 1987; "Man in the Mirror" (#1), "Dirty Diana" (#1), "Another Part of Me" (#11), "Smooth Criminal" (#7) 1988.

FILMS:

Captain Eo (fifteen-minute short for Disney's Epcot Center) 1988.

Me?" laid the groundwork for future music stars to come out of the closet—including George himself. Everything from George's long braids, bowler hat, and baggy whites to the odd little dance steps he performed around that pool became instantly iconic, making him one of the era's most recognizable— and most lampoonable—stars.

> "'Androgynous' is a trendy word, and I *hate* it!" —Boy George, 1984

12. "Goody Two Shoes," Adam Ant (1982). Contrary to popular belief, Adam Ant was not a Billy Crystal character from *Saturday Night Live*. After splitting from his band, Adam and the Ants, this pioneering New Waver had short-lived success as a solo artist, as in this clip, which illustrates the unabashed naughtiness of early videos before MTV's pasteurization in the mid- to late 80s. Ant methodically strips a bookish shrew, only to find her to be a bodacious *Price Is Right* girl underneath, albeit one wearing somewhat less makeup than he is.

13. "Cars," Gary Numan (1980). An early Top 10 New Wave hit whose video is comprised of a slightly dorky guy with heavy eyeliner and rouge in a variety of futuristic settings. This video is the perfect example of the rampant futurism of the early 80s, complete with shiny metallic touches and a space alien star.

14. "Open Your Heart," Madonna (1986). Always pushing the medium forward, Madonna collaborated with French photographer Jean-Baptiste Mondino to create this elaborate minimovie about a young boy's heroine addiction: he worships a sexy stripper. The lush, decadent world inside a strip joint is as otherwordly and beautiful as a pubescent boy might imagine, and Madonna further solidified her role as a sex siren in her studded bustier.

Madonna's stripper persona from her "Open Your Heart" video had a long shelf life: it was employed on the 12" single and—months later—during her world tour, guaranteeing hundreds of magazine covers featuring her studded bustier and short blonde hair, concealed briefly in the video under a feathery blue headpiece.

Culture Club
Boy George, Roy Hay, Michael Craig, Jon Moss

PEAK YEARS: 1983–1984

CLAIM TO FAME: Gender-bending Boy George; outlandish Sue Clowes–designed clothes; George's eventual heroin addiction and long-running affair with Moss.

Gorgeous (Boy) George by Robert Richards.

"America knows a good drag queen when it sees one," Boy George cooed as he and his group accepted a Best New Artist Grammy live via satellite from England (1983). It was the defining moment for a group whose lead singer's outrageous femme look—complete with braids and full glamour makeup—stood in marked contrast with their easy-on-the-ears soul/pop.

Culture Club would never have been popular in America were it not for George's look, and for MTV. When George appeared in the group's first video, "Do You Really Want to Hurt Me?" American teens watched his unapologetic strut and bobbing braids and became fascinated with him.

Boy George's image of no drugs and no alcohol made him a queen you could introduce to Granny, but in 1986 that image disintegrated as George was revealed as a heroin addict. Two friends of his died (one on his premises) before George kicked the habit, but by then he had lost his mass appeal forever.

George is still very active on the club scene and with his own label—More Protein—in England, had a big hit with the title song to the film *The Crying Game* in 1992, and made a bundle on his 1995 autobiography, but his glory days were between 1983 and 1984, an almost unbelievably short time for someone who is remembered by absolutely every 80s kid.

ALBUMS:

Kissing to be Clever (#14), *Colour by Numbers* (#2) 1983; *Waking up with the House on Fire* (#26) 1984; *From Luxury to Heartache* (#32) 1986.

SINGLES:

"Do You Really Want to Hurt Me?" (#2), "Time (Clock of the Heart)" (#2), "I'll Tumble 4 Ya" (#9), "Church of the Poison Mind" (#10), "Karma Chameleon" (#1) 1983; "Miss Me Blind" (#5), "It's a Miracle" (#13), "The War Song" (#17) 1984; "Mistake No. 3" (#33) 1985; "Move Away" (#12) 1986.

Who's Gonna Drive Ya Home Tonight? The Best Cruising Songs of the 80s

1. "Drive," the Cars (1984).

2. "Cars," Gary Numan (1980).

3. "I Can't Drive 55," Sammy Hagar (1984).

3. "I Drove All Night," Cyndi Lauper (1989).

5. "The Pros and Cons of Hitchhiking," Roger Waters (1984).

15. "Words," Missing Persons (1982). Not a day went by that MTV didn't play a Missing Persons video, which didn't help them achieve stardom. Lead singer Dale Bozzio was the frontwoman, her platinum hair teased to the rafters and her slender body wrapped in plastic, tinfoil, and aluminum strips.

> "In the 80s, I think I was best naked. And now that I'm forty, I still think that I'm best naked."
> —Dale Bozzio (Missing Persons), 1995

16. "Like a Prayer," Madonna (1989). After several years in which prominent vid artists were forced to edit their sexually explicit clips in order to make it onto MTV, Madonna took another tack, incorporating Catholic imagery, burning crosses, and an interracial kiss in the single most notorious video of the 80s. Catholic groups (ignoring the video's rather passionately religious bent) were so outraged that Madonna's deal with Pepsi got nixed. It was worth it.

For her "Like a Prayer" video, Madonna went brunette, which symbolized getting back to her roots. For the single (top), even though a sultry image of a praying Madonna with dark hair had been commissioned, she relegated it to the flip side. For the cover (except on the promotional single showed at bottom), Madonna chose a simple painting by her brother, Christopher Ciccone, of the original Madonna.

17. "I Ran," A Flock of Seagulls (1982). The weirdest hairdo on video—possibly in *history*—made its debut with this New Wave group, whose lead singer combed his hair up the sides of his head and down the center to obscure his face. In the video, the group plays instruments around a revolving camera in a setting that was supposed to look like something out of the twenty-first century, but which today looks like something out of, um, 1982.

> "We just got told, 'You're gonna make a video this afternoon.'"
> —A Flock of Seagulls, 1995

18. "Our Lips Are Sealed," The Go-Go's (1981). The charm of the most successful all-female band of all time came through loud and clear in this no-frills clip, which follows them around Los Angeles. They wind up twisting in a huge fountain, splashing each other, and overenthusiastically lip-synching their retro surf song. This is vintage chubby Belinda, before she slimmed down into an Ann-Margret nymphet.

> "I have sex in front of people all the time."
> —Belinda Carlisle in the notorious "Go-Go's Gone-Gone" videotape, 1982

19. "Beat It," Michael Jackson (1983). Following hot on the heels of "Billie Jean," this classic dance video is a clever re-creation of *West Side Story*, with nimble Jacko leading a gang of balletic hoods in intricate dance formations that rival the ones in the movie he's aping. The formula worked so well, he returned to it more than once, and sister Janet returned to it even more frequently.

> "I'm convinced no one is going to remember his songs. He's going to be a statistic, like Rudy Vallee."
> —Elvis Costello on Michael Jackson, 1989

Jacko's appearance in his "Beat It" video was his most classic—a leather jacket, floods, and preppie dancing loafers. "Beat it" was such a catchphrase it was marketed on buttons, shirts, and bumper stickers, its omnipresence making more than one 80s parent wishing Michael Jackson would practice what he preached. This bestselling button makes use of Michael's image as a master dancer, as if to say "Pin this on and you, too, can moonwalk."

Cyndi's true colors were somewhat obscured by the outfits she sported in her "True Colors" video, all of which were used to promote her album and singles. In this case, the aim may be "outrageous," but there is a prepared nature that wasn't there before. Sure, she's wearing a dress made of newspapers, but each piece has been neatly scissored, and her teased-up hair is sprayed into place instead of being truly wild and unruly.

20. "True Colors," Cyndi Lauper (1986). Lauper proved to be a true drama queen with her second video, an impressively acted story of a cute blonde

The Go-Go's
Belinda Carlisle, Jane Wiedlin, Charlotte Caffey, Kathy Valentine, Gina Schock

PEAK YEARS: 1982; 1984

CLAIM TO FAME: All-female rock band, reinventing beatnik chic and surf genre.

The Go-Go's formed in 1978 as a quirky, musically untrained group of California girls whose wealthy parents got them started in the music biz, but by 1981 they were a quirky, musically untrained group of California girls with a boss debut album that hit the top of the charts, the first all-female band ever to accomplish that feat.

Led by chunky-but-cute Belinda Carlisle, the diva lead singer, and by retro elf Jane Wiedlin, the girls wrote their own material and came up with a number of memorable 80s hits like "We Got the Beat" (1982), their signature tune and manifesto.

The Go-Go's were initially helped by the fledgling video form: their debut single, "Our Lips Are Sealed" (1981), was immortalized by a cute video. Their "Vacation" (1982) video had them (through the art of backdrops) water-skiing en masse, and their last hit, "Turn to You" (1984), sported a video in which the girls performed in drag and in which the Belinda character's love interest was played by Rob Lowe.

Lowe and Carlisle shared another thing in common: both would eventually have embarrassing candid videos of themselves publicized. Lowe's was his infamous 1989 episode, in which he screws a girl while another man watches, but Belinda's (and Kathy's, since the butch Go-Go was in there, too) was far worse: it shows a plump, completely bombed Carlisle saying to the camera that we should all masturbate more often and that she used to sleep around, and it shows a demented roadie attempting to pleasure himself while a pathetic groupie is urged to "help him out." The prostrate guy later has an object rammed up his ass while he's unconscious. It's *charming*, real Disney fare.

It was this sort of behind-the-scenes "partying" that helped destroy the freshest, most exuberant rock band of

Jane Wiedlin and (especially) Belinda Carlisle had some solo successes outside The Go-Go's. They were packaged similarly—by stressing their sophisticated allure, a concept that had been impossible to stress in marketing the scruffy Go-Go's. Belinda Carlisle's first album and single pictured her as a sleek, Ann-Margretish kitten, and Jane Wiedlin's solo efforts made use of her dark beauty, portraying her as a sexy imp.

the decade. In 1984 they went their separate ways and feuded until 1990, when they had a small reunion tour.

The Go-Go's reunited again in 1994 for a mildly successful tour and for the release of a live CD, which sucked. It occurred only after Belinda Carlisle's hugely successful solo career (and Jane Wiedlin's minor one) was gone-gone.

Belinda transformed into a svelte, redheaded vixen for her solo effort, but the others remain very much the same, if not a little wiser and a tad jaded. Charlotte formed the band the Graces in 1989. Jane collaborated with Sparks on the fab 80s HiNRG tune "Cool Places" (1983) and had one big solo hit with the monotonous "Rush Hour" (1988).

GO-GO'S ALBUMS:

Beauty and the Beat (#1) 1981; *Vacation* (#8) 1982; *Talk Show* (#18) 1984.

GO-GO'S SINGLES:

"Our Lips Are Sealed" (#20) 1981; "We Got the Beat" (#2), "Vacation" (#8) 1982; "Head over Heels" (#11), "Turn to You" (#32) 1984.

BELINDA CARLISLE ALBUMS:

Belinda (#13) 1986; *Heaven on Earth* (#13) 1987; *Runaway Horses* (#37) 1989.

BELINDA CARLISLE SINGLES:

"Mad About You" (#3), "I Feel the Magic" 1986; "Heaven Is a Place on Earth" (#1) 1987; "I Get Weak" (#2), "Circle in the Sand" (#7), "I Feel Free" 1988; "Leave a Light On" (#11) 1989.

girl who dyes her hair shocking orange and shaves latticework into it and how she handles the surprised reaction of her beau. The big picture of the story is about the travails of being unusual in a highly usual world, a theme near and dear to Lauper's heart. This video (with appearances by her real-life mom and real-life beau/manager Dave Wolff) further established her outsider status and helped her gain her first number-one hit.

21. "Karma Chameleon," Culture Club (1983).

Gender-bending Boy George and Co.'s biggest hit single was illustrated with a curiously all-American video, in which the group plays con artists plaguing a steamboat on the mighty Mississippi around the time of Mark Twain's boyhood.

22. "Planet Earth," Duran Duran (1982).

Expressionistic video that was Duran Duran's first, featuring the boys in full makeup, playing instruments on a narrow field surrounded by a presumably bottomless pit. Most smoldering is Simon LeBon being lowered into flames; most laughable is Nick Rhodes with white hair and kohled eyes. The first in a long line of videos that made the Fab Five premier video artists.

23. "Who's That Girl?" Eurythmics (1984).

Annie Lennox plays an icy chanteuse in a 60s platinum blond wig, performing for a crowd of sophisticates that includes Boy George groupie Marilyn. The androgyny thing is played to the hilt, with Lennox also appearing as a man. Through the wonders of trick photography, the male and female Annies end the video with a touching kiss.

24. "Rio," Duran Duran (1983).

Another winning clip from revolutionary vid whizzes Duran Duran, in which the band—by then less androgynous and more wholesome-looking—slices through the ocean on a catamaran. Arresting touches include a fluorescent drink in a champagne glass being submerged in the sea, stud Roger Taylor in a high-cut bikini being pinched by a very faux lobster, and an equally scantily clad LeBon tumbling off the dock as the camera tilts artificially.

The thrilling Jacko at the dawn of his love affair with militaristic garb, by Robert Richards.

25. "Thriller," Michael Jackson (1984).

The first video of gargantuan proportions, costing in the million-dollar range, featuring a cast of thousands, and directed by a hot movie director (John Landis). In this short film (which was subsequently edited down for frequent airings on MTV), Michael Jackson plays a soft-spoken Valentino in red leather who turns into a werewolf with the full moon. Close-ups of Jacko with yellow, wolfen eyes and gleefully gory scenes of dancing corpses—not to mention Vincent Price's voice-over—combine to make this either totally gross or outrageously campy, but also completely unique.

26. "Faith," George Michael (1987).

Practically speaking, videos are intended as marketing tools, and one surefire way to help market a song is to develop a strong image for it. Under those terms, "Faith" is one of the shrewdest videos ever made. It presents a jukebox (a symbol of a bygone era of rock 'n' roll), a guitar (the ultimate rock phallic symbol and the one tool no rock idol should be without), and George Michael's wiggling behind (no comment) set to the tune of "Faith," a song that became the biggest hit of 1987. I wonder why?

The simple images in this video—offset by a stark white background—were so indelible that in order to shake them, Michael gave us "Freedom '90" (1990), in which he detonated a jukebox and sang out against the commerciality of shaking your ass.

Duran Duran
Simon LeBon, Nick Rhodes, Andy Taylor, John Taylor, Roger Taylor

PEAK YEARS: 1983–1984
CLAIM TO FAME: Cute boys who wore makeup, music video godlings, all married models.

Simon was the lead singer, all pouty and blond (at the time). Nick wore more mascara and foundation than Elizabeth Taylor and physically resembled her by the late 80s. John was the prettiest, hands down. Roger was the strong, silent one. Andy had long hair and always seemed uncomfortable with Duran's teeny-bop following.

Referred to as the Fab Five, these British lads took the world by storm with a steady stream of imaginative, stylish music videos that set a tough standard for others to follow. They initially looked dark and exotic in their "Planet Earth" video (1981), but gradually transformed into a band of uniformly pretty boys by the time of their first big smash, "Hungry Like the Wolf" (1983).

They had scandalized with their "Girls on Film" video (1982), which showed, among other things, a white woman riding a black man and naked breasts galore, continued the trend with the brazenly sexual "Wolf" (in which lead singer LeBon and a woman skirmish in the jungle to the strains of her orgiastic moans), then settled into more restrained fare.

At the time of the single release for "Save a Prayer," Duran squared wanted to project an image of mousse and makeup; they didn't mind being seen as pretty boys. But the three members who made up Arcadia opted for a more musical approach. They were no less prettified, but the sleeve art for "Election Day" seemed to be saying, "Hey, we play instruments!" So? Pull down your pants.

By the time they sank to doing a James Bond theme—the number-one smash "A View to a Kill" (1985)—things were not well with this band band. Andy and Roger jumped ship, and various interesting musical splinter groups were formed. The Power Station featured Andy and John; Arcadia was made up of Simon, Roger, and Nick; and John also had a solo hit with the theme from the Kim Basinger/Mickey Rourke S/M thriller *9 1/2 Weeks* (1986).

To add to the confusion in 1986, Simon, Nick, and John made Duran Duran into a trio and in 1988 condensed their name to DuranDuran, raking in another four hits in that form, of which "Notorious" (1986) was the only one to make it big.

DuranDuran continued to record into the 90s, enjoying a pair of hits in 1993 with new addition Warren Cuccurullo (yes, the guitarist from that other great 80s band Missing Persons), but they were clearly a careless memory by decade's end.

DURAN DURAN ALBUMS:
Duran Duran (#10, in 1983) 1981; *Rio* (#6) 1983; *Seven and the Ragged Tiger* (#8) 1983; *Arena* (#4) 1984; *Notorious* (#12) 1986.

DURAN DURAN SINGLES:
"Hungry Like the Wolf" (#3), "Rio" (#14), "Is There Something I Should Know" (#4), "Union of the Snake" (#3) 1983; "New Moon on Monday" (#10), "The Reflex" (#1), "The Wild Boys" (#2) 1984; "Save a Prayer" (#16), "A View to a Kill" (#1) 1985; "Notorious" (#2) 1986; "Skin Trade" (#39) 1987.

DURANDURAN ALBUMS:
Big Thing (#24) 1988.

DURANDURAN SINGLES:
"I Don't Want Your Love" (#4) 1988; "All She Wants Is" (#22) 1989.

THE POWER STATION ALBUMS:
The Power Station (#6) 1985.

THE POWER STATION SINGLES:
"Some Like It Hot" (#6), "Get It On" (#9), "Communication" (#34) 1985.

ARCADIA ALBUMS:
So Red the Rose (#23) 1985.

ARCADIA SINGLES:
"Election Day" (#6) 1985; "Goodbye Is Forever" (#33) 1986.

Wham!
George Michael, Andrew Ridgeley

PEAK YEARS: Wham!: 1984–1986; George Michael: 1984–1988
CLAIM TO FAME: Wham!: George Michael; George Michael: Elton John-esque songwriting, rapid distaste for own material shortly after release of next project, fluffy blond, then dark '50s pompadour hair, shaking butt in "Faith" video.

Wham! exploded onto the charts in 1984 with a worldwide smash called "Wake Me Up Before You Go-Go," a song they'd written as teens in England and one from which George Michael has since divorced himself. In fact, it wasn't long after Wham! made it big that George started getting "featuring" credits, and it wasn't long after that that he dumped Ridgeley in favor of a solo career.

Wham! made all the girls scream, and they screamed even harder at George Michael alone—his greatest success would come from 1987 to 1988 with *Faith*, one of the Top 10 albums of the decade. Andrew Ridgeley, aside from one embarrassing solo album, was never seen or heard from again.

After a chain of spunky pop hits and melodramatic ballads, George scandalized with his horny "I Want Your Sex" single (1987) and its accompanying R-rated video. In the clip, George paints messages on a lovely Asian woman's nude body, and the two engage in rather unlikely, pantomimed intercourse. But George bent over to MTV's concerns, censoring his video so that the message became explicitly antifree love ("Explore monogamy"), which was much more palatable in the age of AIDS.

In fact, the most interesting aspect of the George Michael phenomenon was his discomfort at the whole process. He took his songwriting seriously and rejected all his presolo material as soon as *Faith* was in the can. By the end of the decade (late 1990), he was blowing up the jukebox from "Faith" in his video for "Freedom," a video in which he obstinately refused to appear, for fear that his artistic integrity would be compromised.

We are talking about the guy from Wham! here, the one whose earliest (non-hit) album, *Young Guns,* contained a song called "Young Guns (Go for It!)."

Highfalutin standards aside, the rest of us pretty much liked all of his music and had a hard time seeing what made a delightfully dopey song like "Monkey" (1988) any better than "I'm Your Man" (1985), or "Too Funky" (a 90s hit) artistically superior to, well, anything he'd ever written.

But let the diva have his way. We promise only to love whatever you're releasing currently, George, and promise never again to watch our bootlegged video of Wham!'s China tour.

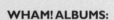

The hits just kept coming for Wham! but the chasm between Andrew's goal of glitzy stardom and George's pretensions as an Artiste were evident in these two record sleeves. Do the poppy tunes "Everything She Wants" and "Freedom" really match such brooding poses?

WHAM! ALBUMS:
Young Guns 1983; *Make It Big* (#1) 1984; *Music from the Edge of Heaven* (#10) 1986.

WHAM! SINGLES:
"Wake Me Up Before You Go-Go" (#1), "Careless Whisper" (billed as "featuring George Michael") (#1) 1984; "Everything She Wants" (#1), "Freedom" (#3), "I'm Your Man" (#3) 1985; "The Edge of Heaven" (#10) 1986.

GEORGE MICHAEL ALBUMS:
Faith (#1) 1987.

GEORGE MICHAEL SINGLES:
"A Different Corner" (#7) 1986; "I Knew You Were Waiting (for Me)" (duet with Aretha Franklin) (#1), "I Want Your Sex" (#2), "Faith" (#1) 1987; "Father Figure" (#1), "One More Try" (#1), "Monkey" (#1), "Kissing a Fool" (#5) 1988; "Heaven Help Me" (duet with Deon Estus) (#5) 1989.

"We know our songs are great, and we believe in presenting them in such a fashion that everybody notices."
—George Michael on the Wham! credo, 1985

27. "Physical," Olivia Newton-John (1981).
Reflecting the workout craze that gripped America from the early 80s, this whimsical video for one of the most popular songs of all time (ten straight weeks at number one) features 70s superstar Olivia Newton-John in her essential gym gear, aerobicizing to the tune of her highly suggestive song. The video's cartoonish quality softens the song's tawdry, man-hungry edge, with Olivia gaping at beefy, more-than-half-naked men. The joke at the end of the video—frequently cut when aired on MTV and elsewhere—was that all the beefy studs walk off holding hands, leaving lusty Olivia in the dust.

28. "Love Plus One," Haircut One Hundred (1982). An influential New Wave band from Britain that never made a major splash in America nevertheless made an MTV splash with this much aired video, in which band members perform in a jungle, swinging from vines and swinging to the rhythm.

29. "Photograph," Def Leppard (1983). The first sign that heavy metal was back: Def Leppard, an obvious take on Led Zeppelin, though the band insisted their name resulted from a booking agent's lame-brained spelling. Their breakthrough video combines head-banging performance clips with a bizarre sequence involving the death of Marilyn Monroe, complete with a convincing impersonator and a chalk outline to imply her demise.

30. "Hot for Teacher," Van Halen (1984). One of the raunchiest videos to pass MTV's censors in the early days, in which children cheer on their sexy teacher as she strips down to her skivvies. You just know that hound dog David Lee Roth had something to do with this.

Stickers were a huge fad in the 80s, and Van Halen was one of the era's biggest rock bands. The merger of the two forms in these puffy stickers shows how many of our tastes are molded at an early age—tots were the main consumers of puffy stickers, which may have been their introduction to hard rock. The stickers showed band members in heavy metal outfits and poses, which started popping up in schools like the mumps.

The same Neanderthal brow that haunted the "Wake Me Up Before You Go-Go" video took center-stage on the sleeve of the single. The brows got smaller as the hits got bigger, and this was one of the duo's only cheery poses, mirroring the upbeat quality of the song and video.

31. "Wake Me Up Before You Go-Go," Wham! (1984). George Michael's first big splash was as a part of the teeny-bop duo Wham! in this, their debut video. George and his buddy Andrew Ridgeley (later unceremoniously dumped) sing on stage in white short-shorts in front of backup singers (two of whom later became the duo Pepsi and Shirley). T-shirts with the logo "Choose Life" predated the pro-life movement slogan, and were meant simply as giddy bits of positivity, which is something this buoyant video *drips*. P.S. Check out George Michael's Neanderthal brow.

32. "Centerfold," J. Geils Band (1981). A number-one smash hit whose video caused much speculation that one of the babes in lingerie was actually original MTV video jockey Martha Quinn. It wasn't, but the urban myth grew.

> **"Would I like to hang out with George Michael? I'd like to *hang* George Michael."**
> **—Robert Smith of the Cure, 1986**

33. "Addicted to Love," Robert Palmer (1986). Feminists gave birth to bouncing baby cows over this slick perfomance piece in which Palmer appears as a nattily dressed smoothie backed by a bandful of highly stylized, mannequinlike beauties. The women are so similar that it's almost impossible to tell them apart, but their dehumanized glares are precisely what make this video a sly commentary on showbiz. This video sparked more parodies than any other, notably by Michelle Shocked (whose 1988 "Green" featured similarly robotic boy toys) and Paula Abdul (whose 1989 "Forever Your Girl" was disturbingly peopled by little girls in tight black outfits and sporting huge, red lips).

34. "Papa Don't Preach," Madonna (1986). Madonna launched the first of her umpteen radical "new looks" with this video, in which she plays both a teenager with a pixie 'do and her own glamorous self. Remember how shocked you were when you saw the formerly trashy Madonna slinking around in black spandex less twenty pounds and looking like a Hollywood star? Madonna also turns in her best silent acting in this video, playing a teenager who bites the bullet and tells her father she's pregnant.

35. "When I Think of You," Janet Jackson (1986). A full-scale video from Janet's pre-skinny days, featuring the overdressed dance diva gyrating and skipping gaily around. The video's infectiously childlike glee helped make the single rise to number one.

Janet's first major single and her first number-one hit were packaged in lookalike sleeves. The uncontrollable strokes that surround the very much in *Control* Janet just served to reinforce her album's message: She's the boss.

Janet Jackson

PEAK YEARS: 1986–1987; 1989
CLAIM TO FAME: Michael's baby sister, Paula Abdul–choreographed dance moves, stints on TV's *Good Times, Diff'rent Strokes,* and *Fame*.

The Janet of the 90s is nothing like the Janet of 1986. In fact, the Janet of the 80s was a whole different animal, a pleasingly plump girl with delightfully vulgar taste in clothes who did her best to ape her brother's dance style and who staged a minirebellion against her powerful, controlling family by striking out on her own with the album *Control* (1986).

Janet Jackson at her tackiest, as a regular on the TV series *Fame* (she's the grinning troll at right).

That Janet was very different from her previous incarnation, an eighteen-year-old who married James DeBarge impulsively, then allowed her family to have the rather dubious union annulled.

Control saw Janet emerging with a unique sound and buoyed by the unfailing grooves of producer-writers Jimmy

"Jam" and Terry Lewis. She was only twenty then, and even though some of her songs were sassy (1986's "What Have You Done for Me Lately?") and some were even raunchy (1986's "Nasty"), her image was—and is—pure as the driven snow.

The massive hits that built Janet Jackson's musical *oeuvre* and her position as one of pop and R&B's biggest divas were helped along by a striking uniformity in their packaging. Her first four singles' sleeves were all variations on her album sleeve, making it easy for fans to identify all JJ product. With later releases like "Let's Wait Awhile" (funny sentiment coming from a chick who got married before she could legally drink) and "The Pleasure Principle," the pattern continued—Janet appeared in the same black catsuit.

Janet emerged in 1989 with her follow-up, *Rhythm Nation 1814,* an equally successful disk that saw her prancing in military gear that nicely echoed her album title's "National Anthem" connection (what's with that Jackson/paramilitary connection?), with a ponytail peeking out of her baseball cap. It was a look that many women in various parts of America liked so much, they still copy it over ten years later. Why?

Unlike most of the biggest stars of the 80s, Janet had no personality at all. She wasn't outrageous, androgynous, opinionated, a vocal powerhouse, or artsy, nor did she have temptestuous affairs. What she did was make music—sweet, danceable, romanceable music—all with some harmless hair extensions and thirty spare pounds.

The Janet of the 90s, of course, is even hotter. Her albums and singles fly out of the box, she has molded herself (literally, in the case of this surgical wondergirl) into a passive sex symbol, and her record deals escalate with every album.

But of the Janet of the 80s, all we can say is that we miss her much.

ALBUMS:

Janet Jackson 1983; *Dream Street* 1984; *Control* (#1) 1986; *Rhythm Nation 1814* (#1) 1989.

SINGLES:

"What Have You Done for Me Lately?" (#4), "Nasty" (#3), "When I Think of You" (#1), "Control" (#5) 1986; "Let's Wait Awhile" (#2), "The Pleasure Principle" (#14) 1987; "Miss You Much" (#1), "Rhythm Nation" (#2), "Escapade" (#1) 1989.

TV:

Diff'rent Strokes 1981–1982; *Fame* 1984–1986.

---

36. "We're Not Gonna Take It," Twisted Sister (1984). Heavy-metal camp. Lead singer Dee Snyder's clown face and frizzy, blond hair, compounded by the over-the-top teen rebellion of this video, made it huge. It fell just shy of being a "novelty hit."

37. "Straight Up," Paula Abdul (1988). A beautifully directed and choreographed black-and-white video that showcases Paula Abdul's looks and her Bob Fosse–like dance moves. A guest appearance by her then beau Arsenio Hall was then hip, though now it is the only part of the video that hasn't aged well. Stunning.

38. "Legs," ZZ Top (1984). The bearded boys of rock 'n' roll made the most of the medium with this tacky (in a good way) tale of a shy young girl's transformation into a flashy, leggy tramp. The formula worked so well (the ZZ Top car, the bevy of harlots, the group standing stoically in sunglasses) that they used it again—in their almost indistinguishable "Sharp Dressed Man" (also 1984).

39. "Black Coffee," Squeeze (1982). A small hit by a hip band that boasts an artful video. The breakup of a relationship is shown in a series of vignettes visible in cubicles of a large, blood-red grid. This clip demonstrated the capacity of music videos to visually tell an interesting story in the space of three or so minutes.

40. "Sunglasses at Night," Corey Hart (1984). The earringed, moussed Hart plays baby Elvis in the slammer in this sexy, sweaty clip. When the door to his cell is slammed in his face, you'll flinch—every time.

The Elvis look Corey Hart was going for in his jailhouse video "Sunglasses at Night" leaked onto the sleeve of the single. His collar-flipping is a quote from Elvis's classic *Jailhouse Rock* pose.

"My fans know I'm sincere and write from the heart."
—Corey Hart, 1986

41. "Burning Down the House," Talking Heads (1983). David Byrne's spooky face projected onto the side of a suburban house.

42. "Love Is a Battlefield," Pat Benatar (1983). Pat Benatar's prostitution epic, wherein she plays a teen (!) runaway who becomes a call girl. When her father kicks her out of the house, his stern shouts punctuate the music, a trend that would occur more and more frequently with highly conceptual videos: the original song is altered to suit the original video. Her mass choreography—done by a cavalcade of women dressed as hookers—gives "Beat It" a run for its money.

43. "Venus," Bananarama (1986). The most successful female act in British history barely made a dent on American charts, except for this number-one remake of the 70s Shocking Pink tune. The video features the three Bananarammers dancing limbo-like toward the camera, peeling off so each has her fair share of screen time; lots of costume changes; and even a woman dressed like a sexy devil. The question is, with three lovely women in

Ten Cutest MTV Video Studmuffins

1. **Corey Hart.** *Screeeam!*

2. **Simon LeBon.** So he was a little prissy—you liked sensitive men. And watching him struggle with that exotic, wailing woman in the "Hungry Like the Wolf" video brought you as close to orgasm as possible with your parents in the house.

3. **Billy Idol.** He brought out the rebel in you, the side that found latex sort of kinky before you grew up and actually *had* sex and realized latex is about as much fun as cough drops.

4. **Rick Springfield.** You "watched him with those eyes," you cut his pictures out of *Teen Beat,* you memorized all the scripts to *General Hospital.* And he played guitar.

5. **Jack Wagner**—the *other General Hospital* heart-throb—was all you ever needed. Was that too much to ask?

6. **The dark-haired guy from Duran Duran.** You could never remember his name, but he looked so appealingly macho next to all the rest of those boys.

7. **Ray Parker Jr.** Just kidding. "Girls Are More Fun"? Than what? Boys? Snakes? Tiffany?

"Like, ohmigod! Rick Springfield is so totally cute!" Jennifer Jason Leigh shows Phoebe Cates her locker in *Fast Times at Ridgemont High.* No idea why she'd also hang a picture of Timothy Hutton, unless it was some sort of alternative punishment to detention.

8. **David Lee Roth.** Sue me, I'm feeling a little reckless tonight.

9. **Morten Harket.** He was the cutest a-ha boy and the one you still dream about even if he *is* born-again and never took on English.

10. **Rockwell.** Somebody *was* watching you, Rockwell.

---

the group, why was a fourth hired to don the devil suit?

> "Andrew Ridgeley was slim, cute, and confident— everything that George Michael wasn't."
> —*Australian Vogue,* 1994

44. "I Want Your Sex," George Michael (1987). MTV heavily censored ex-Wham! lead George Michael's foray into heavy sex. In the final video, Michael engages in sexplay with an Asian model in a platinum wig, blindfolding and rolling in the sheets with her. At video's end, the words "Explore Monogamy" appear, written in lipstick on flesh. This appended message, intended as politically correct lip service to AIDS, made the video

a startlingly contradictory image to accompany a frankly sexual song.

45. "Vacation," The Go-Go's (1982). The Go-Go's on water skis with a highly fake backdrop, plus lots of long shots of actual water-ski ballet.

46. "Rapture," Blondie (1981). Blondie was the first band to create a "video album," for their *Eat to the Beat* collection (1979). "Rapture," like many of their early videos, shows the limitations of the form at that point. Stringbean Deborah Harry wobbles unsteadily (and with no rhythm at all) past an array of surreal activities, including a juggler activated by her gaze.

The Big Band Era

The 80s started out with a rebellion against the disco of the 70s—lots of rockin' bands relying on their instruments as opposed to synthesized sounds. Of course, synthesizers had a real heyday in the 80s, but their aficionados had to go by the code name "New Wave" in order to survive.

The band Blondie, headed up by Chris Stein and his lover, that Garbo of the 70s, Debbie Harry, were the bridge between 70s and the 80s with their progression from punk to disco (the band's first hit was "Heart of Glass," in 1979) to rock ("One Way or Another," "Dreaming" 1979) to New Wave ("Call Me," "Atomic" 1980) to reggae ("The Tide is High" 1980) to rap (the first rap song ever to hit number one, 1981's "Rapture") and then on to oblivion. There has never been another band to chart with such a diversity of songs and to have such incredible successes with so many of them, four number-one singles out of eight charted hits. After nursing Chris through a debilitating disease, Debbie became Deborah and continued her solo career virtually unnoticed by the public at large, though her stylistic and lyrical influences are echoed sharply by Madonna, Courtney Love, and a slew of other 90s rockers.

Following hot on Blondie's heels was another band revolving around sexy blondness, The Police. Not one of those three British boys were natural blonds—all had dyed their hair for attempts at doing TV commercials—but there were never three more artistically intense New Wavers. After warming us up with their big 1979 prostitute hit, "Roxanne," they assaulted the airwaves with hit after hit, bolstered by videos featuring their cute mugs. Most memorable is their schoolgirl/teacher affair song, "Don't Stand So Close to Me," the video that featured Sting disrobing and the three of them dancing like penguins. They built to a head with 1983's "Every Breath You Take," then built back down to a lull, disbanding in 1986. Sting, of course, went on to become an activist for rain forest preservation and for fathering as many babies as possible, in addition to being considered one of the most serious artists of the 90s, whatever that means. Stewart Copeland formed the critically revered band Animal Logic in 1989, and Andy Summers

Deborah Harry's sexy, tousled rocker look of the 70s gave way to a concentrated Garboization in the 80s. Without her band Blondie, her kohled eyes and frigid beauty became motifs of all her single sleeves, in stark contrast to the frequently hot and punky images used to help sell Blondie's big hits.

continued to make experimental music.

The Cars were sort of like the American Police, except ugly. Tall, thin lead singer Ric Ocasek cut a striking figure with his spiked black hair (still working that look circa 1996) and Gothic costumes, and he penned all of their songs. The band's biggest hit was "Drive," which featured Ocasek's future wife, 80s supermodel Paulina Porizkova, in the video as a demented girl, but their signature tune was "Shake It Up," one of the most repetitive songs in rock history (and that's saying a lot). "Shake it up . . . ooh, ooh . . ." After thirteen hits, they parked in 1988.

Genesis was hardly a band exclusively of the 80s. They started out almost as an art-rock band in the late 60s, building a fan base and critical credibility throughout the 70s. By the time the 80s—and MTV—dawned, Genesis consisted of rugrat lead singer Phil Collins, Mike Rutherford (guitar, bass), and Tony Banks (keyboards). Hardly pretty or even young, Genesis was nonetheless boosted by MTV because their videos were usually either creative or fun and simple. Between Phil Collins's solo efforts ("In the Air Tonight" 1981; "You Can't Hurry Love" 1982; "I Don't Care Anymore" 1983; "Against All Odds," "Easy Lover" 1984; "One More Night," "Sussudio" 1985), the hits of Genesis ("No Reply at All" 1981; "Abacab," "Man on the Corner" 1982; "That's All" 1983; "Invisible Touch" 1986) and the hits of Mike + the Mechanics, led by Rutherford ("Silent Running," "All I Need Is a Miracle" 1986; "The Living Years" 1989), Genesis and Co. became one of the hottest groups of the decade. They record erratically today, as do its members.

Bon Jovi started out as a dubious metal band and wound up as a dubious rock 'n' roll band, but they nevertheless ruled the mid- to late 80s. After warming us up with 1984's "Runaway," the band hit the big time with their *Slippery When Wet* album and back-to-back smash hits, including "You Give Love a Bad Name" (1986), "Livin' on a Prayer," "Wanted Dead or Alive" (1987), and "Bad Medicine" (1988). Buoyed by lead singer Jon Bon Jovi's incredible Farrah Fawcett hair and the band's down-to-earth rockin' mentality, they are unstoppable even today, over ten years later.

47. "China Girl," David Bowie (1983). Most famous for Bowie's raunchy roll on the beach with the "China girl" of the title, a segment so revealing that it had to be cut for airing on MTV. At the end, his Asian lover smears her lipstick dramatically, and barbed wire streaks across her image.

48. "White Wedding," Billy Idol (1983). Black-rubbered Billy Idol in a Gothic wedding featuring more babes than brides.

49. "She's a Beauty," the Tubes (1983). A very adult carnival ride with a hypersexual woman and her mile-high ponytail.

> "Why bother to listen to the radio anymore?"
> —Fee Waybill, The Tubes on videos, 1981

50. "She Blinded Me With Science," Thomas Dolby (1983). The real star of the video is the perfectly cast elderly scientist, who mouths, "Science!" with gusto.

51. "What's Love Got to Do With It?" Tina Turner (1984). This video established Tina's new look in her spiky wig and short skirt, jeans jacket, and high heels. All she had to do was strut down the street.

Her wig, her high heels, and her ageless legs were used to project a "new Tina" image in both the video for "What's Love Got to Do With It?" and on the *Private Dancer* album. Tina's attention to coif, her comeback status, and her, well, her *age* made her the singing version of Joan Collins.

52. "Who Can It Be Now?" Men at Work (1982). A memorably insane selection of weirdos arrives at the door, each stranger than the last, but none as strange as this group's bug-eyed lead singer, Colin Hay.

53. "Sledgehammer," Peter Gabriel (1986). Making use of stop animation photography, this relentlessly creative video features Gabriel and all manner of moving shapes jerking across the screen.

54. "Dancing in the Dark," Bruce Springsteen (1984). The Boss performs to a stadium crowd but chooses young Courteney Cox to dance on stage with him.

55. "Saved by Zero," The Fixx (1983). A weary saloon, straight out of *Citizen Kane*, featuring a performance by adorable lounge lizards The Fixx, the same hip Brit band that sang "One Thing Leads to Another."

56. "Wouldn't It Be Good?" Nik Kershaw (1985). Kershaw as space boy, and his suit becomes a pulsating vision of fast-moving images. This spookily spacey video perfectly depicted the weird alienation of adolescence or of being "different" in any way. Kershaw makes a break from his building and endures the shocked stares of neighbors and passersby, which only heightens the euphoria when he makes it to that enormous, signaling satellite dish. "Phone home!"

57. "When Doves Cry," Prince (1984). Prince rising from the tub, and his own image reflected on both sides of the screen against a whited-out backdrop. Sex drenched, yet it's all only implied.

> "We don't second-guess Prince anymore. He's always right. I can't think of when he's ever been wrong."
> —Bob Merlis, Warner Bros. Records, 1985

58. "Pop Muzik," M (1980). A hit the year before, but the video, with bored models bobbing their heads and lip-synching, was a fixture for the entire first year of MTV's existence.

59. "Smalltown Boy," Bronski Beat (1985). A boy cruises another boy at the gym, who seems to return the flirtation. Our hero gets the bejeezus beaten out of him later. Bleak stuff for MTV, but they ran with it, helping to make the song a minor hit.

SMALLTOWN BOY

Bronski Beat's "Smalltown Boy" video shouted "gay" to audiences in the know, but in case you missed their point, their album was called *Age of Consent* (European copies listed ages of consent for homosexual relations in various countries) and the sleeve for the single featured the gay pride symbol: a pink triangle. The sleeve's clever intertwining of the pink triangle, musical clip art, and the band's name served to communicate the group's uncompromisingly gay identification as well as its devotion to music.

Tina Turner

PEAK YEARS: 1984–1986
CLAIM TO FAME: Living legend, biggest comeback of the decade, Phoenix-from-the-flames life after leaving abusive husband, that *hair!* those *legs!*

In the late 70s and early 80s, things looked bad for Tina Turner. As half of the husband/wife team Ike & Tina Turner, she had enjoyed a decade of minor hits that culminated with the major hit "Proud Mary" (1971), all of which had influenced other musicians of the caliber of the Rolling Stones. She even claimed to have taught Mick Jagger how to dance while touring as an opening act for the Stones.

But after divorcing Ike—whose horrifying abuse of her she would document in her 1987 autobiography *I, Tina*—Tina was penniless and unemployed, stuck in that unenviable category of "living legend and borderline homeless person."

After performing and recording for years with no payoff, she finally hit it big in 1984. *Real* big.

First came the cheesy video for her smoking Al Green cover, "Let's Stay Together," in which a leggy Tina was lustily stroked by somnambulistic girl backup dancers. It became her first solo Top 40 hit and preceded her breakthrough album, *Private Dancer.* The first "star" video off that LP was "What's Love Got to Do With It?" in which Tina strolled down the streets of Manhattan in a leather mini, fishnets, and a jeans jacket, topped off by her outrageous spiked wig. The look was so distinctive, it would be five years before she would alter it, but by then she had already won an armful of Grammys and gold records for a string of incredible singles.

Tina didn't really like "What's Love Got To Do With It?" so she had to eat crow when it went ballistic as the biggest hit of her life, but she racked up another eleven hits over the next six years, conquered the movie world with an effective role as "Auntie Entity" in the third Mad Max film, *Mad Max: Beyond Thunderdome,* and toured the country in style.

Years were shaved off Tina's mug in this otherwise realistic painting on the "We Don't Need Another Hero (Thunderdome)" single sleeve, but her connection to wild wigs remained intact—her white mane seems to go on and on and on.... Note that although Mel Gibson is the star of the film, and he appears in front, it's Tina's sexual prowess that was used to help sell this record—she dominates the sleeve with her trademark hair, even if the style is decidedly different from her usual wigs.

Her follow-up album wasn't nearly the success of *Private Dancer,* and ensuing albums ranked lower and lower, but Tina had shown one last time that she was simply the best, even—especially—without mean old Ike around. She continues to record and perform, a surefire contender in the future for the Marlene Dietrich Endurance Award.

ALBUMS:
Private Dancer (#3) 1984; *Break Every Rule* (#4) 1986; *Foreign Affair* (#31) 1989.

SINGLES:
"Let's Stay Together" (#26), "What's Love Got to Do With It?" (#1), "Better Be Good to Me" (#5) 1984; "Private Dancer" (#7), "Show Some Respect" (#37), "We Don't Need Another Hero (Thunderdome) (#2), "One of the Living" (#15), "It's Only Love" (duet with Bryan Adams) (#15) 1985; "Typical Male" (#2), "Two People" (#30) 1986; "What You Get Is What You See" (#13), "Break Every Rule" 1987; "The Best" (#15), "Steamy Windows" (#39) 1989.

FILMS:
Mad Max: Beyond Thunderdome 1985.

60. "Don't Come Around Here No More," Tom Petty and the Heartbreakers (1985). A frightening interpretation of *Alice in Wonderland,* with Petty as the "Mad Hatter." When "Alice" turns into a cake that's greedily devoured by the denizens of the video, and when Petty swallows her whole at the end, your stomach turns.

61. "Smooth Operator," Sade (1985). Sinewy Sade as a cabaret singer (what a stretch) in a smoky video loaded with ambience.

62. "Express Yourself," Madonna (1989). Madonna coopts *Metropolis* in one of the most expensive videos ever made and one of the most arresting showcases for her beauty and body. A tasteful near nude scene and shots of Madonna crawling across the floor like a cat in heat make this video crackle with sexuality, and the production values put Hollywood blockbusters to shame.

63. "Goodbye to You," Scandal (1982). Patty Smyth fronted this duo with her video-pleasing exuberance and sassy delivery. The video looks as if every frame were fried in butter, with hot effects and snappy editing that almost made this song a major radio hit as well.

Madonna

PEAK YEARS: 1985–1987; 1989
CLAIM TO FAME: Biggest star in the world, dance/pop music, scandal, silver screen flops, wealth, attitude.

The so-called Material Girl was confident to the point of egomania, prolific, capitalistic, and devil-may-care.

Born and raised in a middle-class Michigan environment, she decided early in life to distinguish herself from her siblings and from everyone else on the planet. She won a dance scholarship to the University of Michigan, then dropped out to pursue a multimedia career in New York City.

Madonna has appeared on more magazine covers than any other personality in history. Even on her first cover (the New York party paper *Island*, 1983) her fondness for Hollywood idols (imitating Garbo) was evident, but her dark hair would not return in a big way until *Like a Prayer*. For most of the 80s, Madonna was identified with platinum blonde hair (as on *Ciao 2001*). Both covers communicate Madonna's special affection for staring defiantly back at the camera and she's touching her face in both, but look at the difference a little dye makes—she goes from striking to stroking.

According to her own legend, she arrived in Times Square in 1978 with $35 to her name, having told the cabdriver to "take me to the middle of everything." She bounced from dive to dive, eventually trying out a singing career with bands like The Breakfast Club (who would go on to sing "Right on Track" in 1987).

She struck gold on the Sire label with back-to-back smash dance singles, and though her self-titled debut album took over a year to hit the Top 10, it went on to sell over five million copies. Her follow-up was definitive proof that Madonna was an s-t-a-r: *Like a Virgin* introduced her as the most notorious sex siren of the age and among the most reliable producers, writers, singers, and performers of pop anthems. By cooing the word "virgin," she commandeered the airwaves with a number-one hit that topped the charts for six straight weeks. In 1985 *everyone* was *dying* to see Madonna shimmy through her sold-out *Virgin* tour.

Her trademark was controversy. From her trash-chic couture (1983)—which inspired millions of teenage girl "Madonna wannabes" to mimic her appearance—to the emergence of nude photos from her artist's-model days (1985), from her abortion-themed "Papa Don't Preach" single (1986) to her closer-than-close friendship with bisexual comedienne Sandra Bernhard (1989), Madonna stirred things up on a regular basis, turning more people off than on, but always staying in the eye of the storm.

Let's face it: Without Madonna, you might never have seen a pack of six-year-olds in fishnets, chanting, "You've got to prove your love to meee!"

Beyond the shock value, Madonna was the strong woman who helped usher in the age of the female pop star, all the while sporting underwear as outerwear and evoking sex symbols of the politically incorrect past. Her voice, fragile but full of personality, was likened to "Minnie

Mouse on helium" and was assailed by mostly male rock critics as being the worst in the business. *Rolling Stone* claimed she'd slept her way to the top, which didn't stop them from featuring her on their cover more times than any other woman.

Madonna surprised them all by crossing over to big-screen success in the title role of *Desperately Seeking Susan* (1985). She then surprised herself by flopping miserably in her next two starring roles, opposite hubby Sean Penn in 1986's *Shanghai Surprise* (one of the worst films of the 80s) and in a Judy Holliday–esque role in the screwball *Who's That Girl* (1987). Her name became a punch line in La-La Land.

Madonna closed the decade by starring in *Speed-the-Plow* on Broadway (1988) and filing for divorce from bad-boy Penn (1989), whose violent antics with shutter-bugs and movie extras had landed him in jail and the "Poison Penns" in the gossip rags for the duration of their union. She received raves for her 1989 album, *Like a Prayer,* which ushered in a new, softer, more mature Madonna, one who would eventually skip town just like all of her other personae. Like a chameleon? Like a *schiz!*

Madonna is probably the most important artist of the 80s (as voted by *Musician* magazine in 1989) and was the second richest female artist (after Oprah Winfrey), pulling in over $100 million for the decade. She continued her success and artistic influence into the 90s, even though her popularity waned slightly. Madonna, who taught us that "expressing yourself" takes precedence over pleasing

others, tossed away the adoration of the first wave of wanna-bes just as easily as she'd discarded the "boy toy" look that first brought her to their attention.

Face facts: You may hate some of her shenanigans, but you'll always take her back. She's too much fun to resist.

Madonna's 1985 Virgin Tour was such a hot ticket that her manager (Freddy DeMann, who'd previously handled Michael Jackson) had to bump it up from small venues to major arenas.

ALBUMS:

Madonna (#8) 1982; *Like a Virgin* (#1) 1984; *True Blue* (#1) 1986; *Who's That Girl* soundtrack (four songs; supervised soundtrack) (#7) 1987; *You Can Dance* (the first remix album) (#14) 1987; *Like a Prayer* (#1) 1989.

SINGLES:

"Everybody," "Physical Attraction" (both twelve-inch dance singles only) 1982; "Holiday" (#16), "Borderline" (#10) 1983; "Lucky Star" (#4), "Like a Virgin" (#1) 1984; "Material Girl" (#2), "Crazy for You" (#1), "Angel" (#4), "Dress You Up" (#5) 1985; "Live to Tell" (#1), "Papa Don't Preach" (#1), "True Blue" (#3), "Open Your Heart" (#1) 1986; "La Isla Bonita" (#4), "Who's That Girl" (#1), "Causing a Commotion" (#2) 1987; "Like a Prayer" (#1), "Express Yourself" (#2), "Cherish" (#2), "Oh Father" (#20) 1989.

FILMS:

A Certain Sacrifice 1980; *Vision Quest* (singing cameo) 1985; *Desperately Seeking Susan* 1985; *Shanghai Surprise* 1986; *Who's That Girl* 1987; *Bloodhounds of Broadway* 1989.

64. "I'm Still Standing," Elton John (1983). Elton dons all his outlandish sunglasses one last time, prancing absurdly with half-naked boys and girls covered in fluorescent body paint.

65. "Just a Gigolo/I Ain't Got Nobody," David Lee Roth (1985). Roth's infamous collection of stereotypes and caricatures, this time with hilarious celebrity impersonators (doing Billy Idol, Cyndi Lauper, Michael Jackson, and others).

66. "99 Luftballons," Nena (1984). A child's red balloon accidentally starts World War III.

67. "Stray Cat Strut," the Stray Cats (1983). The rockabilly band, a stray cat, and their annoyed, elderly neighbor.

68. "Money for Nothing," Dire Straits (1985). Computerized, 3-D animation illustrates the stock guys who harrumph at various thinly veiled celebrity slams. The refrain in the song—ironically—is "I Want My MTV!" MTV embraced this cynical ditty, displaying something that approached self-deprecation.

69. "I Love Rock and Roll," Joan Jett and the Blackhearts (1982). Joan Jett is tougher than—and wrapped in—leather in this black-and-white clip.

70. "The Safety Dance," Men Without Hats (1983). A roving band of medieval-looking dancers gallops through the countryside, spreading the joys of dance.

The video had a medieval air, but the single for "The Safety Dance" looked like a 50s sock hop into the song's traditionalist roots.

71. "Don't Stand So Close to Me," The Police (1981). Sting plays the teacher who fancies his girl students a little *too* much, to the point where he feels he must remove his shirt (er . . . ?).

72. "Melt with You," Modern English (1983). Harsh lighting as a silhouetted, interracial couple dances in 40s gear.

73. "Round and Round," Ratt (1984). Milton Berle cameos in drag in this heavy-metal video.

74. "Hello," Lionel Richie (1984). High camp as Richie plays artist's model to a young blind woman who winds up sculpting his ugly mug to perfection.

75. "She Works Hard for the Money," Donna Summer (1983). Donna as a waitress. Thank God it's fry-day.

76. "The Look of Love (Part One)," ABC (1982). A postmodern *Gigi*, with New Wavers ABC in straw hats and walking canes.

77. "Girls," Dwight Twilley (1984). In direct contrast with the song, the video features a conga line of bare-assed jocks exiting a locker room. For MTV they shot the scene in underwear.

78. "Pressure," Billy Joel (1982). Like the Maxell ad, a vacuum is at work here.

Crooners

In the fine tradition of Bing Crosby and Frank Sinatra, the 80s were not bereft of dreamy-eyed guys crooning romantic ballads.

Lionel Richie was King Crooner, with ballads such as "Endless Love" (duet with Diana Ross) (1981), "Truly" (1982), "Hello," "Stuck on You," and "Penny Lover" (1984). "Hello" especially solidified his standing as an adult contemporary balladeer, with its overwrought delivery and what survives as one of the campiest videos in music history. He never had another hit after 1987's musically adventurous "Se La," but he did have rather messy marital problems.

The other big crooner of the decade was Kenny Rogers—an even bigger square—who made megamillions singing catchy, unforgettable nightmares including "Don't Fall in Love with a Dreamer" (duet with Kim "Bette Davis Eyes" Carnes) and "Lady" (written by Richie—Double trouble!) (1980), "Through the Years" (1982), and "We've Got Tonight" (duet with Sheena Easton) (1983). This white-haired gent was little more than a glorified lounge singer, but his earthiness was his appeal. He never had another hit after 1984, but he got into an embarrassingly public divorce in the 90s.

You just can't trust those smooth guys.

79. "Rockit," Herbie Hancock (1983). This musical adventurer created the most astonishingly absurd video of the 80s, complete with a mechanical, birdlike star and a pair of electronically activated mannequin legs strolling through center stage.

80. "Black Cars," Gino Vannelli (1985). Drag queens galore, all going for that Joan Collins look as Vannelli works his Valentino stare.

Using his dark looks—particularly a stock devilish grin—Gino Vannelli conjured up the same sort of naughtiness with this album art as the phrase "Black Cars" evoked on the record.

The Ultimate 80s Song

"Into the Groove," Madonna (1985). Never released as a single, "Into the Groove" has nonetheless become one of Madonna's most popular songs. It was originally recorded for her major film debut, *Desperately Seeking Susan* (1985), and it launched the sexual double entendre "into the groove" as a catchphrase. Commenting as it does on the liberating powers of dance, this song cemented Madonna's place as the dancing queen of the era.

Eighty Quintessentially 80s Songs

I. "Let's Go Crazy," Prince (1984). The ultimate party song.

Prince

PEAK YEARS: 1983–1984
CLAIM TO FAME: Musical genius, *Purple Rain* movie, raunchy concerts/lyrics, freaky purple wardrobe, protégées, diminutive stature.

The raging musical jinni who single-handedly made Minneapolis *the* capital of new music (it was the Seattle of the 80s) burst onto the scene at the beginning of the decade with a string of imaginative funk/pop hits so sexy, you needed condoms just to *listen* to them. His "Little Red Corvette," in which he describes having sex in a car with a woman who's had many other "jockeys" before him, was a breakthrough song, both on the radio and on MTV, where it was represented with a straightforward performance clip. That clip—one of Prince's best videos—introduced his energetic band and scandalized with shots of two women practically making love while playing a keyboard. Or at least it *seemed* to be.

But Prince made his biggest splash in 1984 with one of the best-selling soundtracks of all time, *Purple Rain,* which accompanied the intensely personal film of the same name in which he starred as—give or take—himself. Both were smash hits, and he even copped an Oscar for Best Score,

appearing at the ceremony in a ridiculous purple hooded cape. His successes paved the way for his own record label in 1985, Paisley Park, which churned out albums by such Prince discoveries as Apollonia, Vanity 6, Morris Day and the Time, and Jesse Johnson.

Prince's appeal was in his showmanship and in his unswerving self-confidence. He produced albums the way a stray cat squeezes out kittens, one right after the other. He made so many that when the release of his fabled *Black Album* was canceled in 1988 because of its graphic content, that was okay; he had another entire album ready and released that (*Lovesexy*) instead. His devotion to the craft and manic work ethic made him an artist even non-fans respected, though his increasingly pompous behavior and pretensions tried many others.

Like Madonna, he had a big flop after his breakthrough film. *Under the Cherry Moon* was as monumental a disaster as *Shanghai Surprise,* a laughably arty black-and-white film that opened and closed within the space of two weeks, in contrast with the twenty-four weeks that *Purple Rain's* soundtrack spent at number one on the charts.

Though he wouldn't attempt a film again until 1990's equally disastrous *Graffiti Bridge*, Prince persevered musically and went on to score with chart toppers such as "Kiss," which was remade in 1989 by The Art of Noise with Tom Jones, and "Batdance," the wildly experimental theme to Tim Burton's *Batman*, one of the biggest movies of the decade.

Prince's dirty streak was legendary. Who can forget wide-eyed cafeteria discussions of his uninhibited concerts, where he simulated sex on stage, and songs such as "Darling Nikki" (from *Purple Rain*), which—unlike Cyndi Lauper's "She-Bop"—talked about masturbation in no uncertain terms? His peculiar appearance either left you cold or made you red hot, and his romances were equally offbeat: Vanity, Apollonia, Sheena Easton, and Kim Basinger were all said to have succumbed to his Napoleonic charms.

Everyone agrees that Prince is outrageous and in possession of a genuinely dirty mind, but if that's true, it's also true that his music influenced nearly every R&B artist working. How could it not? Half of them were singing songs he'd written.

In the 90s Prince goes by a funky little omnisexual symbol that I really don't feel like having the typesetters mess with, since it's so obnoxious on his part in the first place.

PRINCE ALBUMS:
Prince (#22) 1979; *Controversy (#21)* 1981; *1999 (#9)* 1982; *Sign 'O' the Times (#6)* 1987; *Lovesexy (#11)* 1988; *Batman* soundtrack (#1) 1989.

PRINCE SINGLES:
"I Wanna Be Your Lover" (#11) 1979; "Little Red Corvette" (#6), "1999" (#12), "Delirious" (#8) 1983; "Sign 'O' the Times" (#3), "U Got the Look" (duet with Sheena Easton) (#2), "I Could Never Take the Place of Your Man" (#10) 1987; "Alphabet St." (#8) 1988; "Batdance" (#1), "Partyman" (#18), "The Arms of Orion" (duet with Sheena Easton) (#36) 1989.

PRINCE AND THE REVOLUTION ALBUMS:
Purple Rain (#1) 1984; *Around the World in a Day (#1)* 1985; *Parade (#3)* 1986.

PRINCE AND THE REVOLUTION SINGLES:
"When Doves Cry" (#1), "Let's Go Crazy" (#1), "Purple Rain" (#2), "I Would Die 4 U" (#10) 1984; "Take Me with U" (duet with Apollonia) (#25), "Raspberry Beret" (#2), "Pop Life" (#7) 1985; "Kiss" (#1), "Mountains" (#23) 1986.

FILMS:
Purple Rain 1984; *Under the Cherry Moon* 1986; *Graffiti Bridge* 1990.

Purple Pen
80s Babes Who Sang Prince Songs

One reason Prince-penned songs did so well is that every radio programmer on earth knew he was behind them, guaranteeing lots of airplay. But most of us 80s kids liked "Manic Monday" and "I Feel For You" because they were good songs. They weren't marketed as Prince products; the sleeve art focused on the artists covering the song, as illustrated by this record sleeve, featuring standard head shots of The Bangles. But are they so standard? In each portrait, the women seem to be adapting a decidedly Prince-like stare. Probably went over record-buyer's heads, but let's give them an "A" for effort.

1. Chaka Khan, "I Feel for You" (1984).

2. Cyndi Lauper, "When U Were Mine" (1984).

3. Sheena Easton, "Sugar Walls" (his pseudonym: Alexander Nevermind) (1985).

4. The Bangles, "Manic Monday" (his pseudonym: Christopher) (1986).

5. Elisa Fiorillo, "On the Way Up," (1989–1990).

"When I came to the Lord Jesus Christ, I threw out about 1,000 tapes of mine—every interview, every tape, every video. *Everything*." —Denise Matthews-Smith, a.k.a. Vanity, 1995

2. "Too Shy," Kajagoogoo (1983). Embarrassingly 1983. Perfection.

3. "Obsession," Animotion (1985). An outrageously frank sex song, in which the singer claims she'll be anyone she has to be in order to sleep with the object of her desire.

4. "Heat of the Moment," Asia (1982). Cheesy rock band of the decade.

5. "Don't You (Forget About Me)," Simple Minds (1985). The theme song for *The Breakfast Club*, and don't you worry—we won't.

The huge hit single from *The Breakfast Club* soundtrack benefited from its sleeve design, which featured an image of the movie's overnight stars in their *Breakfast Club* drag.

6. "Greatest Love of All," Whitney Houston (1986). The ultimate wedding song.

The sleeve art for **Whitney Houston's** "Greatest Love of All" was less interested in evoking the concept of undying love as it was in showing off her then-trendy bobbed weave. Her look of innocence and vulnerability is—as you can see—an early indicator of what a bad actress she'd wind up to be.

Whitney Houston

PEAK YEARS: 1985–1989
CLAIM TO FAME: Power voice, daughter of Cissy and cousin of Dionne Warwick, a wig for every occasion, hotly denied rumors of lesbianism.

She is one of the most successful female singers of all time; depending on your criteria, she's ranked high in all categories, right alongside Madonna, Janet Jackson, Mariah Carey, Connie Francis, Diana Ross, and Aretha Franklin.

Whitney Houston took the mid-80s by storm with her deafening roar of a voice (that bitchy Mille Jackson has claimed it is frequently off-key) and model good looks (in fact, she was a teen model).

Houston never wrote a song, but she made each song she sang her own. It's hard to accept that "Greatest Love of All" was a George Benson tune after hearing Houston belt it. She collected Grammys the way some of us collect CDs.

Houston's personal life was a bore until she was forced to confront persistent rumors that she and a close female friend were lovers. She chalked it up to male jealousy and went on about her business, even marrying singer Bobby Brown, one of the most successful R&B artists of the 80s (whose career promptly plummeted after they exchanged "I do"s and she had his child). Houston and Brown announced their divorce in 1995, then reconciled.

The 90s had even better things in store for Whitney: more number-one hits, including the best-selling single of all

Whitney wigs out. On her record sleeves, in her videos, and at public appearances, Miss Houston never thinks twice about donning a wig. In the late 80s, she switched from the snug, caplike wig used to help her outshine the horse on the sleeve for "Saving All My Love For You" to the *Moonstruck*ish hornet's nest she wore to promote "I Wanna Dance With Somebody (Who Loves Me)" and "Love Will Save the Day."

time ("I Will Always Love You," which was later bested in that category) and a sterling film career (*The Bodyguard, Waiting to Exhale*).

In the end, singing is all Houston is remembered for. Her string of number-one hits (seven in a row) was matched only by that of Mariah Carey, and her staying power has been matched only by Madonna. And remember, Whitney had all of her 80s hits from only two different albums. *Gulp.*

Now if only we could teach Whitney how to *dance.*

ALBUMS:
Whitney Houston (#1) 1985; *Whitney* (#1) 1987.

SINGLES:
"You Give Good Love" (#3), "Saving All My Love for You" (#1), "How Will I Know" (#1) 1985; "Greatest Love of All" (#1) 1986; "I Wanna Dance with Somebody (Who Loves Me)" (#1), "Didn't We Almost Have It All" (#1), "So Emotional" (#1) 1987; "Where Do Broken Hearts Go" (#1), "Love Will Save the Day" (#9), "One Moment in Time" (#5) 1988.

7. "What Have You Done for Me Lately?" Janet Jackson (1986). Bitchy, world-weary R&B from a teenage girl.

8. "Born in the U.S.A.," Bruce Springsteen (1984). An embittered cry of rage that twisted into a patriotic anthem.

9. "Bad," Michael Jackson (1987). Really, *really* bad.

Michael Jackson gets down with his "Bad" self on the sleeve for his obnoxious number-one hit, cultivating the image of a poppy gang, which echoes the video's "Beat It"–like street choreography. The men with him are actually his backup band.

Bruce Springsteen

PEAK YEARS: 1984–1987

CLAIM TO FAME: All-American rock, biceps.

Remember when you first heard of Bruce Springsteen? (Not Rick Spring*field*, Bruce Spring*steen*!) It probably wasn't when he was singing "Hungry Heart" at the beginning of the 80s. Your first memory of Bruce is probably of him and his guitar on stage, belting "Dancing in the Dark" to a crowd and inviting a teenybopper up to dance with him.

With *Born in the U.S.A.*, Bruce Springsteen (with his legendary E Street Band) went from being a critical fave and accomplished songwriter (he even wrote the Pointer Sisters' hit "Fire") to being a national institution. The album cover says it all: Bruce's behind tucked into a pair of faded blue jeans, an American flag as the backdrop. It would be downright un-American not to love the Boss.

Springsteen mined seven—count 'em, seven—big hit singles from his breakthrough album and spent the rest of the decade churning out Top 10 hits and starring in low-key performance videos. His first video "acting" was the incredibly hyped "I'm on Fire," in which he emoted impressively as a lovestruck mechanic, making some Hollywood types wish he had a little bit of Prince in him and would be interested in doing movies. However, Springsteen was too focused on making music and performing live to care about such things.

His love life was interesting, though always underplayed in favor of critical praise for his work. He famously dissed rock photographer Lynn Goldsmith, with whom he'd just broken up, by dragging her on stage at Madison Square Garden in 1979 and introducing her to the crowd as "my ex-girlfriend." He married model Julianne Phillips in 1985 but divorced her before the decade was over, then married Patti Scialfa, who had sung backup for the E Street Band. In the video for "Glory Days," Julianne appears as his wife and Patti performs with Bruce and the band.

By 1987 he was so happy with his group that he was billing them, so that his records read "Bruce Springsteen and the E Street Band," but he left them in 1989 to start the new decade with a fresh perspective.

BRUCE SPRINGSTEEN ALBUMS:
The River (#1) 1980; *Nebraska* (#3) 1982; *Born in the U.S.A.* (#1) 1984; *Bruce Springsteen & the E Street Band Live 1975–1985* (#1) 1986.

BRUCE SPRINGSTEEN SINGLES:
"Hungry Heart" (#5) 1980; "Fade Away" (#20) 1981; "Dancing in the Dark" (#2), "Cover Me" (#7), "Born in the U.S.A." (#9) 1984; "I'm on Fire" (#6), "Glory Days" (#5), "I'm Goin' Down" (#9), "My Hometown" (#6) 1985; "War" (#8) 1986.

BRUCE SPRINGSTEEN & THE E STREET BAND ALBUMS:
Tunnel of Love (#1) 1987.

BRUCE SPRINGSTEEN & THE E STREET BAND SINGLES:
"Brilliant Disguise" (#5), "Tunnel of Love" (#9) 1987; "One Step Up" (#13) 1988.

ALPHABET CITY:

MEMBERS OF THE E STREET BAND:
Roy Bittan (keyboards) 1975–1989
Clarence Clemons (sax) 1973–1989
Danny Federici (keyboards) 1973–1989
Vini Lopez (drums) 1973–1975
David Sancious (keyboards) 1973–1975
Gary Tallent (bass) 1973–1989
"Miami" Steve Van Zandt (guitar) 1975–1989
Max Weinberg (drums) 1975–1989

10. "I Can't Wait," Nu Shooz (1986). One of the most infectious bass lines of the era from a squeaky-clean husband-and-wife team.

11. "Never Gonna Give You Up," Rick Astley (1988). From the hit-making stables of Stock, Aitken & Waterman, a baby-faced singer who crooned like Luther Vandross.

12. "Gloria," Laura Branigan (1982). Melodramatic Europop about a woman on the run, this was the first cover version Laura Branigan recorded, but it certainly wasn't the last.

13. "West End Girls," The Pet Shop Boys (1986). Slinky synth-pop from a duo who would become maestros—Neil Tennant and Chris Lowe. Since Tennant used to be editor of England's main teenybop magazine (*Smash Hits*), these guys knew how to work it.

The Pet Shop Boys did not include any cuddly kittens or other pet shop allusions on their debut record sleeve, instead emphasizing the "boys" part of their name. The photo depicts both boys looking like neo-dandies, and Chris Lowe even sports his trademark Boy London cap.

14. "Der Kommissar," After the Fire (1983). A song lifted from Falco's German-language original, about a menacing Russian policeman.

15. "Rock the Casbah," the Clash (1982). A punk classic, from about three years after the form peaked.

16. "867-5309 (Jenny)," Tommy Tutone (1982). A phone number you can remember more readily than your own.

17. "Don't You Want Me?" The Human League (1982). The granddaddy of New Wave pop.

18. "Our House," Madness (1983). Light-headed Brit froth.

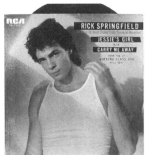

19. "Jessie's Girl," Rick Springfield (1981). With friends like Springfield, how could you ever trust your girl not to fall under his spell?

Rick Springfield may have complained about being mistaken for Bruce Springsteen, but his label didn't mind the company. On the sleeve of his signature hit, he appears in a very Boss-like working man's sleeveless T, pouting like a blue-collar guy down on his luck.

The British Invasion

In 1982, with the chart-topping success of The Human League's "Don't You Want Me?" America's musical tastes suddenly took on a very British flavor, rivaling the so-called British invasion of the early 60s.

Along with The Human League, bands like Wham!, Duran Duran, Culture Club, Eurythmics, Dexy's Midnight Runners, and Tears for Fears invaded radio station playlists.

The music was generally referred to as "New Wave," but what exactly did that *mean*? New Wave seemed to refer to synthesized music with a decidedly cool beat to it, performed by meticulously styled musicians born and working abroad.

Whatever it meant, the second British invasion was very over by the late 80s, when England's biggest acts (including Australian-born Kylie Minogue) could barely dent the American charts.

20. "She-Bop," Cyndi Lauper (1984). Maybe Whitney was wrong about the greatest love of all.

21. "Hot Girls in Love," Loverboy (1983). One of the biggest bands of the 80s singing on a subject that is timeless—hot girls.

Loverboy used shiny leather and stern images to surround themselves with the machismo they knew teenaged boys would admire and teenaged girls would giggle over. Little did they know that everyone would be giggling *at* their campy outfits just a few years later.

22. "Jungle Love," The Time (1985). Sure to start a line dance.

23. "Come Go with Me," Exposé (1987). Miami nice from the all-girl band that helped to popularize the Miami sound.

24. "Hold Me Now," The Thompson Twins (1984). One of the most influential and dance oriented of off-the-wall British pop outfits, this one featuring the odd white chick in a Foreign Legion cap and the black guy with no eyebrows.

As you can see, The Thompson Twins didn't believe in rapid image changes. Alannah kept her platinum hair oddly shaved (sometimes topping it off with a legionnaire's hat) and the band frequently contributed similar poses to their record sleeves, as illustrated by these two big hits.

Miami Amour

The all-Cuban Miami Sound Machine got America's love affair with the Miami sound rolling with their spirited "Conga" in 1985, then followed it up with a series of hits over the next three years, including "Bad Boy" (#8), "Rhythm Is Gonna Get You" (#5), and "1-2-3" (#3). By then, lead singer Gloria Estefan (along with her hubby, producer/percussionist Emilio Estefan) had ditched the band and gone on to become a major diva.

Meanwhile dance music had found itself a new sound to embrace, and whole sections were devoted to Cuban-flavored HiNRG/disco from acts such as Company B ("Fascinated," [#21] 1987), the Cover Girls ("Because of You" [#27]. 1988; "My Heart Skips a Beat" [#38] 1989), and Sweet Sensation ("Sincerely Yours" [#14], "Hooked on You" [#23] 1989).

Company B looked like circus clowns on their self-titled album, a far cry from Gloria Estefan's earthy appeal.

Miami Sound Machine's rhythm got us, but Gloria Estefan was used like a regular *Playboy* bunny to incite lust-addled teenagers to buy these singles.

None of these acts found major, lasting success, but Exposé did. Jeanette Jurado, Gioia Bruno, and Ann Curless formed one of the hottest female acts of the 80s, scoring hit after hit, even though individually they were anonymous. Their first seven songs all hit the Top 10, including—all from 1987—"Come Go with Me" and "Point of No Return," #5 hits that helped define the Miami sound, and power ballads "Let Me Be the One" (#7) and "Seasons Change" (#1). They lost steam by the early 90s but, after replacing Gioia, continued with lesser hits.

The Miami Sound hasn't survived at the top of the charts, making these hits sound all the more distinctly mid- to late 80s.

Exposé had a number-one hit with their ballad "Seasons Change," the sleeve of which was a subdued, hand-colored image that conveniently used Gioia's arm to create the illusion of a tiny waist for Jeanette (far left).

25. "Somebody's Watching Me," Rockwell (1984). Paranoia and the worst voice of the 80s.

26. "Touch Me (I Want Your Body)," Samantha Fox (1986). Everyone's favorite shameless hussy.

Sam Fox's body was the key to marketing her "Touch Me (I Want Your Body)." She was shown on the record in shorts cut so high the crotch probably tickled her belly button, and a tiny T-shirt that left her unnaturally enormous breasts free to droop invitingly. To cinch the sale, limited copies of the single folded out into a poster. Instant Top-5 hit."

27. "Every Breath You Take," The Police (1983). Kind of like Sting meets Lionel Richie.

28. "Walking on Sunshine," Katrina and the Waves (1985). The feel-good song of the 80s.

29. "Two of Hearts," Stacey Q (1986). Cyndi Lauper wannabe with Jody Watley fashion sense. This song stayed on playlists for months thanks to its catchy, stuttered, "I-I-I-I-I."

Stacey Q imitated Cyndi Lauper's baby punk looks with her ratted hair, but also portrayed herself as a glamorous model, wearing wacky fashions and posing like she was hawking Versace, as illustrated by an array of her hit records.

Twenty-five Best Band Names of the 80s

1. Kajagoogoo
2. Animotion
3. Bananarama
4. The Blow Monkeys
5. Fine Young Cannibals
6. A Flock of Seagulls
7. Talk Talk
8. Fun Boy Three
9. Golden Earring
10. Orchestral Manoeuvres in the Dark
11. Pretty Poison
12. Swing Out Sister
13. Frankie Goes to Hollywood
14. Band Aid
15. The Fabulous Thunderbirds
16. Oingo Boingo
17. Johnny Hates Jazz
18. Spandau Ballet
19. Romeo Void
20. Sigue Sigue Sputnik
21. Haircut One Hundred
22. Curiosity Killed the Cat
23. Aztec Camera
24. Transvision Vamp
25. Violent Femmes

30. "Electric Avenue," Eddy Grant (1983). Reggae rears its dreadlocked head.

> "I like to jar people occasionally—musically surprise them." —Daryl Hall, 1985

31. "Maneater," Hall and Oates (1982). The biggest duo of the 80s. No, *really*.

32. "(I Just) Died In Your Arms Tonight," The Cutting Crew (1987). White trash angst.

33. "Shattered Dreams," Johnny Hates Jazz (1988). How does Johnny feel about pop?

In stark contrast to their punk rock–sounding name, Johnny Hates Jazz presented themselves on this sleeve as neo-crooners, slick, blue-eyed soulmeisters who look like they might actually love jazz.

34. "Rumors," The Timex Social Club (1986). An antirumor song was never so gossipy—this one dishes Tina Turner and Michael Jackson.

35. "I Beg Your Pardon," Kon Kan (1989). Sampling goes mainstream.

36. "Fresh," Kool and the Gang (1985). Introducing the term "fresh," meaning "good."

37. "Valley Girl," Frank Zappa (1982). The documentation of the archetype of the 80s. Like, fer sher.

Without dressing up or *trying* to look the part, Moon Unit Zappa embodied the classic Valley Girl type on the sleeve of her New Wave duet with her father Frank.

New Order
New Forms Postdisco

In the wake of disco, several similar forms emerged and distinguished themselves in the 80s.

Most dominant was rap, the most important mass culture musical movement of the 80s. After years of underground popularity among urban black practitioners, rap crossed over big time, so that by the end of the 80s it was incorporated in some form into a majority of popular songs.

Rapping is speak-singing, chanting rhythmically over a killer groove. You don't have to be able to carry a tune to rap, but you'd better have rhythm.

The first rap song to break the Top 40 was the Sugarhill Gang's 1980 hit "Rapper's Delight." They rapped over an instrumental track of Chic's 1979 hit "Good Times," a common practice that would make for interesting legal issues as the decade rolled along. The first rap song to hit number one was, ironically, by a white, blond woman: Debbie Harry and her band Blondie hit the mark with 1981's "Rapture." Grandmaster Flash and Run-D.M.C. were rap's pop pioneers, but they soon gave way to a flood of even bigger acts (Public Enemy, L.L. Cool J, Salt 'N Pepa, and so on).

By the late 80s it was routine for nonrap songs to have rap interludes.

Scratching was also popular, as in the phrase "rappin' and scratchin.'" To scratch was to run the record needle across an album, creating a jarring series of sounds to be incorporated into or work against a song's rhythm. Scratching reached its nadir with Chaka Khan's "I Feel for You" (1984), which featured both an extended rap by Grandmaster Melle Mel and copious scratching. The fad ended within two years of that hit, and once CDs became the norm, scratching seemed hopelessly dated.

Replacing disco was a very close cousin, house music. House is heavily repetitive disco-type dance music that blends Chicago black funk with Eurobeats. The term originated with Chicago's club Wherehouse, where it was invented (but don't tell London that; they think *they* invented it). It has survived in modified forms through the 90s, from deep house (gospel tinged) to acid house (psychedelic, with listeners urged to drop acid while dancing) to industrial to techno and other only slightly different musical types. Face it: Disco never died, it just moved to the house next door under an assumed name.

Rap and house started a new craze in music: sampling. To sample is to electronically capture a piece of audio (either music or lyrics or just noise) and incorporate it into a track. "Me So Horny" (1988) by 2 Live Crew brought sampling to the fore with its shocking and perversely brilliant theft of a line of dialogue from a Vietnamese prostitute in Stanley Kubrick's film *Full Metal Jacket* (1987). From there it seemed every new dance song contained samples.

Similar to house, HiNRG was a nebulous late 80s term meant to encompass pop music with many beats per minute (bpm), soft alternative music (Depeche Mode, the Cure), and songs that weren't too disco, too "housey" (like "Theme from S'Express," S'Express 1988) or too "pat" (like "Bad," Michael Jackson 1987). Examples of HiNRG tunes are "Chains of Love," Erasure (1988), "The Rumour," Olivia Newton-John (1988), and "Sweet and Low," Deborah Harry (1989). It was yet another 80s attempt to disguise evolved disco as something else, like the neutral term "dance music."

38. "Major Tom (Coming Home)," Peter Schilling (1983). An unauthorized sequel to Bowie's 70s "Space Oddity."

39. "Walk This Way," Run-D.M.C. (1986). The first major rap hit by rap's founding fathers, featuring a career-reviving appearance by Aerosmith.

40. "Abracadabra," The Steve Miller Band (1982). Whips crackin' at the refrain.

41. "Jump (for My Love)," The Pointer Sisters (1984). Led to leapfrog on dance floors everywhere.

42. "Sister Christian," Night Ranger (1984). Mall rock.

43. "Islands in the Stream," Dolly Parton and Kenny Rogers (1983). The best pair in country. And Kenny Rogers, too!

44. "Bette Davis Eyes," Kim Carnes (1980). The real Bette Davis absolutely adored this witchy song about a heartless woman with enormous eyes.

Bette Davis eyes and Kim Carnes hair—a deadly combination. Kim Carnes could have opted for a classic Bette Davis still to promote her single, but she chose an image that reminded us who was in charge, a haunted portrait of herself.

45. "Cum on Feel the Noize," Quiet Riot (1983). Party hardy.

46. "Caribbean Queen," Billy Ocean (1984). He mispronounces the title and still goes to number one.

47. "Pump Up the Volume," M/A/R/R/S (1988). Urban dance rap . . . made by British boys.

Free Samples
Most Frequently Sampled Sounds in House Music

1. Alison Moyet's throaty laugh from Yazoo's "Situation."

2. Karen Finley's outraged "Drop that ghetto-blaster!"

3. "House music all night long, house music all night long."

4. "I am ready, and I am out the door."

5. High-pitched "whoo!" followed by baritone "yeah!" ad infinitum.

6. "Get on down and *party*."

7. Girly-voiced, "The music just *turns me on*."

8. "The roof, the roof, the roof is on fire!"

9. Sirens.

10. Porn movie moans.

Heavy Metal
It's Not Just for Burnouts Anymore

In the ten years since the trailblazing debut of Led Zeppelin and the advent of "heavy metal," the form had almost disappeared until a slew of enterprising 80s bands, unafraid to wear makeup (since they grew up listening to Kiss and since Duran Duran made it cool anyway) chalked up a series of short-lived success stories.

Along with metal stars Quiet Riot and the Scorpions, Mötley Crüe blazed a trail of glory through the 80s. The Crüe featured a colorfully trashy lineup including Vince Neil on lead vocals, Tommy Lee on drums, Nikki Sixx on bass, and Mick Mars on guitar. Neil was involved in a drunk-driving accident that killed another rocker and later married a mud wrestler. Lee married 80s *Dynasty* vixen Heather Locklear, divorced her, and married 90s *Baywatch* vixen Pamela Anderson—do you sense a pattern? Nikki Sixx married a *Playboy* Playmate. Mars kept his nose clean. They reimmortalized "Smokin' in the Boys Room" in 1985, and mostly sang about babes. Neil took off in the early 90s, not a moment too soon, since the Crüe just weren't what they used to be.

Poison was sort of a cut-rate Mötley Crüe, which is hard to imagine, made up of lead singer Bret Michaels, Bobby Dall (bass), Rikki Rocket (drums), and C. C. DeVille (guitar). Their first hit, 1987's "Talk Dirty to Me," raised shameless metal to new heights and helped propel their *Look What the Cat Dragged In* album to the upper reaches of the charts. Apparently these guys never saw the humor in Rob Reiner's movie *This Is Spinal Tap*.

48. "Hold On to the Nights," Richard Marx (1988). Whiny, infectious power ballad sung by the man who was the absolute, no-holds-barred, number-one holder of the title Hair from Hell.

49. "Shout," Tears for Fears (1985). A stirring tune about the joys of primal scream therapy.

50. "Love Will Tear Us Apart," Joy Division (1980). The influential single from the group that would become New Order, popular just before the group's original lead singer hanged himself.

51. "Hurts So Good," John Cougar (1982). The pleasure of pain.

Alternative Nation

It was a cold day in hell if you heard Siouxsie and the Banshees being played on Top 40 radio in the 80s.

With the advent of New Wave came a darker form that blended punk into the synthetic beats. This sort of music—basically, anything even mildly unusual that didn't quite make it on Top 40 radio and that was adored by kids wearing black—became classified under the umbrella term "alternative music." Alternative to what, we're not sure. I mean, do you really think it's an either/or proposition? Did Siouxsie fans necessarily reject the Police, Prince, or Eurythmics?

Regardless, alternative music flourished despite missing the mark with the masses. Mostly British bands like Joy Division/New Order, Depeche Mode, the Morrissey-driven Smiths, and The Cure built enormous subpop followings that made them top album acts, concert draws, and—by the early 90s—late-blooming Top 40 success stories.

Joy Division defined alternative dance music with its revolutionary 1980 single "Love Will Tear Us Apart," which set both the staccato, midtempo beat and wildly melancholy timbre that would characterize alternative music in the 80s. The fact that their lead singer, Ian Curtis, had committed suicide just before the single peaked in England only added to the song's poignancy. The fact that the song was almost unheard in the United States until years later just made it cooler to American alternative fans.

NEW

ORDER
—
SUBSTANCE
1987

To stress the "substance" message, New Order's up-till-then greatest hits package was shipped in a barren white sleeve with imposing black titles.

After Curtis's suicide, Joy Division (which had once been called Warsaw) changed its name to New Order and created several extremely influential albums full of cunning electrobeats, including *Substance 1987,* an anthology of their work that helped introduce them to increasingly bigger audiences stateside. They had hits in Britain with singles such as "Blue Monday" (1983, remixed and reissued in 1988 and 1995), "True Faith" (1987), and "Fine Time" (1988), all of which were the epitome of cool for American college types. For some inexplicable reason, fraternity parties embraced New Order; though the title of New Order's 1986 album was *Brotherhood,* it's unlikely that the affection was mutual.

Sort of like New Order with hormones and even bleaker, the four-man band Depeche Mode made much stronger inroads into the masses. With lead singer David Gahan's bone-chilling baritone and Martin Gore's fragile, aggressively provocative lyrics, Depeche Mode forged a career out of adolescent tears. From 1981's *Speak and Spell,* with their parallel to "Love Will Tear Us Apart" ("New Life"), Depeche Mode ("fashion in a hurry" or "fast fashion" in French) has mined depression and edgy moroseness to fill its albums with songs that only the poppier alternative types went for—and they were legion.

Depeche Mode went the opposite route from New Order's near-anonymous album sleeves, preferring to show themselves in all their gothic glory, complete with makeup and the all-important hairstyling.

Depeche Mode offered the United States a collection of their earlier work by issuing *Catching Up With Depeche Mode* (1985), a must-have 80s album for its shameless "Blasphemous Rumours" (about a sixteen-year-old girl who slashes her wrists). They had their first U.S. hit with "People Are People," a plaintive request for humanity that foreshadowed Rodney King's "Can't we all get along?" with its confession that the band can't understand what makes a man hate another man.

With *Music for the Masses* (1987), DM explored S/M with "Master and Servant," a major club hit that sewed up their college following so tightly that the arrival of their 1990 *Violator* album had them filling huge concert halls and landing three singles in the Top 40. They were—and are—still referred to as "alternative."

The Cure was another top alternative act, recognizable for lead singer Robert Smith's Joan Crawford lipstick and Don King hairdo and for his strangely appealing caterwauling singing voice. Their first album, in 1980, *Boys Don't Cry* (and the title track), established them as major album artists in the United Kingdom, and their despairing singles made them—like Depeche Mode—grist for the critics and hugely popular among universally despairing Brit teens.

Like Depeche Mode before them and New Order after, The Cure, too, used an early anthology to alert America to their existence: *Standing on a Beach* (1986). It worked. Their next, *Kiss Me Kiss Me Kiss Me,* was supported by a stadium tour that all the cool kids went to, if only to sing along to "Just Like Heaven." That tour made use of elaborate projected images, a trend that was soon essential for a successfully arty stage show in the late 80s.

**"If I hear Morrissey's down or depressed, I'll send him a bunch of flowers."
—Pete Burns of Dead or Alive, who must've gone bankrupt buying pansies, 1986**

52. "Girl, You Know It's True," Milli Vanilli (1989). False.

53. "Eye of the Tiger," Survivor (1982). The *Rocky* road to love.

54. "Party All the Time," Eddie Murphy (1985). That comedian sure sings funny.

55. "The Kids in America," Kim Wilde (1982). By a kid in England.

56. "Hangin' Tough," New Kids on the Block (1989). Tough talk.

57. "I Just Called to Say I Love You," Stevie Wonder (1984). Though the biggest hit of his career, from the film *The Woman in Red*, this annoying cotton candy was definitely a wrong number.

This One's for the Children

As Mötley Crüe sang in 1987, there's nothing like "Girls, Girls, Girls," and the 80s saw a preponderance of underage girl singers. Just as prominent were gaggles of boy wonders making their first billion before age twenty-one...or age eighteen...or...

Ladies first.

Aside from Queen Janet, the eldest and most successful of the girls was Paula Abdul, who was twenty-two when she had her first hit, one of the most perfect singles of the 80s, "Straight Up" (1988). This was after "Knocked Out" and "It's Just the Way That You Love Me" had failed as singles, so Paula had been giving up hope. She had nothing to worry about; the latter was even rereleased and propelled into hit status by her rising star. A former Laker cheerleader and choreographer for the Jacksons' monumental—and monumentally disastrous—*Victory* tour and for Janet Jackson, Paula is visible in Janet's "Nasty" video. After three of her first four hits landed at number one by the end of 1989, Paula had locked up the title of biggest girl sensation of the 80s, and just in the nick of time.

Even younger and more innocent was Debbie Gibson, the blond sixteen-year-old whose first hit was "Only in My Dreams" in 1987. Her debut album, *Out of the Blue,* was made up of material she'd written and composed herself, a fact that didn't particularly impress in light of "Shake Your Love." But she also came up with knockout ballads such as "Foolish Beat" (1988; a shameless ode to Wham!'s "Careless Whisper") and "Lost in Your Eyes" (1989) and ended the decade on *seemingly* strong legs. Hint: She hasn't gone anywhere since.

Debbie Gibson became a star out of the blue. Check out the progression on her single sleeves, from pre-pubescent to tasteful teen to provocative, mysterious woman. Her label wanted her to have an expanded adult contemporary market.

Debbie's fragrance, Electric Youth, was promoted with cheesy neon T-shirts that were sold alongside the perfume itself. The funky design seemed so deliberately tacky that many people mistook them for Sonic Youth concert T-shirts.

Tiffany was the white-trash Debbie Gibson, an auburn-haired, Chipmunk-sounding singer famous for touring malls in the late 80s. Laugh if you will, but it paid off for a while. Her remake of Tommy James and the Shondells' "I Think We're Alone Now" and sickly sweet ballad "Could've Been" were huge hits, as was her remake of the Beatles' (!) "I Saw Her Standing There," which she phallusized into "I Saw *Him* Standing There" (1988). Her career disintegrated at the end of the decade amid legal wrangling with her mother.

The first of the all-boy groups of the 80s was Menudo, an irresistible pack of ankle biters all under the age of sixteen (which is the translation of the group's Spanish name). These bubbly Latin guys broke hearts across the Spanish-speaking world, failing to hit it big with non-Spanish-speaking teens in America. They were, nevertheless, an enormous phenomenon, selling millions of singles.

Nonetheless, it was Menudo and the Jackson 5 that black producer/entrepreneur Maurice Starr had in mind when he put together his first all-boy music group, New Edition, in 1982. New Edition were Ricky Bell, Michael Bivins, Ronald DeVoe (the three of whom formed the hugely popular Bell Biv DeVoe in 1990), Bobby Brown, Ralph Tresvant, and Brown replacement Johnny Gill. Brown, Gill, and Tresvant (in order of relative success) all had enormous solo careers. Obviously Starr knew what he was doing.

Boston-based New Edition immediately won over a huge black audience and before long had also cracked into a crossover pop audience with their smash "Cool It Now" (1984). After a few smaller hits, the group disbanded and went on to bigger and better things on their own.

Meanwhile Starr decided that instead of forming a black group and then struggling for crossover appeal, why not form a white group and go for the big bucks right away? The fact that the resulting group, New Kids on the

Block, out sold the arguably more talented New Edition is enough to make even the most jaded cynic cluck his tongue.

New Kids on the Block became a merchandising smorgasbord, as illustrated by this, their official board game. Most of their fans bought it if only for the photos used as game pieces.

New Kids on the Block—also five cute boys, also from Boston—became one of the biggest-selling acts in pop history in the late 80s. Formed in 1984 by Starr, they had to chill until New Edition was laid to rest before Starr could devote his full attention to grooming them. *Hangin' Tough,* their first hit album (the second they recorded), sold over eight million copies in the States alone, propelled by powerhouse singles like "Please Don't Go Girl," "You Got It (the Right Stuff)," "I'll Be Loving You (Forever)," and the mock-rock title track. Like Duran

Duran before them, their second album was so big that it led to a resurgence of sales in a first, unnoticed album.

Characterized by lead singer Jordan's strained falsetto balanced with Donnie's rapping (he was the sole tough cookie in a group of animal crackers), the group gained a teenage following as devoted as Beatles fans, who purchased New Kids on the Block merchandise for two solid years.

Rather than allow the Kids to develop musically, Starr cashed in, pushing the release of a Christmas album (which are always unhip) for the end of 1989.

By the time their next album was released in 1990, the Kids were losing steam. By 1994 they had changed their name (to NKOTB), tried their hand at misogynist rap songs ("Dirty Dawg"), and broken up. Aside from budding producer Donnie Wahlberg—older bro of early 90s flash-in-the-pan Marky Mark—and accomplished singer Joe, these kids seem far less likely than New Edition to have future hits.

Yet another teen sensation was The Jets, a group of Samoan siblings who harmonized their way into the Top 40 with hits like "Crush on You." When they attempted to mature their image—as on the cover of "Sending All My Love," which featured the girls in gowns and the boys in tuxes or suits—The Jets' Top 40 status crashed.

See! Hear!
Ten Must-Have Soundtracks of the 80s

The 80s yielded some of the best-selling and most fondly remembered movie soundtracks of all time. This was the decade where the music industry finally realized that entire cool albums could be created as soundtracks for movies they have no connection to. Also, it became unthinkable to plan a youth-oriented film that didn't lend itself to a killer soundtrack. Some films—*Fame* (1980), *Flashdance* (1983), *Footloose* (1984), *Dirty Dancing* (1987)—seem to have been created as excuses for soundtracks.

1. *Purple Rain* (1984). *The soundtrack of the 80s, from a time when we all thought Prince was as cool as *he* thinks he is and when his movie career seemed almost as promising as Madonna's. This was a near perfect album for many, and all the rest of us bought it anyway. Aside from the Jimi Hendrix–y title track, it spawned the number-one hits "When Doves Cry," "Let's Go Crazy," "I Would Die 4 U," and the Apollonia duet "Take Me with U." That's five—count 'em, five—big hits from the same soundtrack, and he could've

released more if he hadn't had about sixty-five other albums waiting to be released.

2. *Beverly Hills Cop* (1985). Remember when Eddie Murphy was funny? This soundtrack to his funniest and best movie was packed with hits, including Patti LaBelle's scorching "New Attitude," Glenn Frey's "The Heat Is On," the Pointer Sisters hit "Neutron Dance," and the ultimate 80s theme: the instrumental "Axel F" by Harold Faltermeyer.

3. *Footloose* (1984). Everyone had a copy of this hit machine, whether for Kenny Loggins's title track, Deniece Williams's pre-Abdulian "Let's Hear It for the Boy," the cheesy Ann Wilson (Heart)/Mike Reno (Loverboy) duet "Almost Paradise," or Bonnie Tyler's "Holding Out for a Hero."

4. *Flashdance* (1983). Sort of like *Fame II,* yet another HiNRG fun meal with Irene Cara's "Flashdance . . . What a Feeling" and Michael Sembello's frenetic "Maniac." This even has a Donna Summer song, "Romeo," that might have kept her going a bit stronger in her postdisco period had it been released.

5. *Valley Girl* (1982). A totally, like, tubular album of songs by bands such as Culture Club, and one of the most valuable movie soundtracks of the decade since it went out of print almost instantly and wasn't available on CD for another thirteen years.

6. *Miami Vice* (1985). A testament to the once hot following of that very 80s TV show, this soundtrack became a sensation in 1985, fueled by Jan Hammer's enigmatic instrumental theme and Glenn Frey's atmospheric "You Belong to the City." This was selling for five cents in rummage sales across the country by 1989.

7. *Top Gun* (1986). Another Kenny Loggins smash, "Danger Zone," helped propel this collection to the top, that and an Oscar-winning ballad by Berlin, "Take My Breath Away." After "Sex" it was quite a shock to see Terri Nunn crooning on a runway, but *hey*—we're easy.

Two of the biggest hits from the *Top Gun* soundtrack illustrate how strongly the singles were tied together to ensure a year of hits. The artists were photographed with the same serious expression the film's star Tom Cruise wore in many print ads, and the film's logo was repeated in exactly the same position.

8. *Dirty Dancing* (1987). Mellow collection of romantic songs tied to the most romantic film of the decade. "(I've Had) The Time of My Life" by Bill Medley and Jennifer Warnes started the ball rolling, followed in rapid succession by Eric Carmen's "Hungry Eyes" (his biggest hit in ten years) and even lead actor Patrick Swayze's "She's Like the Wind." The big joke was that if she was like the wind, did that mean she blew all day long?

9. *The Big Chill* (1983). An albumful of 60s hits to accompany the biggest baby boomer flick of the decade. This made converts of lots of 80s teens, who later gave the Beatles another Top 40 hit when "Twist and Shout" was released from the *Ferris Bueller's Day Off* soundtrack in 1986.

10. *True Stories* (1986). "Wild Wild Life" came from this hallowed place, an enigmatic album of the songs that appeared in the Talking Heads' experimental film of the same title. You had to have this in your collection if you expected to get into a decent college.

58. "Don't You Want Me?" Jody Watley (1987). The former Shalamar side-bar and aspiring solo diva sported hoop earrings big enough for Bengal tigers to leap through.

Jody Watley repopularized enormous hoop earrings with her appearance in the video for "Don't You Want Me?" and on the single's record sleeve. But buying the earrings didn't guarantee you the miniscule waist and cheek bones for days.

59. "Blue Monday," New Order (1985/1988). No frathouse would be complete without it, much to New Order's eternal shame.

60. "Edge of Seventeen (Just Like the White Winged Dove)," Stevie Nicks (1982). You scratch your throat just listening to her itchy emoting.

61. "Africa," Toto (1982). Makes that continent seem as appealing as a Disney ride.

62. "Elvira," The Oak Ridge Boys (1981). Before Cassandra Petersen coopted "Vampira" and became "Elvira, Mistress of the Dark," the Oak Ridge Boys sang this, one of the biggest country crossover hits of the decade.

63. "Back on the Chain Gang," The Pretenders (1983). Complete with the rhythmic grunts of a prison chain gang.

64. "The Sweetest Taboo," Sade (1985). Is it interracial love she's singing about? Or a specific sex act? She could sing about teddy bears and make it sound hot.

65. "Nobody," Sylvia (1982). The most labored double entendre of all time (but it totally works), about a woman who knows her lover is cheating because whenever he gets off the phone, she asks who he was talking to and he replies, "Nobody."

66. "The Politics of Dancing," Re-Flex (1984). Re-Flex for president!

67. "Muscles," Diana Ross (1982). Michael Jackson wrote this ode to…his snake, Muscles. What did you think this was about?

68. "Push It," Salt 'N Pepa (1987). Breaking new ground in female rap.

69. "Rock You Like a Hurricane," The Scorpions (1984). The heaviest and hottest of metal.

70. "Perfect Way," Scritti Politti (1985). Their name may mean "political writing," but there's nothing political about this perfect piece of pop confection.

71. "Tell It to My Heart," Taylor Dayne (1987). The cater-wauling diva from hell.

Unrecognizable today as a buxom blonde, Taylor Dayne began her career as a precociously tressed femme fatale and made sure that her killer crimp was prominently featured on all her records. Why, Taylor? Don't you wish you'd gone with a nice smile?

72. "Oh, L'Amour," Erasure (1986). The first single of one of England's most revered dance duos, who arose from the ashes of Yazoo.

73. "We Don't Have to Take Our Clothes Off," Jermaine Stewart (1986). A direct reference to AIDS, though the singer *does* suggest that cherry wine is essential to having fun.

74. "Mr. Roboto," Styx (1983). Japan and technophobia.

75. "Don't Forget Me (When I'm Gone)," Glass Tiger (1986). A blatant rip-off of "Don't You (Forget About Me)," but this was nonetheless a great choice for a prom theme.

Glass Tiger had dreams of becoming major teen idols, so were photographed under optimal lighting conditions and posed just so perfectly that they seem about to break on the sleeve of their Simple Minds–influenced "Don't Forget Me (When I'm Gone)" single.

76. "Rapper's Delight," the Sugarhill Gang (1980). The very first rap Top 40 hit.

77. "With Or Without You," U2 (1987). The rock ballad that confirmed U2 as the world's greatest rock and roll band.

U2er The Edge was the only band member shown on the cover of the band's breakthrough number-one song "With or Without You," illustrating the song's solitary aura.

78. "A Girl in Trouble (Is a Temporary Thing)," Romeo Void (1984). Classic one-hit wonder that's a scary tale of the girl most likely to stab you in the back.

79. "Owner of a Lonely Heart," Yes (1983). Dinosaur rock outfit Yes returns in style with the biggest hit of their career.

80. "Sweet Child O' Mine," Guns n' Roses (1988). He sounds like Janis Joplin and looks like a bum. He's Axl Rose, heir to the rockin' throne vacated by Led Zeppelin's Robert Plant.

Once Is Certainly Enough
One-Hit Wonders

The 80s rival any other decade for the sheer number of artists to have one and only one Top 40 hit in America.

How exactly does one become a one-hit wonder? It seems almost impossible that an act could excite us enough to entice us into running out and buying their bloody single, then leave us cold with all of their successive releases.

1. Big Country, "In a Big Country" (1983). Just like rappers, this Scottish band plugged their own name in their hit.

2. Autograph, "Turn Up the Radio" (1985). Heavy-metal band that seemed to be urging us to turn up the radio so we could hear their only hit while it lasted.

3. Philip Bailey (with Phil Collins), "Easy Lover" (1984). The former lead singer for Earth, Wind & Fire had a hard time recharting after this big easy.

4. Buckner and Garcia, "Pac-Man Fever" (1982). At the height of the Pac-Man craze, anything related to the munching yellow dot would sell. Here's proof.

5. The Breakfast Club, "Right on Track" (1987). Named not for the quintessential 80s film but for the band's ten-dency to meet and discuss ideas over breakfast. Madonna used to be a member and was probably kicking herself that she missed out on this number-seven smash. . . .

6. Charlene, "I've Never Been to Me" (1982). Weirdly moralistic song that tells women to marry and have children to fulfill themselves. This advice comes from a great big slut (not Charlene, but the singer in the song) who also relates wild adventures like bedding preacher men, screwing on yachts, and making love in broad daylight. A minor hit in the 70s first, it was re-released in 1982, then revived again on the soundtrack to *The Adventures of Priscilla, Queen of the Desert* in 1994.

7. Musical Youth, "Pass the Dutchie" (1983). British kids who changed the song from "Pass the Kouchie," which refers to marijuana. A dutchie is also a pot, but a cooking pot.

8. Kate Bush, "Running Up That Hill" (1985). One of England's biggest stars only had one hit in America. There's no telling why we picked this song over all of her other equally compelling material, but one reason may be its video, which is a modern dance showcase.

9. Double, "The Captain of Her Heart" (1986). Mind-numbingly lilting ballad sung phonetically by Swedes. Kill me now.

10. General Public, "Tenderness" (1985). Salt-and-pepper duo singing a saccharine song about a spicy relationship that requires a pinch of sugar. I need a glass of water.

11. Regina, "Baby Love" (1986). Diana Ross would've been rolling in her grave if she were dead, because this "Baby Love" sounded strictly Madonna.

12. Enya, "Orinoco Flow (Sail Away)" (1989). The most New Age–y song ever to receive Top 40 airplay. The best song ever written about the tides and, like, how they affect you.

13. Laid Back, "White Horse" (1984). This Danish group had an unlikely hit with club bait "White Horse," a song with very few words that still managed to be about the joys of cocaine.

14. Levert, "Casanova" (1987). This smooth R&B song by the progeny of the O'Jays was their only big bang.

15. Tracy Chapman, "Fast Car" (1988). This black folkie's debut was much ballyhooed, but after collecting that cursed Best New Artist Grammy, she took off in the fastest of all cars to obscurity. Until 1996!

16. Mary Jane Girls, "In My House" (1985). Funky all-girl studio group formed by Rick James. They were styled as hookers, and the house they're singing about is not a home.

17. Bobby McFerrin, "Don't Worry, Be Happy" (1988). Annoying song made up entirely of sounds emitting from McFerrin's mouth with vapid message set to a Caribbean beat. This guy dominated that year's Grammy Awards, then disappeared off the face of the Earth.

18. Alison Moyet, "Invisible" (1985). Hefty lead singer from early 80s dance scions Yazoo had only this minor hit here. The title is ironic because she definitely is *not* invisible.

19. Gloria Loring/Carl Anderson, "Friends and Lovers" (1986). Soap star dabbles in pop music and scores huge hit. This smarmy song would have us believe that friends can become lovers without damaging their friendship. Lots of bitter, friendless folks and their ex-lovers refused to make any of her ensuing songs into hits.

20. Gregory Abbott, "Shake You Down" (1986). Slick soul singer with reptilian eyes and *Miami Vice* wardrobe had a huge hit with his polite invitation to knock boots.

The influence of *Miami Vice* was clear on Gregory Abbott's "Shake You Down" pose. He was presenting himself as a smoothie, and copying Philip Michael Thomas's look helped that image along nicely. For the duration of his only Top 40 hit.

Twelve Essential Dance Singles of the 80s

1. "Physical," Olivia Newton-John (1981). Get off it—*everyone* bought this one. Whole roller rinks came and went during the ten weeks this thing topped *Billboard*'s charts. What a way to ring in the 80s! This is going to be the best decade ever!

Besides the biggest hit of her career ("Physical"), Olivia Newton-John had successes in the early 80s with songs like "Make a Move on Me," "Twist of Fate," and "Heart Attack," sampling as many images as possible on these sleeves. She appears as the contemporary seductress, the rock 'n roller ... even as James Dean!

2. "Angel/Into the Groove," Madonna (1985). Sneaky Madonna made you buy the queerball "Angel" remix (who needs to hear an audience chanting her name as the bass?) in order to get ahold of the B-side.

3. "Tainted Love," Soft Cell (1982). You resisted buying this one (too out there), but you eventually took the plunge, never realizing the song segues into a cover of "Where Did Our Love Go?" or that you'd play this twelve-incher until your turntable died.

4. "True Faith," New Order (1987). Like the song's title, the music was an almost religious experience on the dance floor, a baptism in perfectly spaced synth beats.

The Ultimate Album of the 80s

Thriller, **Michael Jackson (1982).** Everybody—I mean *everybody*—had a copy of this classic piece of pop pre-*HIStory.* The album lived up to its title in execution (the production made this a nonstop joyride of poppy R&B) and in effect: all the kids went crazy for this hit machine, and at least half of them fell in love with the soft-spoken black figure on the cover. Critics tripped over themselves proclaiming this one of the best pop albums ever, and Jacko won more Grammys in one night than most of his rivals could expect to win in their entire careers.

5. "Wake Me up Before You Go-Go," Wham! (1984). Choose Wham!!

6. "You Spin Me Round (Like a Record)," Dead or Alive (1985). No idea if that was a guy or a girl, but *hey.*

> "On reflection, I think the 80s were a horrible—an *abysmal*—time."
> —Pete Burns of Dead or Alive, 1995

7. "Call Me," Blondie (1980). Your older brother used to like this weird, punkish band, but then suddenly you were buying their latest *disco* single. Seeing Richard Gere's butt in the movie this came from (*American Gigolo*) only helped make this one of those songs even your folks unwilling-ly knew all the words to.

> "I was adopted when I was three months old through an agency (my first agent)."
> —Deborah Harry, 1982

8. "Let the Music Play," Shannon (1983). Brilliant ode to dance music with a sweet whip effect, but let's hope she didn't quit her day job.

9. "Fascinated," Company B (1987). Your mom: "*What* did that girl just sing? She's fascinated by your '*love toy*'?" You: "Oh, *Mother!*"

10. "The Pleasure Principle," Janet Jackson (1987). Only Janet could stretch "principle" into nine syllables.

11. "I Wonder If I Take You Home," Lisa Lisa and Cult Jam with Full Force (1985). How many people does it take to make a song, anyway?

Lisa Lisa and Cult Jam (sorry, no Full Force pictured!) liked to take the personal approach on their records. As shown here, Lisa Lisa typically donned a leather jacket or another simple outfit and presented herself as she was—a pretty homegirl with more spunk than attitude.

12. "The Safety Dance," Men Without Hats (1983). Alienating people who can't dance . . . what a concept!

Ten Albums You Threw Out in Embarrassment in 1990 That You'd Give Anything to Have Back

1. *Colour by Numbers,* Culture Club (1983). All the cooler for its British spelling of the word "color" and for the fact that it was a virtual drag queen singing songs even your dad couldn't help humming.

2. *Rebel Yell,* Billy Idol (1984). From the rockin' rebellion of the title track to the moony Bing Crosby crooning on "Eyes Without a Face," a great 80s album that still sounds good.

3. *Falco 3,* Falco (1986). Not just a novelty album, though the major hit—"Rock Me Amadeus"—was a commercially sound response to the hit film *Amadeus.*

4. *Hunting High and Low,* a-ha (1985). High drama and higher cheekbones.

The Aid-ies

Look at all the friendship Dionne Warwick and her close, close friends are displaying on this record sleeve. You'd almost believe that Elton, Stevie, and Gladys—who received only the credit "& Friends"—are thrilled about being second banana to their musical inferior. But it was all for a good cause—AIDS.

The 80s are frequently lambasted as the age of greed, yet millions of dollars were raised from a variety of charitable efforts in the music industry, from Dionne Warwick's single "That's What Friends Are For" (1985), which raised money for AIDS, to an array of charitable megaconcerts.

The biggest event was Live Aid (July 13, 1985), a bicontinental rock extravaganza featuring most of the biggest music stars on the planet, performing to raise $40 million to combat the famine in Ethiopia. Over 1.5 billion people around the world watched, and it seemed every major recording artist appeared. Actually, some had passed on the opportunity—including Huey Lewis and the News—fearing that the money raised might not make it to those in need. In fact, technical difficulties and the uncooperative government of Ethiopia *did* hinder a large part of the relief effort.

Previously, the singles "Do They Know It's Christmas?" (1984) and "We Are the World" (1985) had also been released to aid the hungry of Ethiopia, and the single "Dancing in the Street"—a charged duet by David Bowie and Mick Jagger—was debuted at Live Aid.

This bright idea, originated by Live Aid organizer and Boomtown Rats lead singer Bob Geldof, inspired other efforts, including Artists United Against Apartheid (a call to avoid performing in racially segregated South Africa), Northern Lights (the Canadian effort against hunger), and Farm Aid (to aid American farmers).

> "Here is a specific desire to affect consciousness, to make people aware of the plight of Africa, and to raise funds that will hopefully lead to food and pharmaceuticals, equipment and drugs and vitamins, to help out these people."
> —Bill Graham, U.S. promoter of Live Aid, 1985

---

5. *Word Up!* **Cameo (1986).** Almost too funky to stand.

6. *Different Light,* **The Bangles (1986).** The group got campy long before their straightforward rock and pop did.

7. *Valotte,* **Julian Lennon (1984).** Like father, and you'll probably think son's okay, too.

8. *Make It Big,* **Wham! (1984).** That's usually how it works.

9. *True Colours,* **Split Enz (1980).** Cutting-edge New Wave so sharp, you could put somebody's eye out with that thing.

10. *Naked Eyes,* **Naked Eyes (1983).** Beautifully orchestrated pop bolstered by the most successful remake of the classic "Always Something There to Remind Me" and mournful "Promises, Promises."

People Have the Power: Ten Sociopolitically Conscious Songs of the 80s

1. **"Do They Know It's Christmas?" Band Aid (1985).** Hunger in Ethiopia ("We Are the World" by U.S.A. for Africa [1985] also addressed hunger in Ethiopia, but—as usual—the United States merely imitated something started in England).

2. **"Luka," Suzanne Vega (1987).** The abused child who lives upstairs from you.

3. **"Hands Across America," Voices of Freedom (1986).** American homelessness, poverty, and hunger. The release of this song coincided with a failed effort to form a symbolic human chain across the country.

4. "Beds Are Burning," Midnight Oil (1988). Worker's rights.

5. "Sisters Are Doin' It for Themselves," Eurythmics with Aretha Franklin (1985). Feminism.

6. "Sun City," Artists United Against Apartheid (1985). Apartheid in South Africa.

7. "The War Song," Culture Club (1984). The Falkland War.

Commandant Boy George demonstrates some loopholes in the "Don't Ask, Don't Tell" policy on the sleeve for his group's "The War Song."

8. "Russians," Sting (1986). U.S.–Soviet relations.

9. "Sign 'O' the Times," Prince (1987). AIDS and crack, and this was the first song to specifically address either.

The world wondered if that was Prince in the slinky outfit on the single for "Sign 'O' the Times" but it was only a backup singer. The large heart was a deliberate attempt to encourage the former guess, but the legs should've been a giveaway—Prince's are a little knobbier.

10. "19," Paul Hardcastle (1985). The horrors of Vietnam.

If you thought American kids were too apolitical in the 80s, how about the fact that "19" was a major hit despite being about the Vietnam War and despite being packaged with arresting images of that bitter conflict? The bold numeral in the center of the sleeve was the average age of the combat soldier in Vietnam.

Performers in U.S.A. for Africa and How They Got the Gig

IT'S MY ORIGINAL IDEA THAT YOU'RE ALL STEALING FROM, BUT AT LEAST IT'S FOR A GOOD CAUSE

1. Bob Geldof

I WROTE IT, I'D BETTER BE IN IT

1. Michael Jackson
2. Lionel Richie

I'M A LEGEND IN MY OWN TIME

1. Ray Charles
2. Bob Dylan
3. Smokey Robinson
4. Diana Ross (see also next category)
5. Paul Simon
6. Bruce Springsteen
7. Tina Turner
8. Stevie Wonder

I'M A LEGEND IN MY OWN MIND

1. Lindsey Buckingham
2. Waylon Jennings
3. Billy Joel
4. Bette Midler
5. Kenny Rogers
6. Dionne Warwick

I'M GENEROUS, I'M FAMOUS, I'M OLD, AND I HAD NOTHING BETTER TO DO

1. Harry Belafonte

MY BROTHER SAID I COULD BE IN IT

1. Jackie Jackson
2. La Toya Jackson
3. Marlon Jackson
4. Randy Jackson
5. Tito Jackson

BELIEVE IT OR NOT, WE'VE SOLD MORE RECORDS THAN GOD

1. Hall and Oates
2. Kenny Loggins

I'M HERE JUST IN CASE WAYLON JENNINGS IS A NO-SHOW

1. Willie Nelson

IT WAS A VERY GOOD YEAR FOR ME

1. Cyndi Lauper
2. Huey Lewis & the News
3. The Pointer Sisters

I KNOW PRINCE

1. Sheila E.

SOMEONE OWES ME FAVORS

1. Kim Carnes
2. James Ingram
3. Al Jarreau
4. Jeffrey Osborne
5. Steve Perry

YOU'D BE SURPRISED HOW LAX SECURITY WAS THAT DAY

1. Dan Aykroyd

Ten Performers Conspicuously *Not* in U.S.A. for Africa

1. Prince
2. Madonna
3. Janet Jackson
4. Pat Benatar
5. Donna Summer
6. James Brown
7. Grace Jones
8. Frank Sinatra
9. Rebbie Jackson
10. Dolly Parton

Movies or Moviola

Robert Downey, Jr. chills out in *Less Than Zero* (1987).

The 80s, like the 50s, were a time when movies were threatened by TV.

In the 50s the introduction and popularization of TV lured millions of viewers away from their local cinemas. In the 80s potential moviegoers not only had regular TV, they also had dozens of cable channels, some devoted to showing recent hit movies.

An even greater threat to the cinema was the home videocassette recorder (VCR), which allowed the playing of prerecorded movies on television sets. Soon all TV sets were manufactured to be "cable ready," and neighborhood video stores started popping up like toadstools in the 80s, offering thousands of movies. Video movies could be viewed at the renter's leisure, with no lines for popcorn.

But the 80s still saw massive numbers of people—primarily teens—forking over four bucks (or more!) to take in the latest movies. Blockbusters (*Rambo: First Blood Part II*, *Beverly Hills Cop*, *Return of the Jedi*) regularly did more than $100 million in business at the box office, and a movie starring a space alien so ugly that he was cute—*E.T. The Extra-Terrestrial*—became the highest-grossing film of all time (at over $300 million in ticket sales worldwide).

Movies in the 80s became slicker, with increased special effects capabilities. Have you watched 1977's *Star Wars* recently? Effects that seemed impressive at the time now look quaint. By 1986 even the fourth *Star Trek* installment (*Star Trek IV: The Voyage Home*) rated better, with many convincing space scenes and a time travel sequence that would have had Luke Skywalker's head spinning.

Aside from realism, 80s movies took on the values of the yuppies, who along with teens flocked to films. Movies became infinitely more expensive as production values soared. That didn't necessarily mean that 80s movies *only* looked good, but it did mean that even horrifyingly bad movies were likely to be fun to look at (like the Tom Cruise vehicle *Legend*, 1986). Some might call that superficial, but at least a good-looking, bad movie wasn't worthless.

Some wags have even gone so far as to claim that the 80s were all about style over substance. If anything, the 80s proved that style and substance are not mutually exclusive. Just ask any painter you know; the brush strokes can be just as important as the figure and as any message the painting may have.

Aside from the rapid stylization of movies—spurred on by increasingly lavish music videos—movies in the 80s were more and more frequently targeted at teens. Teen exploitation flicks (*Porky's*, 1982), goofy horror movies (led by the *Friday the 13th* and *A Nightmare on Elm Street* series), music-drenched romances (*Footloose*, 1984; *Dirty Dancing*, 1987), and smarter, less condescending teen comedies (*Fast Times at Ridgemont High*, 1982) and dramas (*The Breakfast Club*, 1985) dominated the marquee for the entire decade.

Even films that were not as obviously geared toward teens, such as the 1986 smash *Top Gun*, owed much of their success to the teen audience, lured into the theaters by killer soundtracks, overheated sexual situations, and slam-bang effects. More adult-oriented hits such as *Tootsie* (1982), *Broadcast News*

Nudity in the movies became commonplace in the 80s, as graphically illustrated by David Naughton in *An American Werewolf in London* (1981).

(1987), and *Driving Miss Daisy* (1989) were few and far between, even if these were always the films that garnered the awards.

Another important trend in 80s cinema was the continued push toward breaking former screen taboos. Nudity on film was an outrage in the early 60s, but by the time Adrienne Barbeau bared her moneymakers for 1982's *The Swamp Thing*, the Motion Picture Association of America (MPAA) yawned and granted the film a mild PG rating, meaning that anyone could go see it, but that parents were forewarned.

Eddie Murphy's highly successful film debut with Nick Nolte in *48HRS.* (also 1982) had everyone talking about his mile-a-minute use of the dreaded "f-word" (that's "fuck," for the uninitiated), a trend that only escalated with time. A movie could coast by with a PG rating if "fuck" was uttered only once or if nudity was brief and nonexplicit, but some filmmakers, knowing that the eighteen-and-over stipulation of R-rated movies was never enforced, had no qualms about creating violent and/or profane and/or extremely sexual movies and having their films labeled with an R. The R rating was viewed by teens as a seal of approval, a sign that a movie was interesting enough to be worth seeing.

Several envelope-pushing films that received PG ratings (*Gremlins* and *Indiana Jones and the Temple of Doom*, both 1984, among them) led to the MPAA's creation in 1984 of a brand-new rating especially for the 80s: PG-13. This new rating meant nothing more than "This is a particularly hard PG. Enjoy the movie, kids."

Family-oriented hits like *E.T.* were rare. Disney, the all-time champ of kid fare, went adult, financing its first R-rated film under its Touchstone branch, the Bette Midler hit *Down and Out in Beverly Hills* (1986). Disney's 80s full-length animated features paled in comparison with the products of their golden age (the 30s and 40s), and the studio wouldn't have another cartoon classic until the end of the decade, with 1989's *The Little Mermaid*. Instead, in the 80s we

got the annoying *The Fox and the Hound* (1981) and the lifeless *The Black Cauldron* (1985).

There was a minor revival of westerns in the 80s, which simmered until 1990's megashit, er, -hit, *Dances with Wolves*, after which that genre seemed once again viable to filmmakers. In theory.

For the most part, despite all the technical innovations and stretching of the limits of permissibility, hit makers in the 80s stuck with the tried and true: lots of comedies, some searing dramas to make the critics drool, and traditional elements like romance and great music to sweeten the pot.

In compiling the following list of quintessentially 80s movies, I took several things into consideration:

1. Recognizability: How instantly recognizable and memorable a movie is to the average person who survived the 80s.

2. Characteristically 80s elements: Are Molly Ringwald or Tom Cruise in the movie? Does the movie boast two number-one hits on its soundtrack? These and other 80s-esque elements were tallied.

3. Impact: Did this movie inspire a dozen imitators? Sequels? Rip-offs? TV series? Lunchboxes?

You'll notice that I did not necessarily consider whether or not the movie is any good, but I must admit that most of these eighty films (eighty-one, counting the ultimate 80s movie) are at the very least worthwhile in some way. But because bad movies are sometimes just as memorable (and popular) as good ones, I've included a list of the worst of the worst, along with quite a few other categories to make sure that most of the really memorable movies of the 80s are represented.

Note: The first time a movie title appears in this section—except in filmographies—the following stats are given, as per this example: *Iceman* [title], (1984) [year of release in parentheses], Fred Schepisi [director/culprit], PG [rating]. Timothy Hutton, Lindsay Crouse, John Lone, Josef Sommer, *Danny Glover*, David Strathairn [appended cast].

All names of cast members in italics signify, "What?! Are you sure? I don't remember him/her being in that movie!" For example, can you believe that Danny Glover was in *Iceman*? That's the kind of item you leave off your résumé.

The Ultimate 80s Movie

***The Breakfast Club* (1985),** John Hughes, R. Molly Ringwald, Ally Sheedy, Judd Nelson, Anthony Michael Hall, Emilio Estevez, Paul Gleason, John Kapelos.

Was there ever any doubt?

The most quintessentially 80s movie of the decade was directed by one of the most quintessentially 80s directors, John Hughes. Hughes struck gold—both at the box office and artistically—with his second film, this hilarious and insightful look at the opposing worlds of five very different teenagers.

The jock kisses the flake.

The setup is unlikely: Five teens are condemned to spend an entire day's detention locked in their suburban high school's library . . . on a Saturday. They are forced to get to know each other because of their situation, have a blast, bond, and then part.

Trendy homecoming queen (??) "Claire" (Molly Ringwald, though Ally Sheedy was originally up for the part) has a charmingly spoiled outlook; she doesn't even see her own haughtiness. "Bender" (Judd Nelson) has a chip on his shoulder the size of Nell Carter, an abused burnout who in turn abuses everyone else. He's especially vicious toward "Claire," on whom he has a passionate and unwelcome crush.

In a star turn, Ally Sheedy plays "Allison," a reclusive, high-strung cast-off who dresses in black and seems on the verge of hysteria with her arch mannerisms and lack of social skills. Anthony Michael Hall plays "Brian," the ninety-eight-pound weakling brainiac, and Emilio Estevez has the quiet role of conservative jock "Andrew."

The brilliance of the film is that though the characters are classic 80s stock types, they are fully developed because of their actions while in detention and because of their individual narration of why they are in detention in the first place.

Most poignant is "Brian," who painfully describes taking a shop class, thinking it'd be an easy A, thus guaranteeing that he'd maintain his perfect 4.0. Instead his clumsiness shatters his perfect GPA, making him suicidal. He was caught with a gun at school . . . a flare gun. He's so nerdy, he can't even kill himself in style.

"Andy" has a similarly powerful soliloquy, describing the horrifying prank he was egged into pulling on another guy during gym class. How many other movies make you cry over a jock's remorseful blubbering about how he taped together a defenseless guy's (exceptionally hairy) butt cheeks?

"Claire" got caught cutting class to go shopping, but more pathetically, "Allison" is in detention because she didn't have anything else to do.

In *The Breakfast Club* the modern pressures of being adolescent are etched into a backdrop of frivolity. We get to see "Bender" crawling around inside the drop ceiling (eventually dropping through it), the entire group dashing through the halls while the ultimate high school soundtrack blares, and a madcap pot-smoking episode that leads to a memorable dance montage, wherein we see that really difficult 80s dance where you rotate your ankles and move across the floor. This became one of the last mainstream films to get away with a no-regrets drug scene in the "Just Say No" 80s.

In the end, the burnout French-kisses the prom queen, the jock falls in love with the recluse (who, in timeless Hollywood tradition, is made over from frump to freak), and the brain writes an essay for the entire group, explaining why detention sucks—finally rebelling against the insanity of a system that had him suicidal over a lousy grade. It's classic rebellion, but since it's seen through a diversity of eyes, every teen who watched this movie could relate and experience the elation of abandoning social mores and defying authority. Which, of course, was not a popular thing to actually *do* in the button-down 80s.

This movie captures the archetypes of the 80s, and its performers were themselves classic 80s actors. Hating every minute of it, the five actors (along with non–*Breakfast Club*–bers Sean Penn, Demi Moore, and Rob Lowe) were dubbed "the Brat Pack" (a takeoff on the 60s "Rat Pack" led by Frank Sinatra) by the media, making it difficult for them to land more sophisticated roles, except in rotten movies (including Demi, whose roles got better even if she didn't).

Of the *Breakfast Club* Brat Packers, only Emilio Estevez went on to maintain any sort of high-profile acting career—there is no justice in this world!— while his fellow Brat Packers watched their careers

> "Demented and sad, but social."
> —Judd Nelson, *The Breakfast Club*, 1985

go down in flames before the 90s rolled around. Ally Sheedy picked up a heavy drug habit and also battled anorexia; Anthony Michael Hall beefed up in Joe Piscopo fashion, losing his gangly cuteness; Judd Nelson had trouble acting his age; and Molly Ringwald chucked it all and moved to France after a triumphant return in *Pretty in Pink* and several bombs.

But at least they made *The Breakfast Club*, one of the most important and moving teen films of all time and the quintessential moviegoing experience of the 80s.

Eighty More Quintessentially 80s Movies

1. *Risky Business* (1983), Paul Brickman, R. Tom Cruise, Rebecca DeMornay, Curtis Armstrong, *Bronson Pinchot.*

Tom Cruise arrived on the scene with this monster sleeper hit from 1983, playing a sexy suburban teenager (he was twenty-one at the time) left home alone by his doting parents.

The Breakfast Club Brat Pack
An 80s Filmography

Molly Ringwald

FILMS:
The Tempest 1982; *Packin' It In, Spacehunter: Adventures in the Forbidden Zone* 1983; *Sixteen Candles* 1984; *P.K. and the Kid, The Breakfast Club* 1985; *Johnny Appleseed, Pretty in Pink* 1986; *The Pick-Up Artist, King Lear* 1987; *Fresh Horses, For Keeps* 1988; *Strike It Rich* 1989.

TV:
Surviving (teen suicide) 1986.

Ally Sheedy

FILMS:
Bad Boys, WarGames 1983; *Oxford Blues* 1984; *The Breakfast Club, St. Elmo's Fire, Twice in a Lifetime* 1985; *Blue City, Short Circuit* 1986; *Maid to Order* 1987; *The Heart of Dixie* 1989.

TV:
The Best Little Girl in the World (anorexia) 1981; *We Are the Children* (famine) 1987.

Emilio Estevez

FILMS:
Tex 1982; *The Outsiders, Nightmares* 1983; *Repo Man* 1984; *The Breakfast Club, St. Elmo's Fire, That Was Then . . . This Is Now* 1985; *Maximum Overdrive, Wisdom* 1986; *Stakeout* 1987; *Young Guns, Never on Tuesday* (cameo) 1988; *Men at Work* 1989.

TV:
In the Custody of Strangers (drunk driving) 1982; *Nightbreaker* (atomic bomb effects) 1989.

Judd Nelson

FILMS:
Making the Grade 1984; *The Breakfast Club, St. Elmo's Fire, Fandango* 1985; *Blue City, The Transformers* (voice) 1986; *From the Hip, Dear America* (voice) 1987; *Relentless, Far Out Man* 1989.

TV:
The Billionaire Boys Club (greed), *Moonlighting* (guest) 1987.

Anthony Michael Hall

FILMS:
Six Pack 1982; *National Lampoon's Vacation* 1983; *Sixteen Candles* 1984; *The Breakfast Club, Weird Science* 1985; *Out of Bounds* 1986; *Johnny Be Good* 1988.

TV:
Saturday Night Live (regular cast member) 1985-1986.

Ages of Brat Packers—Playing High Schoolers—When They Filmed THE BREAKFAST CLUB

Molly Ringwald, 16

Ally Sheedy, 22

Emilio Estevez, 22

Judd Nelson, 25

Anthony Michael Hall, 16

Tom Cruise fails to keep his dad's Porsche from a date with Lake Michigan in *Risky Business*.

What's the first thing you'd do if your parents left you home alone? Dance in your underwear and dark sunglasses while lip-synching Bob Seger's "Old Time Rock and Roll"? Good answer! Cruise does just that in a star-making scene that also turned him into an international sex symbol overnight. Fitting, since his name (he was christened Thomas Cruise Mapother IV) makes him sound more like a porn star than a legit actor.

In the movie, Cruise decides to get risky and call a sex service. Boys will be boys, but transvestites will be transvestites, and since the one who shows up is not Tom's cup of tea, s/he sends for Rebecca DeMornay, who fits the bill. DeMornay also takes his parents' crystal egg, a bizarre and apparently valuable item that Cruise spends a lot of time trying to get back. Instead he winds up running a brothel out of his parents' home and doing it so well that he's recruited by Harvard.

The movie is a delicious send-up of yuppie values, leaving us with a wealthy and unrepentant Cruise and memories of his hot sex scene with DeMornay in a

> "Sometimes you just gotta say, 'What the fuck.'" —Tom Cruise, *Risky Business*, 1983

subway car. It's also—along with *The Breakfast Club*—one of the best teen films ever made for its black wit and savage parody.

Best 80s flashback: Check out Tom's center-parted hair!

2. *Airplane!* (1980), Jerry Zucker and Jim Abrahams, PG. Robert Hays, Julie Hagerty, Lloyd Bridges, Peter Graves, Robert Stack, Leslie Nielsen, Stephen Stucker, Kareem Abdul-Jabbar, Lorna Patterson, Jill Whelan.

> "I like my coffee black. Like my men." —precocious little girl, *Airplane!* 1980

The funniest movie of the 80s and the first in a string of hit-or-miss, broad comedy projects from Zucker and Abrahams (*Police Squad!* [TV] 1982; *Top Secret!* 1984) that is definitely all hit and no miss.

Airplane! hilariously skewers 70s plane disaster flicks (most closely the campy *Airport 1975*) at every turn, with the crew and many passengers suffering from food poisoning (it was the fish), a former pilot suffering from performance anxiety (Hays), dim-witted stewardesses (Hagerty and Patterson), and a ground crew capped off by the flaming Stucker, who is more concerned with a sale at Penney's than the welfare of the ill-fated airplane.

The rule of the day is absurdity: Lloyd Bridges plays an air traffic controller addicted to every substance known to man, Hays and Hagerty flashback to their budding romance in Vietnam complete with an anachronistic, late 70s *Saturday Night Fever* dance number, and the automatic pilot is an inflatable doll that sexually molests hapless Hagerty.

The movie is full of one-liners that have invaded daily speech ("And don't call me Shirley") and brilliant, deadpan performances to nurse tearful gales of laughter out of even the biggest sourpuss you know.

3. *Raiders of the Lost Ark* (1981), Steven Spielberg, PG. Harrison Ford, Karen Allen, Wolf Kahler, Paul Freeman, John Rhys-Davies, Denholm Elliott.

The biggest adventure movie of the decade is Spielberg's perfect *hommage* to the B-movie action flicks of the 40s and 50s, full of nonstop chills and the most arresting first ten minutes of any movie you've ever seen (with the possible exception of *Betty Blue*, 1986)—Harrison Ford infiltrates the inner sanctum of an ancient treasure chamber, only to have to outrun poison arrows, booby traps, and a runaway boulder.

> "Snakes. Why did it have to be snakes?" —Harrison Ford, *Raiders of the Lost Ark,* 1981

Set during World War II, the main adventure has "Indiana Jones" (Ford) assisting the U.S. government by trekking to Asia in search of the fabled Ark of the Covenant, an object alluded to in the Bible and purported to hold the secrets to ruling the world. "Indy" must locate it before Hitler's agents do—the fate of the entire planet is at stake!

Our hero's chemistry with ex-flame "Marion Ravenwood" (Allen) is palpable as they outsmart various foreign agents and eventually locate the Ark, only to be captured. The Nazis greedily open the Ark . . . and promptly melt into goo, their punishment by God for tampering with an artifact they should have left alone.

It's hard to imagine a more exciting movie, and its enormous success paved the way for all of Spielberg's—and Ford's—monster hits that followed.

4. *Flashdance* (1983), Adrian Lyne, R. Jennifer Beals, Michael Nouri, Belinda Bauer, Lilia Skala, Cynthia Rhodes, Sunny Johnson.

Talk about the American dream!

Jennifer Beals plays a hardworking welder (don't ask) who supplements her income and builds up her thighs by stripping. This is no ordinary stripping, however. The strippers at her club are drenched by buckets of water and dance around while soaking wet, which is apparently such a turn-on that full nudity isn't necessary—we never get to see bare bodies.

"Alex" (Beals) is in love with "Nicky" (Nouri), her boss, who loves her and supports her entrepreneurial goals. His understanding of his lover's career drive makes for a very 80s romance, one that at the time was considered trashy but upon reviewing is almost impossibly sweet and old-fashioned.

Without a doubt, *Flashdance*—which also boasted a prize soundtrack and Oscar-winning title song— was the movie that most influenced fashion in the 80s. For years, every woman had several artistically torn sweatshirts in her wardrobe, until even men started wearing them. A sweatshirt that bares your shoulder remains the single most recognizably 80s fashion statement.

The elaborate dancing in *Flashdance* was choreographed by Jeffrey Hornaday, who would later stage some of Madonna's concerts, and this film definitely resembles a music video. Beals didn't do her own legwork—dancer Marine Jahan stood in for her, sporting a curly wig.

The most memorable scene is Beals's workout, immortalized by Giorgio Moroder's music video "Maniac," wherein we see her huffing and puffing and her (or Jahan's) buns jiggling to the beat.

5. *Purple Rain* (1984), Albert Magnoli, R. Prince, Apollonia, Morris Day, Clarence Williams III, Olga Karlatos.

The biggest filmed ego trip imaginable, but it's still really good.

Prince went big-time with the release of this surprise hit and its accompanying soundtrack. He stars

"The Kid" (Prince) likes what he sees in *Purple Rain*.

in the film as a mysterious loner, a rockin' rebel who wants nothing less than to be the biggest singing star in the world, or at least in Minneapolis, where the movie is set.

Purple Rain single-handedly built Prince into a living musical legend on par with Jimi Hendrix, won him an Oscar for Best Original Song Score, and earned him millions of fans who couldn't figure him out but knew he was a musical genius.

6. *Footloose* (1984), Herbert Ross, PG. Kevin Bacon, Lori Singer, Chris Penn, John Lithgow, Dianne Wiest, *Sarah Jessica Parker*.

A high-concept movie with heart, about a midwest town so backward that its elders have made dancing illegal. Never have screen teens had something so basic to rebel against. I mean, the kids in *Rebel Without a Cause* were all a little psycho, but the *Footloose* kids just want to dance.

Kevin Bacon is our hero, butting heads with evil minister John Lithgow (in one of his many 80s creep

Kevin Bacon patiently tries to teach a hick (then-scrawny Chris Penn) how to disco in *Footloose*.

roles) and winning the heart of Lori Singer. He also eventually wins over the town, and dancing is made legal again. Now if only he could get them to legalize pot . . . But that's another movie.

After this movie it would be lots of bombs (*Quicksilver*, 1986; *She's Having a Baby*, 1988; *The Big Picture*, 1989) and just as many years before Bacon would score big again (*A Few Good Men*, 1992), and Singer never matched her success in this feel-good extravaganza. Maybe she should try dancing again.

7. *Fatal Attraction* (1987), Adrian Lyne, R. Michael Douglas, Glenn Close, Anne Archer, Stuart Pankin, Ellen Foley, *Fred Gwynne*.

Michael Douglas, who always seems to play philandering jerks so realistically, plays the ultimate pig in this frightening morality tale. He cheats on his beautiful wife (Archer) with an alluring (?) fellow yuppie (Close), which leads to some hot (and yet funny), knock-down, drag-out sex scenes, but which also leads to Close stalking him and his family.

His one-night stand from hell gets Closer and Closer to attacking his family, until Douglas finally spills the beans and his wife sides with him, telling Close off. *Not* the best way to handle things.

Close is the perfect villainess, deranged and yet seemingly fragile, bringing the concept of stalking into the mainstream and drawing attention to the alarming increase of that modern crime.

One reason this movie cleaned up at the box office has to be its obvious link to AIDS—having one-night stands could kill you starting in the 80s, and Close personified that fact, a fear that gripped every adult. That concept also plays into the delight that audiences are intended to feel when Close gets her comeuppance in a very scary, if slightly gimmicky, ending.

It's also tempting to believe that some audiences found Close's character especially loathsome because she is a seemingly tough, together career woman, whereas Archer is admired as a housewife. Though career women were making headway in the 80s, hard-core traditionalists sympathized more strongly with the latter.

The original ending actually had Close slashing

her wrists, a dark finish that made her much more pathetic and sympathetic, and one which was apparently deemed too layered for the masses. Instead we got a false ending straight out of *The Terminator*, with Close exhibiting the staying power of an Energizer bunny. But both versions will scare the life out of you, which is precisely the point.

8. *Valley Girl* (1983), Martha Coolidge, R. Nicolas Cage, Deborah Foreman, Colleen Camp, Frederic Forrest.

A lost gem, this movie illustrates the life of one of the most colorful personality types of the 80s, the airheaded Valley Girl, played by Deborah Foreman.

Valley boy, he's a valley boy: Nicolas Cage is the original Valley boy to Deborah Foreman's *Valley Girl*.

Frank Zappa's "Valley Girl" song, his only Top 40 hit, inspired the movie, but this is more than another MTV-influenced, ninety-minute music video.

Foreman falls for the exact wrong boy, Nicolas Cage, who is a hood from the wrong side of town. Their very different lifestyles clash, cleverly illuminating the Val culture of the 80s in all its shallow, somehow inevitable glory.

This movie had the most sought after obscure soundtrack of the 80s, notable for its early use of New Wave music by everyone from Culture Club to The Waitresses.

9. *Raging Bull* (1980), Martin Scorsese, R. Robert De Niro, Cathy Moriarty, Joe Pesci, Frank Vincent, Nicholas Colasanto.

A film that many critics call the best of the 80s and possibly one of the best American films ever made . . . but it didn't win the Oscar because its director is too much of a maverick.

Scorsese adapted the life story of boxer Jake LaMotta into this elaborately filmed, black-and-white melodrama featuring more gut-wrenching boxing scenes than all the *Rocky*s combined, plus the best performance of De Niro's career.

This masterpiece garnered a lot of attention for De Niro's ultra-Method tactics, which included gaining (and eventually losing) fifty pounds so he could realistically portray LaMotta at his peak and at his nadir.

Probably the most artistically breathtaking film ever to inspire a *Playboy* centerfold, a layout by LaMotta's fiftysomething ex-wife, Vicki, portrayed in the movie by Cathy Moriarty. We didn't fuck his wife, but we saw her naked.

10. *Dirty Dancing* (1987), Emile Ardolino, PG-13. Patrick Swayze, Jennifer Grey, Cynthia Rhodes, Jerry Orbach, Jack Weston, Jane Brucker.

The most romantic movie of the 80s, starring Jennifer Grey in her best role to date as a naive JAP who falls in love with a sexy dancer (Swayze) at a predominantly Jewish resort in the Catskills. Her father hates Swayze, believing he knocked up his dance partner (Rhodes), who underwent an abortion that Grey funded with Daddy's money.

Grey, whose nickname in the film—"Baby"—is all too fitting, has a lot of growing up to do, which she does quite nicely while managing to win the big dance contest with Swayze.

You're blind if you don't see the depth of these characters' star-crossed love, but if you don't remember how popular its 60s soundtracks (there were two!) were, you're just plain deaf.

Dance fever! Jennifer Grey and Patrick Swayze boogie oogie oogie in *Dirty Dancing*.

11. *Ferris Bueller's Day Off* (1986), John Hughes, PG-13. Matthew Broderick, Mia Sara, Alan Ruck, Jeffrey Jones, Jennifer Grey, Cindy Pickett, Edie McClurg, *Charlie Sheen*.

Teen films are usually about rebellion. What else? But here is a teen movie about rebellion wherein the rebel is interested only in having good, clean fun and getting away with it. He's not trying to change the world, reject his parents, lash out at society. "Ferris Bueller" (Broderick) just wants to have a good time. And he does.

"Ferris" convinces his love interest, the blank-eyed Mia Sara, and his best buddy, nerdy Alan Ruck, to play hooky by spending a day joyriding in Ruck's father's priceless vintage Ferrari, taking in all that Chicago has to offer.

Along the way they dine at an elegant restaurant, take in a Cubs game, visit the Art Institute, and watch "Ferris" lip-synch "Twist and Shout" and "Danke Schoen" atop a parade float, all the while narrowly avoiding detection by his father. The principal of his school has a vested interest in taking the perennially absent "Bueller" down a peg and spends the entire film trying to catch him, only to be thwarted by the family dog and "Ferris"'s sister, played by Jennifer Grey, who mistakes him for an intruder.

Full of laughs and great, to-the-camera narration by Broderick, this film captures the joy of adolescence and the beauty of Chicago in one fell swoop. Sit through the credits for a great scene involving Gummi Bears.

Whoopi Goldberg has never approached the impact she had with her virgin screen performance as "Celie" in Steven Spielberg's *The Color Purple*.

12. *The Color Purple* **(1985),** Steven Spielberg, PG-13. Whoopi Goldberg, Danny Glover, Oprah Winfrey, Margaret Avery, Adolph Caesar, Rae Dawn Chong.

An adaptation of one of the most widely read books of the 80s, Alice Walker's *The Color Purple*, a touching story of the various forms of oppression experienced by several black women in the early part of the century and their individual responses to it.

Spielberg opted for sunny choreography, which some critics felt "Disneyized" the disturbing story, but he also pulled powerhouse performances out of an immensely talented cast. The movie was criticized by the NAACP for casting black men in such a negative light, a ridiculous generalization that did not sit well with the black men starring in the movie.

Whoopi Goldberg made an amazing debut in the film, deserving an Oscar as Best Actress, an honor she lost to Geraldine Page. Margaret Avery shamelessly campaigned to win for Best Supporting Actress but still lost, and Oprah Winfrey seemed destined for silver screen stardom but gave it away for even more lucrative success as the ultimate talk show host of the 80s.

Simply, a powerful movie full of unexpected laughs, plenty of tragic moments, and an ending that leaves you sobbing.

13. *E.T. The Extra-Terrestrial* **(1982),** Steven Spielberg, PG. Debra Winger (E.T.'s voice), Henry Thomas, Dee Wallace, Drew Barrymore, Robert MacNaughton, Peter Coyote, C. Thomas Howell, Sean Frye.

The most successful movie of all time, this fun fantasy follows the travails of E.T., a space alien who falls to planet Earth accidentally and longs to go home.

Henry Thomas plays the boy who takes E.T. under his wing and whose siblings (including future coke abuser Drew Barrymore) help E.T. in his effort to "phone home."

The character E.T. was so beloved by children around the globe that he was made into this hot-selling plush toy. This toy's soft, cuddly texture was in sharp contrast to E.T.'s scaly, reptilian skin, but matched the alien's warm heartlight.

Reese's Pieces got lots of exposure as one of E.T.'s favorite foods (after M&M's refused to allow Spielberg to use their name).

Funny and touching, with the prerequisite bad guys attempting to subject E.T. to scientific tests, this is one 80s movie that everyone on Earth has seen.

14. _Top Gun_ (1986), Tony Scott, PG. Tom Cruise, Kelly McGillis, Val Kilmer, Tom Skerritt, Anthony Edwards, _Meg Ryan, Tim Robbins._

Tom Cruise in an airplane.

A snappy romance that finds Tom Cruise as a young fighter pilot trainee and Kelly McGillis as his winsome love interest, the hottest astrophysics professor of all time.

The preposterous anti-Russkie subplot, in which Cruise actually downs some Russian planes, is pure 80s Reaganism, but what's most memorable are the young actors and Cruise's cocky performance. Unfortunately he repeated that cockiness in most of his movies after realizing it worked once, but there's no denying its effectiveness here.

Flag-waving froth.

15. _Beverly Hills Cop_ (1984), Martin Brest, R. Eddie Murphy, Judge Reinhold, John Ashton, Lisa Eilbacher, Ronny Cox, Bronson Pinchot, _Paul Reiser, Damon Wayans._

After scoring big with _48HRS._, Eddie Murphy hit even bigger with this hilarious cop movie.

Murphy breathed life into "Axel Foley," a streetwise Detroit cop driven to solve the murder of his best pal in ritzy Los Angeles. The resulting culture shock is outrageous, and Murphy's star seemed to be forged from platinum. This movie's phenomenal success made him one of the highest paid stars of the 80s, one whose paycheck would only decrease with bomb (_The Golden Child_, 1986) after bomb (_Harlem Nights_, 1989).

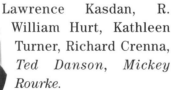

16. _Body Heat_ (1981), Lawrence Kasdan, R. William Hurt, Kathleen Turner, Richard Crenna, _Ted Danson, Mickey Rourke._

This sweltering thriller launched the career of Kathleen Turner, who sweats through her debut with Hurt as a woman who wants her husband offed during the worst heat wave

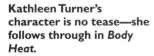
Kathleen Turner's character is no tease—she follows through in _Body Heat._

in Florida history.

Fans of _Double Indemnity_ will fear the worst for dim-bulb Hurt, and they'll be right.

Turner has never topped her sultry performance, and very few films have managed to capture the kind of chemistry she and Hurt conveyed in this update of the film noir genre of the 40s and 50s. It keeps you guessing until the end, and even if you guess right, you won't guess everything.

"You're not too smart, are you? I like that in a man."
—Kathleen Turner, _Body Heat_, 1981

17. _Desperately Seeking Susan_ (1985), Susan Seidelman, PG-13. Rosanna Arquette, Madonna, Aidan Quinn, Mark Blum, Robert Joy, Laurie Metcalf, Steven Wright, _John Turturro_, Richard Hell, Ann Magnuson.

Madonna's music was all over the radio, and her first major film became a surprise hit, helping to launch the first wave of wannabes, who desperately wanted to don lace gloves, mesh hair ties, and funky pyramid jackets.

The movie is actually even better than its fashion statements, a funky screwball comedy that finds housewife "Roberta" (Arquette) wishing she had as exciting a life as the "Susan" whose name keeps popping up in personal ads. A knock on the head transforms "Roberta" into "Susan," just like "Mary Ann" thinking she was "Ginger" on _Gilligan's Island_!

A hip, charming movie (which is a difficult combination to achieve) with a great supporting cast, including Laurie Metcalf as the meddlesome sister-in-law. This film popularized the expression "desperately seeking," which has been desperately overused ever since.

18. _Fame_ (1980), Alan Parker, R. Irene Cara, Barry Miller, Paul McCrane, Anne Meara, Joanna Merlin, Richard Belzer.

They want to live forever, or at least put on a good show.

Irene Cara and seven other students at New York's High School of Performing Arts (which actually exists) work their way through school, all the while banking on stardom.

It's unlikely that many of these kids will "make it," which makes this fun, lively musical thoroughly engrossing.

After this movie hit big, the school it portrays couldn't keep up with new applications, and it even spawned a TV version starring pre-_Control_ Janet Jackson.

19. *Fast Times at Ridgemont High* (1982), Amy Heckerling, R. Sean Penn, Jennifer Jason Leigh, Judge Reinhold, Robert Romanus, Brian Backer, Phoebe Cates, Ray Walston, Forest Whitaker, *Eric Stoltz, Nicolas Cage* (under his given name, Nicolas Coppola).

Judge Reinhold and Phoebe Cates in Amy Heckerling's *Fast Times at Ridgemont High.*

Amy Heckerling hit the nail on the head with her exhilaratingly realistic teen sex comedy with a difference, focusing on SoCal adolescents and their major obsession: sex.

Judge Reinhold gets caught masturbating, Jennifer Jason Leigh loses her virginity, and Sean Penn is the ultimate no-brainer in this extremely funny and razor-sharp look at teen culture in the 80s. Most exciting is Heckerling's flawless ear for then contemporary speech and slang. In 1995 she returned with a similarly hilarious teen movie—*Clueless*—most interesting for being funny despite having absolutely *nothing* in common with real teens.

Take special note of how the movie relies on the mall as a setting, that great, antiseptic shopping center that became a mecca for teens in the 80s.

The first *Ghostbusters* was a smash, so merchandise had been licensed months in advance of the sequel's premiere. The second film was a dud, ensuring there'd never be trading cards featuring a little ghost holding up three fingers. The little ghost seemed to be designed with kids in mind, since he's an obvious salute to that friendliest of ghosts, Casper, with his smirk and non-scary countenance. But these cards didn't sell any better than the movie.

20. *Ghostbusters* (1984), Ivan Reitman, PG. Bill Murray, Dan Aykroyd, Harold Ramis, Rick Moranis, Sigourney Weaver, Annie Potts, Ernie Hudson.

Murray, Aykroyd, Ramis, and Hudson are the Ghostbusters, "experts" on the paranormal who promise to rid your house of unwanted spirits. Only problem is, they've never really had to deal with any-thing too major, so when horrifying ghosts and visible spirits begin to infest Manhattan, the inept Ghostbusters are almost at a loss.

"He slimed me."
—Bill Murray,
Ghostbusters,
1984

21. *Ordinary People* (1980), Robert Redford, R. Mary Tyler Moore, Donald Sutherland, Timothy Hutton, Judd Hirsch, M. Emmet Walsh, Elizabeth McGovern, Adam Baldwin, Dinah Manoff.

Just as the idea of family values began to infiltrate America after the swinging 70s, Robert Redford made this movie, showing blood may be thicker than water, but some blood is indisputably *bad*.

Mary Tyler Moore, who had a few years earlier ended her long-running stint as TV's lovable "Mary Richards," here plays a pathologically unfeeling mother whose obsession over the drowning of her favorite son has driven her surviving son (Hutton) to the brink of insanity.

This movie questions the American dream, the classic family unit (you stand up and cheer when Mommie dearest drives out of her family's lives forever), and the blossoming yuppie lifestyle that had yet to be defined.

The scariest nonhorror movie of the 80s.

22. *Do the Right Thing* (1989), Spike Lee, R. Spike Lee, Danny Aiello, Richard Edson, Ruby Dee, Ossie Davis, Giancarlo Esposito, Bill Nunn, John Turturro, John Savage, Rosie Perez.

Spike Lee had already made a name for himself with thoughtful, provocative, comedic dramas (*She's Gotta Have It*, 1986; *School Daze*, 1988) about the black experience when he unloaded this bombshell on an unsuspecting public.

Do the Right Thing followed the transformation of "Mookie" (Lee) from a passive black employee of a white-owned pizza parlor in an all-black neighborhood to his ultimate destination as a guy who causes the violence that destroys the place.

This shocking movie had audiences debating whether or not "Mookie" did the right thing, even though it was clear that Lee himself wasn't so sure. It also introduced the catchphrase "do the right thing," routinely used literally, which is exactly how not to take the title of this freaky, fascinating movie.

This one made Spike an auteur.

23. *Who Framed Roger Rabbit?* (1988), Robert Zemeckis, PG. Charles Fleischer (voice), Bob Hoskins, Kathleen Turner (voice), Amy Irving (voice), Christopher Lloyd, Joanna Cassidy.

The trend toward technical innovations reached its zenith with this intricate movie, part live action, part animated, in which a bumbling rabbit named Roger (inspired by Bugs Bunny) and a hardboiled P.I. (Hoskins) team up to solve the question posed in the title: Roger's cheating wife, Jessica Rabbit (voiced by Kathleen Turner, except for the singing, which was done by Amy Irving), is mourning the sudden death of her lover, and everyone thinks jealous Roger is to blame.

The resulting adventure is chock full of wonderful cartoon cameos (Betty Boop, Donald and Daffy Duck, Mickey Mouse, and nearly every other animated star in motion picture history). The ingenious merging of cartoons and humans via computer graphics and careful shadowing hinted at the wonders computer art would provide in the 90s.

24. *Rambo: First Blood, Part II* (1985), George P. Cosmatos, R. Sylvester Stallone, Richard Crenna, Charles Napier, Steven Berkoff, Julia Nickson-Soul, Martin Kove.

Stallone was already known for his tired *Rocky* series, and when the sequel to his surprise 1982 hit *First Blood* took off, a new character was born: the indomitable "Rambo."

Attitudes toward Vietnam—and especially toward its long-reviled veterans—shifted sharply in the 80s with the unveiling of the Vietnam War Memorial in Washington, D.C., in 1982. There were new feelings of respect for the warriors of that unpopular war. "Rambo" was one by-product of those feelings, an American soldier of almost mythic abilities and endless patriotism.

In this ridiculous movie, "Rambo" is enlisted to enter Cambodia in search of U.S. soldiers presumed to still be in captivity. MIAs (for "missing in action") were a popular subject in the 80s, and the thought that some of them could still be alive proved irresistible to combat-thirsty filmgoers, teenagers, and Reagan boosters. In effect, *Rambo: First Blood, Part II* represented a one-man restaging of Vietnam . . . where the United States won.

Pretty silly stuff, but also indescribably influential.

Not only did it feed into the heady patriotism of the 80s—when the Cold War still existed—it sparked dozens of similar Vietnam-themed films. It could even be argued that without the *First Blood* series, Oliver Stone couldn't have secured financing for his own, very different Vietnam movie, *Platoon* (1986).

25. *Beaches* (1988), Garry Marshall, PG-13. Bette Midler, Barbara Hershey, John Heard, Spalding Gray, Lainie Kazan, James Read, *Mayim Bialik.*

Sob!

The teariest movie of the 80s, even sadder than the already devastating *Terms of Endearment* (1983).

This modest film became a major video success, and Bette Midler's overwrought song "Wind Beneath My Wings" became her first number-one hit, describing as it did the tragic story of *Beaches*.

In the movie, Midler is a flashy, successful showbiz type, and her best friend, Barbara Hershey, is the quiet housewife. The two have been friends their entire life (complete with flashbacks), and their relationship is heart-wrenchingly strengthened when Hershey's character learns she has a terminal illness.

I'm getting choked up just capsulizing this. . . .

26. *The Blues Brothers* (1980), John Landis, R. John Belushi, Dan Aykroyd, James Brown, Cab Calloway, Aretha Franklin, Carrie Fisher, Ray Charles, Henry Gibson, John Candy, *Twiggy, Pee-wee Herman/Paul Reubens.*

Every frat boy's favorite 80s comedy is this cheesy, bluesy road movie wherein two enigmatic blues musicians (Aykroyd and Belushi) go "on a mission from God" to reassemble their old band. It's a mission that takes them all across the South Side of Chicago and into numerous spontaneous musical sequences with R&B and soul greats.

The music is incredible, and the vignettes—especially Aretha as a waitress belting "Think"—are indelible. Aykroyd and Belushi manage to keep straight faces throughout, and the grand finale is a hoot.

27. *Romancing the Stone* (1984), Robert Zemeckis, PG. Michael Douglas, Kathleen Turner, Danny DeVito, Zack Norman, Ron Silver.

One of many *Raiders of the Lost Ark* imitators is this film, which is worth imitating itself.

A classic adventure in the "Indy" mold, this film follows a repressed romance writer (Turner) as she goes on a cross-continental journey to locate a vast treasure and free her sister from bondage at the hands of greedy treasure hunters. She reluctantly accepts assistance from Douglas, who tries his best to be "Indiana Jones" but really seems more like your dad trying to be cool.

Still, this movie is packed with laughs, sight gags, and some genuinely exciting moments, and Douglas/Turner were one of the only male/female teams of the 80s—they returned together in *The Jewel of the Nile* (1985) and *The War of the Roses* (1989).

A porno film was made with the copycat title *Romancing the Bone.*

28. *9¹/₂ Weeks* (1986), Adrian Lyne, R. Mickey Rourke, Kim Basinger, Margaret Whitton, Karen Young, David Margulies.

Speaking of porno films (see #27) . . .

One of the most controversial films of the decade was this scorching hot ode to S/M, in which Basinger and Rourke bared all. The film follows the sexual experimentation of the couple (both yuppies), which quickly moves toward a full-fledged master/slave relationship.

This movie is so sexually provocative that Basinger later commented that she felt she'd been "raped" in making it, a bizarre comment from an actress paid well and whose career skyrocketed afterward.

For better or worse, *9 ¹/₂ Weeks* opened the doors for many other psychosexual dramas (including Rourke's bomb *Wild Orchid*, 1990) and helped to usher candid exploration of S/M into the mainstream by the early 90s.

29. *Friday the 13th* (1980), Sean S. Cunningham, R. Betsy Palmer, Adrienne King, Harry Crosby, Laurie Bartram, *Kevin Bacon.*

This classic piece of cheese spawned so many laughable sequels that it's almost shocking how good the original actually is.

Setting the standard for teen slasher flicks of the 80s (and borrowing heavily from 1978's superior *Halloween*), this exploitative horror movie takes place at a sleepy summer camp, which has just reopened after twenty dormant years. Previously, kids had been dying mysteriously, starting with the tragic drowning of one "Jason Voorhees." The counselors who arrive to prepare the camp for a new wave of kiddies are much more interested in screwing each other, and—one by one—they are brutally murdered by an unseen killer.

The culprit is "Jason"'s vengeful mother, bitter over the fact that her son drowned while his counselors orgied. But the ending introduces "Jason"'s killer corpse in a truly scary sequence that could be real or could be a nightmare. The sequels are a bit more literal, and one was released for every year of the 80s with the exceptions of 1983 and 1987.

30. *Poltergeist* (1982), Tobe Hooper, PG. JoBeth Williams, Craig T. Nelson, Beatrice Straight, Heather O'Rourke, Zelda Rubinstein, Dominique Dunne.

Far superior to other horror films of the 80s, *Poltergeist* is also a hell of a lot scarier. It's the story of the perfect family and their struggles with supernatural occurrences after moving into a new house in a shiny, happy suburb.

O'Rourke is searing as the eerily cute daughter "Carol Ann," who secretly communicates with spirits via her family's television set.

What follows is a series of shocking effects, including a killer tree smashing through the children's room and attempting to snatch them away and a poolful of uprooted corpses. Seems the developer (for whom daddy Nelson works) intentionally built the subdivision on top of an old cemetery, which sparked all the frightening poltergeist activity.

"They're heeere."
—Heather O'Rourke, *Poltergeist*, 1982

Too bad the Ghostbusters were still two years away; nobody needed them more than these poor saps.

A creepy subtext to the film is that Dunne (daughter of novelist Dominick Dunn), who played the sister, was strangled to death in real life shortly after the film's release and O'Rourke died of an intestinal blockage after lensing the movie's second sequel.

31. *Tootsie* (1982), Sidney Pollack, PG. Dustin Hoffman, Jessica Lange, Teri Garr, Dabney Coleman, Bill Murray, Charles Durning, *Geena Davis.*

Surely Hoffman is the last actor in Hollywood who could pass as a woman.

Hoffman plays a struggling actor who can't land any roles but is immediately cast in a major soap opera when he auditions for a female role in drag.

"Dorothy" becomes a sensation, but Hoffman is much more concerned with his budding love for his costar, down-to-earth soap opera actress (how often do you read that phrase?) Jessica Lange.

Tootsie is hilarious, full of great laughs provided by Garr and Murray and also by the multitude of sticky situations "Dorothy" gets into as a man dressed as a woman. It doesn't even matter that "Dorothy" is singularly ugly; it almost makes her more believable since one sure way to spot a drag queen is by her glamour.

Tootsie enjoyed a brief reign as the most successful comedy of all time, and it ushered in a spate of drag-oriented comedies (*Just One of the Guys*, 1985; *He's My Girl*, 1987) that didn't even attempt to tease out the rich commentary on relationships that *Tootsie* did. Virtually remade as the worthless *Mrs. Doubtfire* (1993) with even more astonishing success at the box office.

32. *A Nightmare on Elm Street* (1984), Wes Craven, R. John Saxon, Heather Langenkamp, Ronee Blakley, Robert Englund, *Johnny Depp*, Charles Fleischer.

Like *Friday the 13th*, this movie launched beaucoup sequels that are still—at last word—ongoing.

Unlike *Friday the 13th*, this movie's villain is not a vindictive child, wronged by his watchers, but a sadistic child molester—"Freddy Krueger"—who's back from the dead to murder teenagers whose parents once murdered him.

His identifying marks are his horribly scarred countenance (he was burned alive, Frankenstein's monster style) and his razor-studded gloves, all the better to carve you to ribbons with, my dear.

Most terrifying about "Freddy" is that he roams the dream world, so there truly is no escape. Once you fall asleep and begin to dream, he appears, pursuing you until he is able to snuff you, something that—in keeping with old wives' tales—leads to death in the waking world as well.

None of the sequels came close to the eerie quality captured by the first installment, but this film's villain was all over the place in the 80s: on TV, reflected in children's Halloween costumes, and featured in a series of books. He was the perfect embodiment

of the kind of antihero so popular in the 80s, right along with "Jason," "Michael" (of the *Halloween* series), and Michael Jackson. . . .

33. *The Terminator* (1984), James Cameron, R. Arnold Schwarzenegger, Michael Biehn, Linda Hamilton, Paul Winfield.

One of the biggest stars of the 80s had his first true blockbuster with this inventive thriller in which a cyborg from the future arrives in the present day to kill one "Sarah Connor," a woman fated to give birth to a great enemy of the bad guys who will eventually rule earth. (No, not televangelists.)

Going through the phone book, heartless machine Schwarzenegger proceeds to kill everyone named "Sarah Connor" except for the right one (Hamilton), who escapes and is aided by another emissary from the future (Michael Biehn) with whom she promptly falls in love.

Non-stop excitement and extremely well acted, this movie featured numerous false endings that became par for the course in the 80s, and inspired a sequel in the 90s in which Arnold opted to play a *good* cyborg.

34. *Terms of Endearment* (1983), James L. Brooks, PG. Shirley MacLaine, Jack Nicholson, Debra Winger, John Lithgow, Jeff Daniels, *Danny DeVito*.

Shirley MacLaine finally—and deservedly—won an Oscar for her portrayal of an aging mom rediscovering the joys of whoopee and reevaluating her antagonistic relationship with her daughter (Winger).

Though MacLaine's dates and romps with her cocky ex-astronaut neighbor (Nicholson) are hilari-

ously enacted, the movie is even more memorable as a two-hanky weepie, since Winger gets cancer and dies.

The movie is like a "disease of the week" TV movie—so popular in the

How many schoolkids were dying to apply *Terms of Endearment* stickers to their Trapper Keepers??? Making these stickers even more grotesque was their inclusion of a Shirley MacLaine photo with its carrot top cropped. What's next? *Madame Sousatzka* T-shirts?

80s—except with real punch, real characters, and even more tears.

35. *Mommie Dearest* (1981), Frank Perry, PG. Faye Dunaway, Diana Scarwid, Steve Forrest, Mara Hoble, Rutanya Aida, Harry Goz.

The campiest movie of the decade came early. Based on Christina Crawford's explosive memoir about the abuse she suffered at the hands of her famous adoptive mom, screen star Joan Crawford, the movie incorporated two elements that were riding high in the 80s.

First, it dealt with a tell-all movie star tale of the sort that the tabloids were exploiting more and more. It also dealt with child abuse, a complex social problem that came out of the closet in the 80s (along with spousal abuse, date rape, eating disorders, and so forth).

Weirdly, though Faye Dunaway's performance ranks as one of the best of the decade (you'll never be able to see Crawford on screen again without marveling at Dunaway's dead-on impersonation), it basically destroyed her career, pigeonholing her as a shrill, melodramatic figure for most of the rest of her filmwork.

The movie is almost like a telefilm, and it's certainly not exquisite to watch, but it *is* hysterically funny, stomach turning, and earnest.

36. *The Lost Boys* (1987), Joel Schumacher, R. Jason Patric, Kiefer Sutherland, Corey Haim, Jami Gertz, Dianne Wiest, Corey Feldman, Barnard Hughes, Edward Herrmann.

Helping to launch "the two Coreys" (Haim and Feldman), this glossy vampire romp stars Patric as your basic teen heartthrob who wants to impress a girl, the alluring Jami Gertz, when he first moves into her hometown of Santa Cruz—the murder capital of the world.

It soon becomes apparent that the rebellious teens who rule the town are actually bloodsuckers, controlled by the unseen head vampire, who winds up being the last person you'd guess (making it the first).

Corey Haim is really funny as Patric's hyper younger brother who has a sexy Rob Lowe poster in his bedroom and who is his brother's only hope in combatting the evil undead. Most hilariously, he tells Patric he's "in trouble" for becoming a vampire.

Vampire movies came back into vogue after this cute nail-biter, and Kiefer Sutherland's star was definitely on the rise. It also provided another "perfect mom" role for Wiest.

37. *Blade Runner* (1982), Ridley Scott, R. Harrison Ford, Rutger Hauer, Sean Young, Daryl Hannah, M. Emmet Walsh, Edward James Olmos, Joe Turkel, Brion James, Joanna Cassidy.

Ridley Scott's futuristic masterpiece about a twenty-ninth-century (why not?) police officer who must round up lethal replicants, humanlike forms that are grown to perform slavish tasks and then die. Except these replicants, led by Hauer, are trying to take as many humans with them as possible.

Visually stunning and definitely influencing all sci-fi pictures to follow, this film featured a great hard-boiled performance by Harrison Ford outside of "Indy" or *Star Wars* pictures. This is one of the most admired science fiction films and also one of the bleakest glimpses into the future you're likely to stumble across at your neighborhood Blockbuster.

38. *Back to the Future* (1985), Robert Zemeckis, PG. Michael J. Fox, Christopher Lloyd, Lea Thompson, Crispin Glover, Wendie Jo Sperber, Marc McClure, *Huey Lewis*.

Time travel is a timeless plot device, and it was used to great effect in this baby boomer bait, a film in which a kid from the 80s travels back in time to the 50s.

Filled with sweet scenes from that simpler era (coonskin caps, soda shops, the works), *Back to the Future* rides on Fox's nervous comic timing and his weird encounters in 50s-land, starting with his own mother having a crush on him. No, this is not a Ken Russell movie.

Zemeckis unwittingly created a movie that allowed America to cherish a return to one of the most repressive—and yet less turbulent—decades, just as he would provide fodder for reactionaries with his 1994 smash *Forrest Gump*. But at least Michael J. Fox's character had a brain, and he had to live for only a week in the 50s, rather than relive all the high and low lights of the past thirty years.

39. *The Big Chill* (1983), Lawrence Kasdan, R. Tom Berenger, Glenn Close, Jeff Goldblum, William Hurt, Kevin Kline, Mary Kay Place, Meg Tilly, JoBeth Williams, *Kevin Costner* (he was the corpse).

This is *The Breakfast Club* for baby boomers, a cute, touching story of several thirtysomething friends who gather to bid farewell to a prematurely deceased compatriot.

The amazing ensemble cast—one of the best of the 80s—spend the movie reminiscing and interacting in the shadow of their friend's death, coming to the realization that their idealistic days as 60s radicals were the best years of their lives, especially now that they are all sell-outs to yuppiedom.

This emotionally complex film correctly identified the yuppie vs. yippie tension that so many 60s survivors were experiencing and prefigured *The Breakfast Club* structurally and *Dirty Dancing* with its enormously popular 60s Motown soundtrack. It also undoubtedly led to the development of one of the quintessential TV shows of the 80s, *thirtysomething* (1987–1991).

40. *Sophie's Choice* (1982), Alan J. Pakula, R. Meryl Streep, Kevin Kline, Peter MacNicol.

Meryl Streep won her second Oscar for her stellar portrayal of "Sophie," a Polish Auschwitz survivor involved with two very different men. One is a wild artist (Kline), and one is a quiet Southern writer (MacNicol), but it is her story of survival that is most gripping and one in which she was once forced to choose between her children—only to lose them both.

This was the movie that made Streep the acting diva of the decade and—after 1981's *The French Lieutenant's Woman*—also featured one of the first of her many accents.

41. *The Road Warrior* (1982), George Miller, R. Mel Gibson, Bruce Spence, Emil Minty, Vernon Wells.

Mel Gibson had received acclaim for his performance in the Australian film *Gallipoli* (1981), but it was this highly imaginative post-Armageddon action film, the sequel to *Mad Max* (1980), that introduced him to American audiences.

As "Mad Max," Gibson had undertaken a *Death Wish*–like act of vengeance against the marauding bandits who murdered his wife and child. That film's cult success led to major interest in this sequel, in which "Max" goes from vigilante to protector, helping a village defend itself against still more postapocalyptic bandits.

The Road Warrior's exciting action sequences and in particular its masterfully edited chases were widely emulated by lesser action films in the 80s, and the film helped make Mel Gibson a major star.

> "He's beautiful, but only on the outside."
> —Susan Sarandon on Mel Gibson

42. *Big* (1988), Penny Marshall, PG. Tom Hanks, Elizabeth Perkins, John Heard, Robert Loggia, Jon Lovitz, Mercedes Ruehl.

The feel-good movie of the 80s was directed by TV's "Laverne" from the 70s, Garry Marshall's little sister, Penny. Marshall had first directed the underrated Whoopi Goldberg comedy *Jumpin' Jack Flash* (1986), but she came into her own with this big hit, which also established Tom Hanks as a romantic and comedic leading man.

The premise of the movie is that a young teen with all the usual teen problems wishes he were "big"—and is inexplicably granted his wish, awakening in the body of an adult (Hanks), but stranded with the life experience and outlook of a boy.

Hanks is hired by a toy company (naturally) and sweetly tries to handle the side effects of being a grown-up: competition at work and the advances of a gorgeous co-worker (Perkins).

This was the *Freaky Friday* of the 80s, except with much more time spent on the lessons Hanks learns trapped in the body of an adult, and much more insight into the pitfalls of adulthood.

43. *Kiss of the Spider Woman* (1985), Hector Babenco, R. William Hurt, Raul Julia, Sonia Braga.

Hurt was the surprise Oscar winner of 1985 for his uncanny portrayal of "Molina," a flamboyantly gay inmate in an oppressive Latin American prison, where he shares a cell with radical "Valentin" (Julia), jailed for his antifascist political beliefs.

Hurt shares his fantasy life, built around a glamorous '40s movie (which may or may not have been a piece of fascist propaganda) *Kiss of the Spider Woman*, which is one of his favorites.

Julia resists Hurt's fantastic tales at first, finding such glitz valueless and even decadent, but he is eventually drawn in, as is the audience, through lengthy black-and-white sequences of that film-within-a-film, starring Sonia Braga as "Marta," the spider woman of the title.

Eventually Julia gives in to the fantasy and also shares a night of passion with Hurt, who sacrifices himself in an effort to save his lover and whom we see at the end entering the fantasy film world he has created.

This film's juxtaposition of reality and fantasy via a nostalgic movie was echoed in Woody Allen's *Purple Rose of Cairo* (also 1985), and it was a film that paved the way for matter-of-fact presentations of homosexuality on screen.

44. *An American Werewolf in London* (1981), John Landis, R. David Naughton, Griffin Dunne, Jenny Agutter, Frank Oz, Brian Glover.

Naughton was already immediately identifiable as the guy singing about being a "Pepper" in that unforgettable Dr Pepper commercial and also from the 1979 TV series *Makin' It*, and though he never did quite make it, he was a delight in this juicy werewolf movie.

The tale is updated as a comic tragedy involving two friends backpacking through Europe as the main characters. When a werewolf attacks them, one (Dunne) dies, and the other (Naughton) is wounded, only to slowly realize that he will soon become a full-fledged werewolf when the moon is full (when else?).

This ghoulishly funny movie has some of the most shocking dream sequences and a really disgusting scene wherein a naked Naughton catches and eats a deer (copied by 1994's *Wolf*), and it helped bolster the rabid return to genre horror in the 80s.

Best parts? Dunne's sporadic, beyond-the-grave visits to his good buddy, with his corporal body rapidly decomposing.

45. *Sixteen Candles* (1984), John Hughes, PG. Molly Ringwald, Justin Henry, Anthony Michael Hall, Michael Schoeffling, Haviland Morris, Gedde Watanabe, *John Cusack, Joan Cusack, Jami Gertz*, Zelda Rubenstein, Brian Doyle-Murray.

The first big John Hughes teen movie was this heartwarming story of a girl (Ringwald) whose sixteenth birthday goes completely unnoticed by her family because her big sister is getting married. Can you get any more suburban princess than that? All the teens in America were sympathizing with Ringwald every step of the way, silently shaking their fists at a world that continually failed to notice them.

Anthony Michael Hall plays the nerd, a Hughes staple role that would later be played by the even more desperately geeky Jon Cryer. Hall's goofily adorable presence and Ringwald's (as always) perfect embodiment of a sulky teenage girl make this work, and it has plenty of guffaws that make it completely watchable every time.

> "I can't believe I gave my panties to a geek."
> —Molly Ringwald, *Sixteen Candles*, 1984

Recommended for viewing every year.

46. *48HRS.* (1982), Walter Hill, R. Nick Nolte, Eddie Murphy, James Remar, *Annette O'Toole, Denise Crosby*.

Eddie Murphy couldn't have asked for a better screen debut after wowing America with his comedy talents on TV's *Saturday Night Live* (1980–1983).

In this thoroughly 80s buddy movie, Murphy plays a convict who is freed from jail for two days only so he can help a surly cop (Nolte) nail a drug lord to the wall. Murphy crackles as the con, peppering his appearance with more dirty words than ever contained in any other mainstream movie, a gambit that translated into big box office.

> "I'm your worst nightmare: a nigger with a badge."
> —Eddie Murphy, *48HRS.*, 1982

The movie's antagonistic buddy relationship was echoed throughout the 80s (*Running Scared*, 1986; *Lethal Weapon*, 1987; *Midnight Run*, 1988).

47. *Dangerous Liaisons* (1988), Stephen Frears, R. John Malkovich, Glenn Close, Michelle Pfeiffer, Uma Thurman, Keanu Reeves, Swoosie Kurtz, Mildred Natwick.

Glenn Close and John Malkovich plotting in *Dangerous Liaisons.*

A major costume drama adaptation of the Choderlos de Laclos novel *Les Liaisons Dangereuses*, in which a conniving, eighteenth-century noblewoman (Close) spars with an equally cunning nobleman (Malkovich).

Malkovich and Close are wonderfully amoral as they ruin the lives of a former virgin (Thurman) and saintly wife (Pfeiffer), indulging in game-playing of the highest degree—yuppies were drooling over the power plays these two executed. Most interesting is that Malkovich finds himself falling in love with Pfeiffer, and he takes great pleasure in the ruination of his former lover (Close) and scheming cohort.

"Sometimes I sing and dance around the house in my underwear. Doesn't make me Madonna."
—Joan Cusack, *Working Girl*, 1988

48. *Working Girl* **(1988),** Mike Nichols, R. Melanie Griffith, Harrison Ford, Sigourney Weaver, Joan Cusack, Alec Baldwin, *Ricki Lake, Nora Dunn.*

Shrill Griffith is the typical 80s working girl of the title, a secretary from Staten Island with high hair and friends (Cusack) with even higher hair, not to mention a dumb-as-hammers boyfriend (Baldwin).

When her yuppie boss (Weaver) must recuperate away from the office, Griffith takes over, makes over, and finally wins over...the affection of the very man (Ford) who once loved her ruthless boss.

This is a sweet love story set against the grim corporate reality of the 80s, one that shows a hard-working girl (who boasts that she has "a head for business and a bod for sin") and her tortuous journey to success.

49. *The Fly* **(1986),** David Cronenberg, R. Jeff Goldblum, Geena Davis, John Getz, anonymous housefly.

One of the worst ideas for a remake (why mess with perfection?) turned out to be a highly credible reinvention of the incredible tale of a misguided scientist who accidentally merges himself with a common housefly, and the sickening results.

Goldblum is the scientist, who is madly trying to develop a *Star Trek*–like way to teleport from one place to another. When a fly gets into the chamber with him, his DNA is bonded with that of the pest, and he slowly, inexorably changes into a human fly.

The transformation will have you tearing your hair out, as a beautiful reporter (Davis) falls in love with a guy doomed to turn into a hideous monster. She's ultimately saved, but not before witnessing his inevitable demise, and not before that memorable scene where she discovers those barbed fly "hairs" protruding from his back.

50. *The Last Temptation of Christ* **(1988),** Martin Scorsese, R. Willem Dafoe, Harvey Keitel, Barbara Hershey, Harry Dean Stanton, André Gregory, *David Bowie*, Verna Bloom.

The most controversial religious film of the decade by one of America's most revered filmmakers, this is a frankly speculative story of the life of Jesus Christ, recasting the figure that Christians believe to be divine as completely human, fallible, and even sexual—though only within the context of Satan's tempting of Christ.

That more Christians didn't realize the depth of Christian spirituality in this movie is a great irony. It's a contribution to spirituality that Scorsese is unlikely ever to make again.

In retrospect, however, this film captures the return to things spiritual that evolved in the late 80s as the early 80s joys of materialism began to rot.

51. *The World According to Garp* **(1982),** George Roy Hill, R. Robin Williams, Mary Beth Hurt, John Lithgow, Glenn Close, Hume Cronyn, Jessica Tandy, Swoosie Kurtz, Amanda Plummer.

The warped film adaptation of John Irving's equally warped book about the classic loser "T. S. Garp"

(Williams), whose overbearing mother runs and nearly ruins his life. Full of scathing parodies (most notably of extreme feminism), this movie introduced Williams as a viable lead, was Close's film debut, and provided an Oscar-nominated opportunity for John Lithgow to play a six-foot transsexual.

52. *The Accused* (1988), Jonathan Kaplan, R. Jodie Foster, Kelly McGillis, Bernie Coulson, Steve Antin.

After early success as a child actress (not to mention as the model in those famous Coppertone ads), Jodie Foster went off to college in the 80s and seemed to disappear from acting. This movie, following a string of comeback misses, put her back on the Hollywood map in a big way, establishing her as a serious actress and winning her an Oscar for her portrayal of a rape victim whose nonvirginal past is used against her at trial.

> "I heard someone screaming, and it was me."
> —Jodie Foster, *The Accused*, 1988

Foster is alluring and feisty as barfly "Sarah Tobias," who is gang-raped on a pinball machine in a story torn from today's headlines. The movie's basis in fact (it was inspired by a 1983 case in which a woman was gang-raped on a pool table in a bar) makes it quintessentially 80s—moviemakers in the 80s turned toward real-life stories for material, altering them only slightly. It is also the most effective movie to date on the issue of rape, itself a hot topic in the 80s, when the concept of "date rape" and outcries against "blaming the victim" were first heard.

53. *On Golden Pond* (1981), Mark Rydell, PG. Henry Fonda, Jane Fonda, Katharine Hepburn, Dabney Coleman, Doug McKeon, William Lanteau.

Henry Fonda finally won his Oscar for this bittersweet film about a tough kid and his equally tough, ancient caretakers, an elderly couple (Fonda and Hepburn, starring together for the first time). The boy unwittingly helps the old coot to better understand his rebellious adult daughter (Jane Fonda) in a film rife with real-life parallels: Jane Fonda's radical politics had

> "Hell, if I hadn't won, I wouldn't be able to walk with my head up anymore."
> —Henry Fonda on winning the Oscar, on his deathbed, 1982

long been a burr under her conservative father's saddle.

On Golden Pond was an enormous hit, demonstrating the viability of films starring actors six decades older than Molly Ringwald. Was it a coincidence that *The Golden Girls* started its umpteen-year TV run just four short years after this film was released?

54. *Platoon* (1986), Oliver Stone, R. Charlie Sheen, Willem Dafoe, Tom Berenger, Francesco Quinn, Forest Whitaker, Kevin Dillon, *Johnny Depp*.

One of the most obnoxious and yet talented directors of the 80s and 90s launched his Vietnam trilogy with this gut-wrenching epic and also earned Oscars for himself and for his very personal movie.

The film's timing was impeccable, tapping into long-simmering dissatisfaction among Vietnam vets and their supporters, who felt they'd been pariahs too long. This film changed all that, making it "okay" to feel sympathy for those warriors, even to revere them.

How did Stone do it? He crafted a movie so harrowing that it made many of its viewers almost feel that they'd lived through the war. Shell-shocked, a new generation of moviegoers would rank this as one of the most profoundly disturbing war movies they'd ever seen.

55. *An Officer and a Gentleman* (1982), Taylor Hackford, R. Richard Gere, Debra Winger, Louis Gossett Jr., David Keith, Lisa Eilbacher, Robert Loggia.

A much less serious side of military life was portrayed in this hot, romantic drama, which allowed Richard Gere once again to show off his derriere and Louis Gossett, Jr. to become one of a mere handful of African-Americans to win an Oscar.

The movie has an unflinching "Be All That You Can Be" tack, since Gere plays an aimless guy who finds himself when he enlists in the navy. This did for the navy what *Top Gun* would later do for the air force.

56. *WarGames* (1983), John Badham, PG. Matthew Broderick, Dabney Coleman, John Wood, Ally Sheedy.

One of the first thrillers to capitalize on that most basic fear of the 80s: technophobia. As PCs invaded homes like pods from *Invasion of the Body Snatchers* most nongeeks were baffled by their power, and the fantastic plot of this movie tweaked that fright with a surgeon's precision.

Broderick is the computer whiz kid, Sheedy his faithful girlfriend. Broderick cheekily breaks into the government's new NORAD missile files and begins playing what at first seems to be a simple game of war . . . except the computer may think it's for real. Could Armageddon be launched with a joystick? This movie made us think so.

57. *Arthur* (1981), Steve Gordon, PG. Dudley Moore, Liza Minnelli, Sir John Gielgud, Geraldine Fitzgerald, Stephen Elliott, *Jill Eikenberry*.

Before political correctness made inebriation unfunny, Dudley Moore scored the hit of his life with this silly farce, in which he plays the perpetually drunken title character.

Prefiguring *Big* ("Arthur" is very childlike, from his predilection for playing with kiddie toys to his irresponsible life), *Arthur* is the story of a happy-go-lucky heir who receives the ultimatum that he must either marry a blue-blooded deb or lose his multimillion-dollar inheritance.

"I wish I had a dime for every dime I have."
—Dudley Moore, *Arthur*, 1981

This stands as one of the only good things Liza Minnelli did during the decade and one of the only good things Dudley Moore has ever done.

58. *Bad Boys* (1983), Rick Rosenthal, R. Sean Penn, Esai Morales, Reni Santoni, Ally Sheedy.

This was the best of the well-made bad boy movies (*Tex*, 1982; *Rumble Fish*, *The Outsiders*, both

Esai Morales confronts the original bad boy, Sean Penn.

1983) and the only one not based on an S. E. Hinton novel.

When Penn kills a rival during a gang war, he gets sent up the river, only to come face-to-face with yet another rival, the guy who raped his girlfriend (introducing Miss Ally Sheedy, in her first movie).

This movie alone proves Penn's acting skills and was a hint of the escalating concern over gangs, soon to be reflected not only in melodramatic movies, but on the nightly news.

59. *Dressed to Kill* (1980), Brian De Palma, R. Angie Dickinson, Michael Caine, Nancy Allen, Keith Gordon, *Dennis Franz*.

One of the most despised and/or beloved directors of the 80s was De Palma, known for his Hitchcock envy and his incessant quoting from other movies within his own work.

To his credit, his *hommages* almost always worked, as they do in this, one of his greatest creations.

Angie Dickinson is a sexually frustrated woman who allows herself to get picked up in a museum and screwed on the backseat of a taxi. She then gets slashed to death in an elevator, and it's up to her son and a friendly whore (Allen) to solve her murder.

Dickinson's tawdry shower scene shows everything that Hitchcock's *Psycho* coyly refused to, and her cat-and-mouse pursuit in the museum goes on forever but is so compelling that it could have lasted even longer.

Not as psychologically taut as De Palma thinks it is, *Dressed to Kill* is nonetheless a near perfect "movie-movie," a good old-fashioned shocker with all the right ingredients to make it a hit in the 80s: shameless nudity, rivers of blood, and a distinctly postmodern flair in its salute to the master of suspense.

60. *The Last Starfighter* (1984), Nick Castle, PG. Lance Guest, Robert Preston, Barbara Bosson, Dan O'Herlihy, Catherine Mary Stewart, Cameron Dye, Wil Wheaton.

One of those surprising gems that sounded like hell to sit through when it was first cast (Robert Preston and Lance Guest?) but ended up as a warmly funny, slightly quirky space comedy.

In the years before the shuttle blew up, America had rediscovered its fascination with outer space.

That fascination is vivid in this comedy, in which Preston plays an alien who recruits video game champ Guest to fight an intergalactic battle. The premise capitalized not only on our interest in the galaxy, but on a universal interest of any 80s adolescent worth his salt: arcade games.

61. *Mask* (1985), Peter Bogdanovich, PG-13. Cher, Sam Elliott, Eric Stoltz, Estelle Getty, Richard Dysart, Laura Dern.

A remorselessly sad movie that combines *The Elephant Man* (1980) with *Terms of Endearment* (1983) to produce a tragedy about a plucky boy born with a horribly disfiguring disease that renders his head an enormous, misshapen mass. He makes the most of his lot, finding love (with ethereal Laura Dern) and giving his rough-and-tumble biker mom (Cher) a reason to live.

Like mother, like son: "Rocky" (Eric Stoltz) and "Rusty" (Cher) have the same tresses in *Mask*.

Eric Stoltz gives a great performance under tons of incredibly realistic makeup, and Cher was considered a shoo-in to walk away with a Best Actress Oscar . . . but failed even to get nominated, one of those inexplicable, shocking oversights of Oscar lore.

Mask is what all those 80s disease-of-the-week telefilms should have been: honest, illuminating, and educational.

62. *The Empire Strikes Back* (1980) and *Return of the Jedi* (1983), Irvin Kershner and Richard Marquand, respectively, both PG. Mark Hamill, Carrie Fisher, Harrison Ford, James Earl Jones (voice), Alec Guinness.

These two sequels to the 70s blockbuster *Star Wars* enjoyed similar blockbuster status, each placing in the top ten highest-grossing films of all time.

In these action-packed space operas we are treated to the ongoing adventures of young "Luke Skywalker" (Hamill), macho "Han Solo" (Ford), and beleaguered "Princess Leia" (Fisher).

The bizarre space creatures (Yoda, Jabba the Hut, R-2D2, C-3PO), thrill-a-minute fights, and high-tech special effects don't overwhelm the genuinely funny and interesting interplay among the characters, who must patch up their differences in order to defeat the evil Dark Side.

The second sequel was originally called *Revenge of the Jedi*.

63. *Less Than Zero* (1987), Marek Kanievska, R. Andrew McCarthy, Jami Gertz, Robert Downey Jr., James Spader.

Not the greatest movie by any stretch, this film is nonetheless vintage 80s since it is a screen adaptation of one of the most widely read pop fiction books of the era, written by then nouveau brat Bret Easton Ellis. It also had a soundtrack that captured the "Die young, stay pretty" atmosphere of 80s L.A. (okay, L.A. of almost any era) and is full of scenes documenting cocaine use, shallow friendships, and out-of-control partying.

The critics found this worthless when it was released, but it's very watchable and contains a strong performance by Robert Downey, Jr., way before anyone was taking him seriously. The movie does pull punches, though, converting Ellis's bisexual protagonist into a straight guy who's horrified when his friend must service men for drug money. The 80s hungered for hedonism but struggled with Republican morals, and the result was *Less Than Zero*.

64. *Aliens* (1986), James Cameron, R. Sigourney Weaver, Michael Biehn, Lance Henriksen, *Paul Reiser*.

The sequel to 1979's claustrophobic space chiller proved to be just as good, in a different, more bombastic way.

Weaver returns as "Ripley," the butch, independent space traveler who was the sole survivor of a vicious alien attack on the freighter in which she worked. Now she returns to destroy the alien forever but is stymied by the cowardly antics of Paul Reiser and her attachment to a little girl.

> **"Get away from her, you bitch!" —Sigourney Weaver, *Aliens*, 1986**

The action is nonstop, and "Ripley" is by far the best movie heroine of the 80s: she's no-nonsense, moral, and can kick some serious alien butt.

65. *Pretty in Pink* (1986), Howard Deutch, PG-13. Molly Ringwald, Andrew McCarthy, Jon Cryer, Harry Dean Stanton, James Spader, Annie Potts, *Andrew Dice Clay*, Margaret Colin, *Dweezil Zappa*.

Molly Ringwald consults her confidante Annie Potts (yes, Annie Potts) at the record store in *Pretty in Pink*. The "pick of the week" at the store was *Different Light* by The Bangles.

Molly plays a white-trash girl who longs to be loved by richie Andrew McCarthy. She gets her big chance, but her poor father (Stanton) can't afford to give her the kind of hip outfits that will impress McCarthy's terminally snobbish pals (headed up by Spader, who always played the teen snob bastard in these adolescent angst movies).

Annie Potts steals scenes as Molly's fast galpal, but what's most memorable (aside from the Psychedelic Furs crooning the title track and OMD's angst-ridden soundtrack contribution, "If You Leave") is the convincing sense of romantic fervor evoked by Molly Ringwald and the accidental exposure of the perils of yup-piedom—ivory tower syndrome could lose you the love of your life (or at least your date for the prom).

Jon Cryer played "Ducky" a little *too* well.

> "It's kind of magical, like being a part of a fraternity of freaks."
> —Andrew McCarthy on being a Hollywood star, 1989

66. *Moonstruck* (1987), Norman Jewison, PG-13. Cher, Nicolas Cage, Olympia Dukakis, Danny Aiello, Vincent Gardenia, Anita Gillette.

Cher won that Oscar she deserved for *Mask* and—shortly after this raging success—gave up making movies for years. This was the perfect vehicle for her, playing an attractive, still young widow who, with the help of a magnificent make-over (and a major wig) transforms into a dazzling beauty.

Her problem is that Danny Aiello, her fiancé, does not make that same transformation—she's much more interested in his little brother (Cage), even if she hates to admit it.

Love and romance and sex seem always to be crapshoots, but by the 80s these things were more complicated than ever, so much so that Cher could not marry a stable man out of convenience, but instead chose a man she truly loved and truly lusted after.

> Nicolas Cage:
> "I'm in love with you."
> Cher:
> "Snap out of it!"
> — *Moonstruck,* 1987

67. *About Last Night . . .* (1986), Edward Zwick, R. Rob Lowe, Demi Moore, Elizabeth Perkins, James Belushi.

The topsy-turvy dating scene of the 80s, with its one-night stands (which for most people were starting to either disappear or become charged with the risk of disease or even death) is presented in this light, funny film. It was based on David Mamet's play *Sexual Perversity in Chicago*, but at the last minute studio heads opted for its final, coy title. Audiences of the 80s weren't quite ready to pay to see anything they thought might be seen as "perverse."

This movie showed Demi Moore's capabilities as an actress and made her such a hot property that she never had to bother acting again.

68. *Die Hard* (1988), John McTiernan, R. Bruce Willis, Bonnie Bedelia, Alan Rickman, Alexander Godunov, Paul Gleason, *Hart Bochner*.

With terrorism a constant plague in the Middle East and with terrorist bombings dotting Europe, it seemed all too believable that some foreign menace could infiltrate the United States and strike on American soil. Ironically, though the villains in this movie are foreign, they are European, not Middle Eastern, and it's cold, hard cash they're after (so the yuppies could grasp the concept).

Bruce Willis plays off his *Moonlighting* persona, keeping the glibness but adding more heroism and grit as a one-man S.W.A.T. team trying desperately to rescue his wife and daughter from the building held hostage by terrorists. Our fear of terrorism was heightened by this movie, though it wouldn't be until the 90s that America would have to deal with real-life terrorists bombing an enormous building on U.S. soil.

69. *Stand by Me* (1986), Rob Reiner, R. River Phoenix, Wil Wheaton, Jerry O'Connell, Corey Feldman, Kiefer Sutherland, Richard Dreyfuss, Casey Siemaszko, John Cusack.

The "Meathead" of the 70s became one of the most consistent directors of the 80s, whether doing parody (*This Is Spinal Tap*, 1984), romance (*The Sure Thing*, 1985), fantasy (*The Princess Bride*, 1987), or even a coming-of-age tale such as this one, based on a Stephen King short story.

Four boys go on a miniadventure to lay claim to the corpse of a missing boy, so they can take the glory for finding him. They never consider how bleak their discovery will be until they have made it, and it's a moving symbol for their loss of innocence.

This is basically *The Big Chill* (it's set in the 50s), except the boomers are in their preteens instead of their late 30s.

Ben E. King's classic song, used to title the movie, became one of the biggest hits of the year when it was reissued, and this movie launched the career of a kid who would be at the forefront of the next group of young actors after the considerably less talented Brat Pack—River Phoenix.

70. *Gremlins* (1984), Joe Dante, PG. Zach Galligan, Phoebe Cates, Hoyt Axton, Polly Holliday, Frances Lee McCain, Keye Luke, Corey Feldman, Judge Reinhold.

Terribly underrated today by critics with short memories (possibly because of its cutesy title?), this wildly energetic pastiche of 50s creature features and the *Star Trek* episode "The Trouble with Tribbles" sparked numerous inferior imitators (*Ghoulies* and *Creepers*, both 1985; *Creepazoids* 1987; and so on).

When a teenager's dad buys him a mysterious creature from Keye Luke, he breaks all the proscribed rules, exposing him to bright light, getting him wet, and feeding him after midnight. The resulting progeny are malicious clones of the sweet-tempered "Gizmo" who wreak havoc with the entire city on Christmas Eve (the same time that *Die Hard* takes place).

This is a movie about movies, with rambunctious gremlins enthralled by classic films that baby boomers cherish, even winding up imprisoned in a theater—doomed by their fascination with *Snow White and the Seven Dwarfs*.

Some of the grosser scenes (a gremlin going "splat" in a microwave comes to mind) led to public outcry about its PG rating. The gremlins are so obviously puppets that it's hard to be truly disturbed. Rather, you rally around the heroes (Galligan and Cates) in the same way you cheered for Steve McQueen in *The Blob*—with utter conviction—and yet gleefully watch the antiheroes (the rebel gremlins) as they attempt to destroy humanity.

Hilarious, creative, and a huge, postmodern wink.

71. *Batman* (1989), Tim Burton, PG-13. Michael Keaton, Jack Nicholson, Kim Basinger, Robert Wuhl, Tracey Walter, Billy Dee Williams, Jack Palance, *Jerry Hall.*

One of the most hyped movies in Hollywood history, *Batman* was being promoted a year before its release. The first bat signal was nothing more than a stylized bat insignia, an effective teaser that would later be copied by almost every major summer movie-to-be, from *Dick Tracy* (1990) to *Casper* and *Cutthroat Island* (both 1995).

But *Batman* was about more than hype. It was also the highly personal vision of auteur Tim Burton, who had made such memorable and unique 80s movies as *Pee-wee's Big Adventure* (1985) and *Beetlejuice* (1988), hits big enough to justify his helming of this megabucks studio gamble.

The character was already legendary and loved, but Burton's direction made *Batman* the movie a dark and sinister affair, with a cruelly frightening "Joker" played by Jack Nicholson, in sharp contrast with Cesar Romero's high-camp interpretation of the character on the 60s TV series.

From its elaborate, surreal, Gothic sets to the uncanny transformation of Nicholson, from Prince's quirky (and yet massively popular) soundtrack to the millions of bat toys and spin-offs created to cash in on the film, this was a major success in every regard.

This movie is a love-it-or-hate-it affair (whoever decided that Michael Keaton should play the title role had you-know-what in the belfrey), but it was one of the true blockbusters of the 80s and an artistically influential piece of filmmaking that led many to consider maverick Burton as one of the hottest and most creative directors working.

72. *Amadeus* (1984), Milos Forman, PG. F. Murray Abraham, Tom Hulce, Elizabeth Berridge, Simon Callow, Roy Dotrice, Christine Ebersole.

One of the most accessible of the historical epics of the 80s, this grand, heady interpretation of the life of Wolfgang Amadeus Mozart (Hulce) as seen through the embittered eyes of his rival Antonio Salieri (Abraham in an Oscar-winning role) was a major box office hit as well as a favorite of the critics.

By the time boyish Hulce got through playing Mozart (so to speak), he'd helped to reinvigorate our image of that seminal figure in music history, exposing his borderline-crazy persona and lust for life. Sales of Mozart's music soared. Too bad it was hundreds of years too late for him to enjoy the renewed attention.

"I hate politics!"
—Tom Hulce,
Amadeus, **1984**

The movie also inspired Falco to record the number-one pop hit "Rock Me Amadeus" (1986), enough reason in itself to rank this film as very important indeed.

73. *Revenge of the Nerds* (1984), Jeff Kanew, R. Robert Carradine, Anthony Edwards, Timothy Busfield, Andrew Cassesse, Curtis Armstrong, Ted McGinley, John Goodman, Bernie Casey.

This movie should have been really stupid, lame, forgettable . . . but it's not. In fact, *Revenge of the Nerds* stands as one of the funniest farces of the 80s, most striking for its all-inclusive portrait of a group of nerds who fight back against popularettes, frat boys, and their ilk.

There are topless scenes, scatological one-liners, and lots of gratuitous drunken bits, but this teen comedy champions the rights of the losers who traditionally pay to go see teen sex comedies, not star in them. The fraternity that the nerds start probably would have accepted Jon Cryer.

74. *"Crocodile" Dundee* (1986), Peter Faiman, PG-13. Paul Hogan, Linda Kozlowski, John Meillon, Mark Blum.

All things Australian (except Olivia Newton-John) became popular when Australian Paul Hogan exported his star vehicle from Down Under (where it had already become the biggest hit of all time). America was quite taken with the earnest Aussie who, after being discovered in the Outback by a sophisticated career woman (Kozlowski) attempts to blend into the New York City social scene.

The result is a great "fish out of water" film, a concept that many braving the rigid social structures of the 80s could relate to. And if the chemistry between Hogan and Kozlowski seems highly believable, believe this: Hogan divorced his longtime wife to marry the pretty young blonde a few years after this—his only successful movie—captivated American moviegoers.

"G'day."
—Paul Hogan,
"Crocodile"
Dundee, **1986**

75. *Blame It on Rio* (1984), Stanley Donen, R. Michael Caine, Joseph Bologna, Demi Moore, Michelle Johnson, *Valerie Harper*.

This is probably the worst movie on this list (well . . . there's always *St. Elmo's Fire*), but there's no denying the instant recognition of that vaguely sexy title (is it the Brazilian connection of "Rio" or the movie's notorious reputation?).

The story is tawdry: an aging man has a wild fling with a close friend's provocative daughter.

Demi Moore here doesn't seem to have those enormous, voluptuous breasts she acquired in the late 80s. . . . Was she a late bloomer?

76. *Beetlejuice* (1988), Tim Burton, PG. Michael Keaton, Geena Davis, Alec Baldwin, Sylvia Sidney, Catherine O'Hara, Winona Ryder, Jeffrey Jones, *Dick Cavett*.

Ostensibly a dopey farce for kids, this movie actually doubles as a strikingly nonsensical commentary on how hard it is living in the real world. Two ghosts—too timid to frighten away the family trespassing in their house—ask a hyperactive poltergeist ("Beetlejuice") to do the deed.

This movie became a huge hit, especially among small children and film buffs, who make strange bedfellows. It also led to a less surreal Saturday morning cartoon (1989).

77. *St. Elmo's Fire* (1985), Joel Schumacher, R. Rob Lowe, Demi Moore, Andrew McCarthy, Judd Nelson, Ally Sheedy, Emilio Estevez, Mare Winningham, Martin Balsam, *Joyce Van Patten*, Andie MacDowell.

The worst Brat Pack movie is so bad that it's almost unwatchable. When Phil Donahue had some of its stars on his show and aired a clip featuring Ally Sheedy emoting in her baby Sandy Dennis sort of way, all he could say afterward—unconvincingly—was, "Now, *that's* acting."

This movie is like *The Little Chill* or even *The Lunch Club*. It follows the soap operatic existences of seven Georgetown grads, whose problems range from sexual dysfunction (McCarthy) to infidelity (Nelson) to blah, blah, blah. Horribly acted (Lowe) and maudlin, this movie is impossible to like.

Coming so soon after *The Breakfast Club* (also 1985) and with such a similar cast, it helped solidify the perception of who was in the Brat Pack. It also established the ensemble casts that Gen Xers would crave in the future (think of it as a direct ancestor of *Melrose Place*).

The title, one of the most memorable of the 80s, refers to a phenomenon involving stars in the night sky. With the notable exceptions of megastar Moore, Estevez, and bit player MacDowell, the cast made like supernovae and burned out while their shine still lingered.

78. *The Karate Kid* (1984), John G. Avildsen, PG. Ralph Macchio, Pat Morita, Elisabeth Shue, Randee Heller, Chad McQueen.

Like the *Kung Fu* (TV, 1972–1975) of the 80s, this spiritually uplifting tale of an underdog (Macchio) who learns karate as a means of recapturing his sense of self scored with an array of audiences, especially among kids. Macchio's eventually fearless confrontation of the biggest bully imaginable is totally believable and the loving advice he receives from his own personal Burgess Meredith (Pat Morita) applies to life as well as to fighting.

A fight movie that manages to advocate peace.

79. *Chariots of Fire* (1981), Hugh Hudson, PG. Ben Cross, Ian Charleson, Nigel Havers, Ian Holm, Alice Krige, Brad Davis, Patrick Magee, Sir John Gielgud.

A rather interminable epic about runners in the 1924 Olympics in Paris that helped make the Olympics major press and audience events in the 80s, egged on by a mystically monotonous theme song by Vangelis that was much parodied.

The movie won an Oscar as the best of 1981, which it certainly didn't deserve since it's another example of overly dry British drama; yet it does capture the romance of international competition, whereas other treatments concentrate on cutthroat athletics.

80. *Repo Man* (1984), Alex Cox, R. Emilio Estevez, Harry Dean Stanton, Sy Richardson, Tracy Walter, Olivia Barash.

Arguably the biggest cult film of the decade, starring future Mighty Duck Emilio Estevez as an apathetic punker who repossesses cars for a living against the backdrop of a futuristic, chaotic world (which we could feasibly be slipping toward).

This tiny movie has garnered a major following for its stylishly edgy production values and sick, un-PC sense of humor.

Ten Quintessentially 80s Directors

1. Steven Spielberg: *Raiders of the Lost Ark* 1981; *E.T. The Extra-Terrestrial* 1982; *Twilight Zone: The Movie* (segment) 1983; *Indiana Jones and the Temple of Doom* 1984; *The Color Purple, Amazing Stories* (TV series pilot) 1985; *Empire of the Sun* 1987; *Indiana Jones and the Last Crusade, Always* 1989.

2. John Hughes: *Sixteen Candles* 1984; *The Breakfast Club, Weird Science* 1985; *Ferris Bueller's Day Off* 1986; *Planes, Tranes & Automobiles* 1987; *She's Having a Baby* 1988; *Uncle Buck* 1989.

3. Rob Reiner: *This Is Spinal Tap* 1984; *The Sure Thing* 1985; *Stand by Me* 1986; *The Princess Bride* 1987; *When Harry Met Sally* 1989.

4. Ron Howard: *Cotton Candy* (TV) 1982; *Night Shift* 1982; *Splash* 1984; *Cocoon* 1985; *Gung Ho* 1986; *Willow* 1988; *Parenthood* 1989.

5. Woody Allen: *Stardust Memories* 1980; *Midsummer Night's Sex Comedy* 1982; *Zelig* 1983; *Broadway Danny Rose* 1984; *The Purple Rose of Cairo* 1985; *Hannah and Her Sisters* 1986; *Radio Days, September* 1987; *Another Woman* 1988; *Crimes and Misdemeanors, New York Stories* (segment) 1989.

6. Martin Scorsese: *Raging Bull* 1980; *King of Comedy* 1983; *After Hours, Amazing Stories* (TV, episode) 1985; *The Color of Money* 1986; *The Last Temptation of Christ* 1988; *New York Stories* (segment) 1989.

7. Lawrence Kasdan: *Body Heat* 1981; *The Big Chill* 1983; *Silverado* 1985; *The Accidental Tourist* 1988.

8. David Cronenberg: *Scanners* 1981; *Dead Zone, Videodrome* 1983; *The Fly* 1986; *Dead Ringers* 1988.

9. Brian De Palma: *Dressed to Kill* 1980; *Blow Out* 1981; *Body Double* 1984; *Scarface* 1983; *Wise Guys* 1986; *The Untouchables* 1987; *Casualties of War* 1989.

10. Joel Schumacher: *The Incredible Shrinking Woman* 1981; *D.C. Cab* 1984; *St. Elmo's Fire* 1985; *The Lost Boys* 1987; *Cousins* 1989.

Ten Quintessentially 80s Actresses

1. Meryl Streep: *The French Lieutenant's Woman* 1981; *Still of the Night, Sophie's Choice* 1982; *Silkwood* 1983; *Falling in Love* 1984; *Out of Africa, Plenty* 1985; *Heartburn* 1986; *Ironweed* 1987; *A Cry in the Dark* 1988; *She-Devil* 1989.

2. Molly Ringwald: (see page 80).

3. Kathleen Turner: *Body Heat* 1981; *The Man with Two Brains* 1983; *A Breed Apart, Crimes of Passion, Romancing the Stone* 1984; *Prizzi's Honor, The Jewel of the Nile* 1985; *Peggy Sue Got Married* 1986; *Julia and Julia, Dear America* (voice) 1987; *The Accidental Tourist, Switching Channels, Who Framed Roger Rabbit?* (voice) 1988; *Tummy Trouble* (voice), *The War of the Roses* 1989.

4. Debra Winger: *Urban Cowboy* 1980; *An Officer and a Gentleman, Cannery Row, E.T. The Extra-Terrestrial* (voice) 1982; *Terms of Endearment* 1983; *Mike's Murder* 1984; *Legal Eagles, Black Widow* 1986; *Made in Heaven* 1987; *Betrayed* 1988.

5. Ally Sheedy: (see page 80).

6. Jami Gertz: *Endless Love, On the Right Track* 1981; *Alphabet City, Sixteen Candles* 1984; *Mischief* 1985; *Solarbabies, Quicksilver, Crossroads* 1986; *Less Than Zero, The Lost Boys* 1987; *Renegades, Listen to Me* 1989.

7. Sally Field: *Smokey and the Bandit Part II* 1980; *Absence of Malice, Back Roads* 1981; *Kiss Me Goodbye* 1982; *Places in the Heart* 1984; *Murphy's Romance* 1985; *Surrender* 1987; *Punchline* 1988; *Steel Magnolias* 1989.

8. Kelly McGillis: *Reuben, Reuben* 1983; *Code of Honor* (TV) 1984; *Witness* 1985; *Top Gun* 1986; *Made in Heaven* 1987; *The House on Carroll Street, The Accused, Unsettled Land* 1988; *Winter People* 1989.

9. Jennifer Grey: *Reckless, The Cotton Club, Red Dawn* 1984; *American Flyers* 1985; *Ferris Bueller's Day Off* 1986; *Dirty Dancing* 1987; *Light Years* (voice) 1988; *Bloodhounds of Broadway* 1989.

10. Jessica Lange: *How to Beat the High Cost of Living* 1980; *The Postman Always Rings Twice* 1981; *Frances, Tootsie* 1982; *Country, Cat on a Hot Tin Roof* (TV) 1984; *Sweet Dreams* 1985; *Crimes of the Heart* 1986; *Far North, Everybody's All-American* 1988; *Men Don't Leave, Music Box* 1989.

Ten Quintessentially 80s Actors

1. Tom Cruise: *Endless Love, Taps* 1981; *Losin' It, The Outsiders, Risky Business, All the Right Moves* 1983; *Legend* 1985; *Top Gun, The Color of Money* 1986; *Cocktail, Rain Man* 1988; *Born on the Fourth of July* 1989.

2. Andrew McCarthy: *The Beniker Gang* (TV), *Class* 1983; *Heaven Help Us, St. Elmo's Fire* 1985; *Pretty in Pink* 1986; *Less Than Zero, Mannequin, Waiting for the Moon* 1987; *Kansas, Fresh Horses* 1988; *Club Extinction, Weekend at Bernie's* 1989.

3. Jack Nicholson: *The Shining* 1980; *Reds, The Postman Always Rings Twice* 1981; *The Border* 1982; *Terms of Endearment* 1983; *Prizzi's Honor* 1985; *Heartburn* 1986; *The Witches of Eastwick, Broadcast News, Ironweed* 1987; *Batman* 1989.

4. William Hurt: *Altered States* 1980; *Body Heat, Eyewitness* 1981; *The Big Chill, Gorky Park* 1983; *Kiss of the Spider Woman* 1985; *Children of a Lesser God* 1986; *Broadcast News* 1987; *The Accidental Tourist, A Time of Destiny* 1988.

5. Arnold Schwarzenegger: *The Jayne Mansfield Story* (TV) 1980; *Conan the Barbarian* 1982; *Conan the Destroyer, The Terminator* 1984; *Commando, Red Sonja* 1985; *Raw Deal* 1986; *Predator, The Running Man* 1987; *Red Heat, Twins* 1988.

6. Michael Douglas: *It's My Turn* 1980; *The Star Chamber* 1983; *Romancing the Stone* 1984; *The Jewel of the Nile, A Chorus Line* 1985; *Fatal Attraction, Wall Street* 1987; *The War of the Roses, Black Rain* 1989.

7. Eddie Murphy: *48HRS.* 1982; *Trading Places, Eddie Murphy: Delirious* (HBO) 1983; *Best Defense, Beverly Hills Cop* 1984; *The Golden Child* 1986; *Eddie Murphy: Raw, Beverly Hills Cop II* 1987; *Coming to America* 1988; *Harlem Nights* (also directed) 1989.

8. Sylvester Stallone: *Victory, Nighthawks* 1981; *Rocky III, First Blood* 1982; *Staying Alive* (director) 1983; *Rhinestone* 1984; *Rocky IV, Rambo: First Blood Part II* 1985; *Cobra* 1986; *Over the Top* 1987; *Rambo III* 1988; *Lock Up, Tango and Cash* 1989.

9. Dustin Hoffman: *Tootsie* 1982; *Death of a Salesman* (TV) 1985; *Ishtar* 1987; *Rain Man* 1988; *Family Business* 1989.

10. Steve Guttenberg: *To Race the Wind* (TV), *Can't Stop the Music* 1980; *Miracle on Ice* 1981; *Diner* 1982; *The Man Who Wasn't There, The Day After* (TV) 1983; *Police Academy* 1984; *Police Academy 2: Their First Assignment, Cocoon, Bad Medicine* 1985; *Police Academy 3: Back in Training, Pecos Bill* (TV), *Short Circuit* 1986; *Surrender, The Bedroom Window, Three Men and a Baby, Amazon Women on the Moon, Police Academy 4: Citizens on Patrol* 1987; *Cocoon: The Return, High Spirits* 1988.

Ten Great Date Movies of the 80s, or Dirty Dancing Was Sold Out

1. *White Nights* (1985), Taylor Hackford, PG-13. Mikhail Baryshnikov, Gregory Hines, Isabella Rossellini, Helen Mirren, Geraldine Page.

Baryshnikov acts! (In tights.)

2. *Racing with the Moon* (1984), Richard Benjamin, PG. Sean Penn, Elizabeth McGovern, Nicolas Cage, Crispin Glover, Dana Carvey, Carol Kane.

A World War II love story so sweet, you're guaranteed to be holding hands throughout.

3. *Children of a Lesser God* (1986), Randa Haines, R. William Hurt, Marlee Matlin, Piper Laurie, Philip Bosco.

Hurt must be Matlin's ears, and she nibbles on his to return the favor.

> "Do you think that we could find a place where we can meet . . . not in silence, and not in sound?"
> —William Hurt, *Children of a Lesser God*, 1986

4. *Urban Cowboy* (1980), James Bridges, PG. John Travolta, Debra Winger, Scott Glenn, Madolyn Smith, Barry Corbin.

This is a hot and steamy country and western romance, and that's no (mechanical) bull.

5. *The Sure Thing* (1985), Rob Reiner, PG-13. John Cusack, Daphne Zuniga, Anthony Edwards, Boyd Gaines, Lisa Jane Persky, *Viveca Lindfors, Nicolette Sheridan, Tim Robbins*.

A charmingly riotous movie for the date with a sense of humor.

6. *Endless Love* (1981), Franco Zeffirelli, R. Brooke Shields, Martin Hewitt, Don Murray, Shirley Knight, Beatrice Straight, Richard Kiley, James Spader, *Tom Cruise*, Jami Gertz.

A touching love story about two crazy kids who just can't stop touching each other.

7. *Somewhere in Time* (1980), Jeannot Szwarc, PG. Christopher Reeve, Jane Seymour, Christopher Plummer, *Teresa Wright*.

Michigan never looked so good as in this time travel romance, set on historic Mackinac Island. Don't ask questions.

8. *Mystic Pizza* (1988), Daniel Petrie, R. Annabeth Gish, Julia Roberts, Lili Taylor, Vincent D'Onofrio, Billy Moses.

A low-budget John Hughes–style movie featuring Julia Roberts before her "cute thing" got out of control.

9. *Vision Quest* (1985), Harold Becker, R. Matthew Modine, Linda Fiorentino, Ronny Cox, Roberts Blossom, Daphne Zuniga, Madonna.

A high school wrestler is crazy for an older woman, proving that age is just a number.

10. *Torch Song Trilogy* (1988), Paul Bogart, R. Harvey Fierstein, Anne Bancroft, Matthew Broderick, Brian Kerwin, Karen Young, Charles Pierce.

The perfect gay date movie: romance, a gay kiss, and extended drag sequences.

Star Fuckers: The Ten Hottest Movies of the 80s

1. *The Postman Always Rings Twice* (1981), Bob Rafelson, R. Jack Nicholson, Jessica Lange, John Colicos, Anjelica Huston, *Christopher Lloyd.*

Had everybody guessing: Did they or didn't they? Just remember that Anjelica was on the sidelines refereeing.

2. *The Hunger* (1983), Tony Scott, R. Catherine Deneuve, David Bowie, Susan Sarandon, Cliff DeYoung, Ann Magnuson, Dan Hedaya, *Willem Dafoe.*

If guys like to see two women making love, guess what they thought about seeing two goddesses?

3. *The Big Easy* (1987), Jim McBride, R. Dennis Quaid, Ellen Barkin, Ned Beatty, John Goodman, Ebbe Roe Smith, Charles Ludlum.

Ellen Barkin in the title role.

4. *Betty Blue* (1986), Jean-Jacques Beineix, R. Beatrice Dalle, Jean-Hughes Anglade, Gerard Darmon.

The movie opens with a lengthy, relentless sex scene and Anglade's matter-of-fact voice-over: "I had known Betty for two weeks."

5. *Bull Durham* (1988), Ron Shelton, R. Kevin Costner, Susan Sarandon, Tim Robbins, Trey Wilson, Robert Wuhl, Jenny Robertson.

The movie is based on balls, plus you get Tim Robbins in a garter belt to satisfy frustrated Ed Wood fans.

6. *The Fabulous Baker Boys* (1989), Steven Kloves, R. Michelle Pfeiffer, Jeff Bridges, Beau Bridges, Elie Raab, Jennifer Tilly.

. . . and the bodacious girl they're after.

7. *9¹/2 Weeks* (1986), Kim Basinger, Mickey Rourke.

The ties that bind.

8. *Romancing the Stone* (1984), Kathleen Turner, Michael Douglas.

They even generated enough body heat for a quickie sequel — *Jewel of the Nile* (1985).

9. *Risky Business* (1983), Tom Cruise, Rebecca De Mornay.

Sometimes you gotta say, "What a fuck!" An incredible sequence on the Chicago el has all the right moves.

10. *Breathless* (1983), Jim McBride, R. Richard Gere, Valerie Kapriski.

Being serious about their craft, they agreed to do the acting only because it was instrumental to the nude scenes.

Ten Movies Featuring the Least Likely Sex Symbols of the 80s

1. *Dangerous Liaisons* (1988), Glenn Close and John Malkovich.

The homeliest, sexiest stars ever to size each other up.

2. *Pretty in Pink* (1986), Molly Ringwald and Andrew McCarthy.

But you see she's not particularly, and they're both a bit young, no?

3. *The Goonies* (1985), Martha Plimpton and Corey Feldman. Richard Donner, PG. Also starring Sean Astin, Josh Brolin, Jeff B. Cohen, Anne Ramsey.

This flick led to pinups for both in teen magazines, apparently to make other adolescents feel better.

4. *Making Love* (1982), Harry Hamlin and Michael Ontkean. Arthur Hiller, R. Also starring Kate Jackson, Wendy Hiller, Arthur Hill, Nancy Olson, Terry Kiser, Camilla Carr, Michael Dudikoff.

Yeah, right.

5. *Terms of Endearment* (1983), Shirley MacLaine and Jack Nicholson.

Sex after forty. And fifty.

6. *Sugarbaby* (1985), Marianne Sagebrecht and Essi Gulp. Percy Adlon, R. Also starring Toni Berger, Wil Spendler, Manuela Denz.

She dolls herself up to get her man but won't give up the waistline. Bravo!

7. *Hairspray* (1988), Ricki Lake and Michael St. Gerard. John Waters, PG. Also starring Divine, Jerry Stiller, Sonny Bono, Deborah Harry, Mink Stole, *Pia Zadora*, *Ric Ocasek*, Ruth Brown, *John Waters*.

Another blow for chubby chasers, and equal opportunity lovin' for those with perpetual bad hair days.

8. *Ghostbusters* (1984), Sigourney Weaver and Rick Moranis.

That ole devil called love.

Who do you think would wind up on top?

9. *Weird Science* (1985), Anthony Michael Hall and Kelly LeBrock. John Hughes, PG-13. Also starring Ilan Mitchell-Smith, *Robert Downey, Jr.*, Bill Paxton.

Don't hate her because she's beautiful, but what's stopping you from loathing Hall, an underage, girl-crazy computer nerd? A May/December of the following year romance.

10. *Rich and Famous* (1981), Jacqueline Bisset and Matt Lattanzi. George Cukor, R. Candice Bergen, David Selby, Hart Bochner, Meg Ryan, Steven Hill, Michael Brandon.

It's hard to believe he'd make such an ass of himself so willingly.

Only When I Laugh: Twenty Funny Films of the 80s

1. *National Lampoon's Vacation* (1983), John Hughes, R. Chevy Chase, Beverly D'Angelo, Imogene Coca, Randy Quaid, Anthony Michael Hall, Christie Brinkley, James Keach, John Candy, Brian Doyle-Murray.

Gag-filled family parody with that scene-stealing southern teen who brags that her daddy says she's the best French kisser in the world.

2. *Hannah and Her Sisters* (1986), Woody Allen, PG. Mia Farrow, Barbara Hershey, Dianne Wiest, Michael Caine, Woody Allen, Maureen O'Sullivan, Lloyd Nolan, Sam Waterston, Carrie Fisher, Max von Sydow, Julie Kavner, Tony Roberts, John Turturro.

One of Woody's funniest. Everyone gets laughs in this movie— even Max von Sydow.

3. *The Man with Two Brains* (1983), Carl Reiner, R. Steve Martin, Kathleen Turner, David Warner, *Sissy Spacek (voice)*, *Merv Griffin*.

Hysterical farce that was an early indication that Kathleen Turner had a sense of humor.

4. *Cannonball Run* (1981), Hal Needham, PG. Burt Reynolds, Farrah Fawcett, Roger Moore, Dom DeLuise, Dean Martin, Sammy Davis, Jr., Jack Elam, Adrienne Barbeau, Peter Fonda, Bert Convy, Jamie Farr.

A holdover from the 70s, a zany chase movie full of stars and personalities and followed by outtakes of DeLuise cracking up during filming. Believe it or not, just as funny now as then.

5. *Women on the Verge of a Nervous Breakdown* (1988), Pedro Almodovar, R. Carmen Maura, Fernando Guillen, Julieta Serrano, Maria Barranco, Rossy De Palma, Antonio Banderas.

Rossy De Palma's face makes this a film you'll giggle through. Actually, just her nose is enough for continual snickers.

6. *A Fish Called Wanda* (1988), Charles Crichton, R. John Cleese, Jamie Lee Curtis, Kevin Kline, Michael Palin.

Cleese spent years perfecting this script, and it brought Jamie Lee Curtis back from the dead.

7. *Eating Raoul* (1982), Paul Bartel, R. Paul Bartel, Mary Woronov, Buck Henry, Ed Begley Jr., Edie McClurg, Robert Beltran.

The joke here is cannibalism. Ha-ha! But funniest is when a poolful of yuppies get unceremoniously electrocuted.

8. *Trading Places* (1983), John Landis, R. Eddie Murphy, Dan Aykroyd, Jamie Lee Curtis, Ralph Bellamy, Don Ameche, Denholm Elliott, Paul Gleason, James Belushi.

Murphy and Aykroyd indulge in that age-old formula: the switch movie. It sparkles here, and Don Ameche went on to a full-scale second career as a cute, funny old geezer.

9. *Caddyshack* (1980), Harold Ramis, R. Chevy Chase, Rodney Dangerfield, Ted Knight, Michael O'Keefe, Bill Murray, Brian Doyle-Murray.

The ridiculously fake gopher, dancing to "I'm Alright," and Bill Murray as the Missing Link.

10. *Married to the Mob* (1988), Jonathan Demme, R. Michelle Pfeiffer, Dean Stockwell, Alec Baldwin, Matthew Modine, Mercedes Ruehl, Joan Cusack, Ellen Foley, *Chris Isaak.*

Michelle Pfeiffer lets her (brown) hair down, cracks bubblegum, and helps make this one of the funniest mob comedies to date.

11. *Police Academy* (1984), Hugh Wilson, R. Steve Guttenberg, Kim Cattrall, Bubba Smith, George Gaynes, Debralee Scott, Michael Winslow, Leslie Easterbrook, Georgina Spelvin.

Too much of a good thing after the umpteenth sequel, but funny as lame cop send-ups go.

12. *A Christmas Story* (1983), Bob Clark, PG. Peter Billingsley, Darren McGavin, Melinda Dillon.

Peter "Messy Marvin" Billingsley trudges resentfully through a bitterly funny Christmas valentine. The "tongue stuck on the icy pole" scene has been known to incapacitate viewers.

13. *Raising Arizona* (1987), Ethan Coen, R. Holly Hunter, Nicolas Cage, John Goodman, William Forsythe, M. Emmet Walsh, Frances McDormand.

Outlandish kidnap comedy that came out of nowhere.

Wyatt Knight sees something glorious through the hole that peeks into the girls' shower room in *Porky's.*

14. *Porky's* (1982), Bob Clark, R. Dan Monahan, Wyatt Knight, Scott Colomby, Tony Ganios, Mark Herrier, Kim Cattrall.

The ultimate teen exploitation comedy. Hard to believe it's Canadian.

15. *Mr. Mom* (1983), Stan Dragoti, PG. Michael Keaton, Teri Garr, Christopher Lloyd, Martin Mull, Ann Jillian, Edie McClurg, Valri Bromfield.

An ode to the latchkey kids, who must put up with a working mom and inept housedad.

16. *Night Shift* (1982), Ron Howard, R. Henry Winkler, Michael Keaton, Shelley Long, Kevin Costner, Richard Belzer, *Shannen Doherty.*

The Fonz and Michael Keaton (in his first movie) run a call girl ring out of a morgue. Dead funny, despite an infamous homophobic jailhouse scene.

17. *Monty Python's The Meaning of Life* (1983), Terry Jones, R. Graham Chapman, John Cleese, Terry Gilliam, Eric Idle, Terry Jones, Michael Palin.

The most consistently funny and politically daring of their movies and sketches, including the infamous "Every Sperm Is Sacred" musical number.

18. *Down and Out in Beverly Hills* (1986), Paul Mazursky, R. Bette Midler, Nick Nolte, Richard Dreyfuss, *Little Richard*, Elizabeth Pena.

Bette Midler and Mike the Dog do double takes.

19. *Three Men and a Baby* (1987), Leonard Nimoy, PG. Tom Selleck, Steve Guttenberg, Ted Danson, Margaret Colin, *Celeste Holm, Nancy Travis.*

Three major, soon-to-become redundant male stars fumble with an infant.

> **"How could something so small create so much of something so disgusting?"**
> —Steve Guttenberg, *Three Men and a Baby,* 1987

20. *Look Who's Talking* (1989), Amy Heckerling, PG-13. John Travolta, Kirstie Alley, Olympia Dukakis, George Segal, *Abe Vigoda*, Bruce Willis (voice).

Okay, maybe it is a little gross (after *The Silent*

Scream, do we really need a talking fetus?), but parents around the globe laugh knowingly.

That Was Acting: Ten Powerhouse Dramatic Films of the 80s

1. *Frances* (1982), Graeme Clifford, R. Jessica Lange, Kim Stanley, Sam Shepard.

The story of Hollywood starlet Frances Farmer, harrowingly portrayed by Lange in the first role for which she received unanimous acclaim.

2. *Glory* (1989), Edward Zwick, R. Denzel Washington, Matthew Broderick, Morgan Freeman, Cary Elwes, Jihmi Kennedy, Donovan Leitch, Jane Alexander.

The unique, panoramic vision of a real-life, all-black unit during the Civil War.

3. *Places in the Heart* (1984), Robert Benton, PG. Sally Field, John Malkovich, Danny Glover, Ed Harris, Lindsay Crouse, Amy Madigan.

White trash surviving the Great Depression.

4. *Driving Miss Daisy* (1989), Bruce Beresford, PG. Jessica Tandy, Morgan Freeman, Dan Aykroyd, Esther Rolle, *Patti LuPone*.

A crotchety old white woman destined to outlive us all and the touching, loving relationship she has with her black chauffeur.

5. *Colors* (1988), Dennis Hopper, R. Sean Penn, Robert Duvall, Maria Conchita Alonso, Trinidad Silva, Randi Brooks.

Way before Rodney King, a scary look at life on the gang-run streets of Los Angeles.

6. *Missing* (1982), Constantin Costa-Gavras, PG. Jack Lemmon, Sissy Spacek, John Shea, Melanie Mayron, David Clennon, Janice Rule.

A conservative father and his liberal daughter-in-law try to locate a missing writer during a South American coup.

7. *Diner* (1982), Barry Levinson, R. Steve Guttenberg, Daniel Stern, Mickey Rourke, Kevin Bacon, Paul Reiser, Ellen Barkin, *Tim Daly*.

Friends meet at their favorite old diner to reminisce.

8. *Gloria* (1980), John Cassavetes, R. Gena Rowlands, Buck Henry, John Adams, Julie Carmen.

A gutsy broad defends the life of a child against the mob.

9. *A Soldier's Story* (1984), Norman Jewison, PG. Howard E. Rollins, Jr., Adolph Caesar, Denzel Washington, *Patti LaBelle*, *Robert Townsend*, Wings Hauser, *David Alan Grier*.

Tense whodunit set in an all-black regiment during World War II.

10. *The Unbearable Lightness of Being* (1988), Philip Kaufman, R. Daniel Day-Lewis, Juliette Binoche, Lena Olin, Derek de Lint.

Day-Lewis's breakthrough role as a terminally shallow doctor.

Meryl Streep appears to have dozed off while filming the terminally tedious *Out of Africa*.

The Good, the Bad, the Boring: Ten Historical Epics of the 80s

1. *Out of Africa* (1985), Sydney Pollack, PG. Meryl Streep, Robert Redford, Klaus Maria Brandauer, Michael Kitchen.

Sleeping!

2. *Gandhi* (1982), Richard Attenborough, PG. Ben Kingsley, Candice Bergen, Edward Fox, Sir John Gielgud, Sir John Mills, Saeed Jaffrey, Trevor Howard, Ian Charleson, *Martin Sheen*, *Daniel Day-Lewis*.

Comatose!

3. *Reds* (1981), Warren Beatty, PG. Warren Beatty, Diane Keaton, Jack Nicholson, Edward Herrmann, Maureen Stapleton, Gene Hackman, Jerzy Kosinski,

"He even took the gramophone on safari."
—Meryl Streep, *Out of Africa*, 1985

George Plimpton, Paul Sorvino, William Daniels, M. Emmet Walsh, Dolph Sweet.

Much more like it. Better *Reds* than dead.

4. *Yentl* (1983), Barbra Streisand, PG. Barbra Streisand, Mandy Patinkin, Amy Irving, Nehemiah Persoff, Steven Hill.

Mildly diverting tale of a girl who tries to pass as a boy so she can study the Talmud, but for this she wants an Oscar?

5. *Quest for Fire* (1982), Jean-Jacques Annaud, R. Everett McGill, Rae Dawn Chong, Ron Perlman, Nameer El-Kadi.

Mesmerizing with no real dialogue, just a made-up, aboriginal speech.

6. *Greystoke: The Legend of Tarzan, Lord of the Apes* (1984), Hugh Hudson, PG. Christopher Lambert, Sir Ralph Richardson, Andie MacDowell, *Glenn Close (voice)*, Ian Holm, James Fox, Ian Charleson.

Most interesting thing about this is watching Glenn Close's voice come out of Andie MacDowell's mouth—MacDowell's Texas accent was deemed too strong.

7. *The Right Stuff* (1983), Philip Kaufman, PG. Ed Harris, Dennis Quaid, Sam Shepard, Scott Glenn, Fred Ward, Charles Frank, Barbara Hershey, Kim Stanley, Veronica Cartwright, *Jeff Goldblum*, Harry Shearer.

The golden age of space travel made this an appealing throwback.

8. *Ragtime* (1981), Milos Forman, PG. Howard E. Rollins Jr., James Cagney, Kenneth McMillan, Brad Dourif, Mary Steenburgen, Debbie Allen, Jeff Daniels, Moses Gunn, Donald O'Connor, Mandy Patinkin, *Norman Mailer*.

Just plain bad.

9. *The Bounty* (1984), Roger Donaldson, PG. Mel Gibson, Anthony Hopkins, Sir Laurence Olivier, Daniel Day-Lewis, Edward Fox, Liam Neeson.

Time for a mutiny.

10. *Valmont* (1989), Milos Forman, R. Colin Firth, Meg Tilly, Annette Bening, Fairuza Balk, Sian Phillips, Jeffrey Jones, Henry Thomas.

Pointless, coming on the heels of the superior adaptation, *Dangerous Liaisons* (1988), though it was fun to see the kid from *E.T.* all grown up.

Creature Features: Twenty Groovy Horror Movies of the 80s

1. *Hellraiser* (1987), Clive Barker, R. Andrew Robinson, Clare Higgins, Ashley Laurence, Sean Chapman, Oliver Smith.

Wonderfully scary and so campy that you'll roll your eyes at almost every part of it, this imaginative and spooky movie deserved better than the lame sequels it got.

> **"Jesus wept."**
> **—Andrew Robinson,**
> ***Hellraiser*, 1987**

2. *The Re-Animator* (1985), Stuart Gordon, R. Jeffrey Combs, Bruce Abbott, Barbara Crampton.

Captures H. P. Lovecraft's wild-eyed insanity to a tee, with relentless gore and purposefully bad acting.

3. *Near Dark* (1987), Kathryn Bigelow, R. Adrian Pasdar, Jenny Wright, Bill Paxton.

A sexy vampire movie Anne Rice wishes she had written.

4. *Fright Night* (1985), Tom Holland, R. William Ragsdale, Chris Sarandon, *Amanda Bearse*, Roddy McDowall, Stephen Geoffreys.

This playful *hommage* to creature features also manages some truly frightening moments as characters you think will escape undeath don't.

5. *The Howling* (1981), Joe Dante, R. Dee Wallace, Patrick Macnee, Dennis Dugan, Christopher Stone, John Carradine, Slim Pickens.

Gore galore and a great, pessimistic ending.

6. *Evil Dead* (1983), Sam Raimi, R. Bruce Campbell, Ellen Sandweiss, Betsy Baker.

Low-budget nightmare that asks: How much blood is too much blood?

7. *The Company of Wolves* (1985), Neil Jordan, R. Angela Lansbury, David Warner, Micha Bergese, Tusse Silberg, *Danielle Dax*, *Stephen Rea*.

A bizarre, hypersexual retelling of "Little Red Riding Hood."

8. *The Thing* **(1982),** John Carpenter, R. Kurt Russell, Wilford Brimley, T. K. Carter, Richard Masur, Keith David, Richard Dysart. You think you know someone . . .

9. *Altered States* **(1980),** Ken Russell, R. William Hurt, Blair Brown, Bob Balaban, *Drew Barrymore.*

Mad scientist screws up big-time while in a sensory deprivation tank.

10. *Child's Play* **(1988),** Tom Holland, R. Catherine Hicks, Alex Vincent, Chris Sarandon, Dinah Manoff, Brad Dourif.

Introducing Chucky, the absolute last doll anyone would buy for their child in the first place. Blamed in Britain for inspiring prepubescents to murder a toddler.

11. *Christine* **(1984),** John Carpenter, R. Keith Gordon, John Stockwell, Alexandra Paul, Harry Dean Stanton, Kelly Preston.

Americans have love affairs with their cars, and here's one who loves back . . . but jealously.

12. *Creepshow* **(1982),** George A. Romero, R. Ted Danson, Hal Holbrook, Adrienne Barbeau, Viveca Lindfors, E. G. Marshall, Stephen King, Leslie Nielsen, Carrie Nye, Fritz Weaver, Ed Harris.

Cockroaches. Lots of them.

13. *Scanners* **(1981),** David Cronenberg, R. Stephen Lack, Jennifer O'Neill, Patrick McGoohan.

Head rush!

14. *Dead Zone* **(1983),** David Cronenberg, R. Christopher Walken, Brooke Adams, Tom Skerritt, Martin Sheen, Herbert Lom, *Colleen Dewhurst.*

A disturbing prescient and the megalomaniacal man who will stop at nothing to become president.

15. *Silent Night, Deadly Night* **(1984),** Charles E. Seller, R. Lilyan Chauvin, Gilmer McCormick, Toni Nero.

The most controversial horror film of the 80s, because the killer was Old Saint Nick.

16. *Dead Ringers* **(1988),** David Cronenberg, R. Jeremy Irons, Genevieve Bujold, Heidi von Palleske.

Every woman's worst nightmare: a gynecologist with an ax to grind.

17. *Twilight Zone: The Movie* **(1983),** Steven Spielberg, John Landis, George Miller, Joe Dante, PG. Dan Aykroyd, Albert Brooks, Vic Morrow, Kathleen Quinlan, John Lithgow, Billy Mumy, Scatman Crothers, Kevin McCarthy, *Selma Diamond, John Larroquette, Burgess Meredith.*

For the opening sequence, in which sweet, funny Dan Aykroyd asks, "Do you wanna see something *really* scary?"

18. *Terror Train* **(1980),** Roger Spottiswoode, R. Jamie Lee Curtis, Ben Johnson, Hart Bochner, *David Copperfield, Vanity.*

More because of the outfits than the brutal slayings.

19. *The Shining* **(1980),** Stanley Kubrick, R. Jack Nicholson, Shelley Duvall, Scatman Crothers, Danny Lloyd, Joe Turkel, Barry Nelson.

You'll pee your pants when Jack axes his way through the door.

20. *Wolfen* **(1981),** Michael Wadleigh, R. Albert Finney, Gregory Hines, Tommy Noonan, *Edward James Olmos.*

The only thing worse than a werewolf is a werewolf with its master's degree, as in this story of a race of übercanines with brains as big as their fangs.

Action Figures: Ten Big Action Flicks of the 80s

1. *Indiana Jones and the Temple of Doom* **(1984),** Steven Spielberg, PG. Harrison Ford, Kate Capshaw, Ke Huy Quan, Amrish Puri.

Not as good as the original, but better than most adventure movies, and you can never have too many exotic bug scenes.

2. *Robocop* **(1987),** Paul Verhoeven, R. Peter Weller, Nancy Allen, Ronny Cox.

But does he eat doughnuts?

3. *Action Jackson* (1988), Craig R. Baxley, R. Carl Weathers, Vanity, Craig T. Nelson, *Sharon Stone*.

Blaxploitation returns!

4. *Escape From New York* (1981), John Carpenter, R. Kurt Russell, Lee Van Cleef, Donald Pleasence, Isaac Hayes, Adrienne Barbeau, Harry Dean Stanton, Season Hubley.

In the future, New York is nothing but a giant prison for the worst criminals on earth. Some scenes almost seem contemporary. Took fifteen years for the sequel to arrive.

5. *First Blood* (1982), Ted Kotcheff, R. Sylvester Stallone, Richard Crenna, Brian Dennehy, Jack Starrett.

A Vietnam vet versus a cop. Right-wingers didn't know whom to side with.

6. *Commando* (1985), Mark L. Lester, R. Arnold Schwarzenegger, Rae Dawn Chong, Dan Hedaya, Vernon Wells, James Olson, David Patrick Kelly, *Alyssa Milano*.

The first Arnie movie that had intellectuals saying, "But it was good."

7. *Iron Eagle* (1985), Sidney J. Furie, PG-13. Louis Gossett Jr., Jason Gedrick, Tim Thomerson.

Saving your dad from Middle Eastern captors. With luck, he'll increase your allowance.

8. *Red Dawn* (1984), John Milius, PG-13. Patrick Swayze, C. Thomas Howell, Harry Dean Stanton, Powers Boothe, Lea Thompson, Charlie Sheen, Ben Johnson, *Jennifer Grey*.

The Reds have invaded America! But why bother with the Midwest?

9. *Conan the Barbarian* (1982), John Milius, R. Arnold Schwarzenegger, James Earl Jones, Max von Sydow, Sandahl Bergman, Mako.

A real stretch for Arnie.

Even barbarians know it's polite to share, as Arnold Schwarzenegger demonstrates to a wary (and bikini-ed) Sandahl Bergman in *Conan the Barbarian.*

10. *Sudden Impact* (1983), Clint Eastwood, R. Clint Eastwood, Sondra Locke, Pat Hingle, Bradford Dillman.

"Dirty Harry" surviving in the 80s by hunting down a woman (Locke) who is herself hunting down the rapists who assaulted her and her sister. Can't we all get along?

> "Go ahead...make my day."
> —Clint Eastwood, *Sudden Impact*, 1983

Happy Campers: Twenty Camp Flicks of the 80s

1. *Clash of the Titans* (1981), Desmond Davis, PG. Harry Hamlin, Sir Laurence Olivier, Maggie Smith, Claire Bloom, Ursula Andress, Burgess Meredith.

What's more delightful—the phony underwater scenes? the Claymation Medusa? or the enormous buzzard that Harry Hamlin hitches a ride on?

2. *The Beastmaster* (1982), Don A. Coscarelli, PG. Marc Singer, Tanya Roberts, Rip Torn, John Amos, Josh Milrad.

Because of Tanya Roberts, some critics called this *The Breastmaster*.

3. *The Lonely Lady* (1983), Peter Sasdy, R. Pia Zadora, Lloyd Bochner, Bibi Besch, *Ray Liotta*.

Not so lonely after she's raped with a garden hose. Proof positive that as an actress, Pia is a great singer.

4. *Victor/Victoria* (1982), Blake Edwards, PG. Julie Andrews, James Garner, Robert Preston, Lesley Ann Warren, Alex Karras, John Rhys-Davies.

Camp on purpose and brilliantly so, with Warren as a bottled-blond siren and Andrews playing a woman posing as a man posing as a woman.

> "I'm horny."
> —Lesley Ann Warren, *Victor/Victoria*, 1982

5. *The Blue Lagoon* (1980), Randal Kleiser, R. Brooke Shields, Christopher Atkins, Leo McKern, William Daniels.

Brooke Shields gets pregnant on a desert island and decides to keep the baby.

6. The Seduction (1982), David Schmoeller, R. Morgan Fairchild, Andrew Stevens, Michael Sarrazin, Vince Edwards, Colleen Camp (appropriately enough), Kevin Brophy.

How many stalkers do you know who look like Andrew Stevens?

7. Can't Stop the Music (1980), Nancy Walker, PG. Valerie Perrine, Bruce Jenner, Steve Guttenberg, Paul Sand, The Village People, *Leigh Taylor-Young.*

Hey, I know—let's have Rosie, the Quicker Picker-Upper, direct a movie with the Village People!

8. Angel (1984), Robert Vincent O'Neil, R. Donna Wilkes, Cliff Gorman, Susan Tyrrell, Dick Shawn, *Rory Calhoun.*

High school honor student by day, hooker by night. Most kids just get a dollar for every A.

9. Bolero (1984), John Derek, R. Bo Derek, George Kennedy, Anna Obregon, Andrea Occhipinti, Olivia D'Abo.

Grounds for divorce.

10. Body Double (1984), Brian De Palma, R. Craig Wasson, Melanie Griffith, Greg Henry, Deborah Shelton, Guy Boyd, *Dennis Franz.*

With references to every movie Hitchcock ever made. No, wait—to every movie ever made.

11. Angel Heart (1987), Alan Parker, R. Mickey Rourke, Robert De Niro, Lisa Bonet, *Charlotte Rampling.*

Rourke and Bonet chicken out.

Apparently, Lisa Bonet didn't see 9 1/2 Weeks before signing to do *Angel Heart* with Mickey Rourke—a different world, indeed.

12. Butterfly (1982), Matt Cimber, R. Pia Zadora, Stacy Keach, Orson Welles, Edward Albert, James Franciscus, Lois Nettleton, *June Lockhart.*

Incest, Orson Welles, and Lassie's mom.

13. Swamp Thing (1982), Wes Craven, PG. Adrienne Barbeau, Louis Jourdan, Ray Wise, *Adam West.*

Swamp Thing, I think I love you.

14. Reform School Girls (1986), Tom De Cimone, R. Wendy O. Williams, Linda Carol, Pat Ast, Sybil Danning.

Women in prison, a dying genre in the 80s.

15. S.O.B. (1981), Blake Edwards, R. William Holden, Julie Andrews, Robert Preston, Richard Mulligan, Robert Webber, Shelley Winters, Robert Vaughn, Larry Hagman, Stuart Margolin, Loretta Swit, Craig Stevens, Robert Loggia, *Rosanna Arquette*, Marisa Berenson.

Supposedly campy on purpose, but you have to wonder.

16. Sheena: Queen of the Jungle (1984), John Guillermin, PG. Tanya Roberts, Ted Wass, Donovan Scott.

Tanya: Queen of the Howler.

17. Toxic Avenger (1986), Michael Herz, R. Mitchell Cohen, Andree Maranda, Jennifer Baptist.

Hilarious eco satire that doubles as no-brain tripe.

18. Polyester (1981), John Waters, R. Divine, Tab Hunter, Edith Massey, Mink Stole, Stiv Bators, David Samson.

With Odorama, not something you might desire from a Divine movie.

19. Tarzan, the Ape Man (1981), John Derek, R. Bo Derek, Miles O'Keeffe, Richard Harris, John Phillip Law.

Bo Derek plays a virgin. No, not like an instrument.

20. American Anthem (1986), Albert Magnoli, PG-13. Mitch Gaylord, Janet Jones, Michelle Phillips, Michael Pataki.

Olympic flame.

Gay Pride: Ten Gay and Lesbian Movies of the 80s

1. Parting Glances (1986), Bill Sherwood, R. Steve Buscemi, John Bolger, Richard Ganoung.

The first feature film about AIDS, but what makes it so memorable is its low-key exploration of 80s gay relationships, a frequent side effect of AIDS films.

2. *My Beautiful Laundrette* **(1986),** Stephen Frears, R. Gordon Warnecke, Daniel Day-Lewis, Saeed Jaffrey, Roshan Seth.

A ferocious gay love story set amid the race and class conflicts of Thatcher London.

3. *Maurice* **(1987),** James Ivory, R. James Wilby, Hugh Grant, Rupert Graves, Mark Tandy, Ben Kingsley, Denholm Elliott, Simon Callow, Helena Bonham Carter.

Repressed British blueblood finds platonic love with a schoolmate and nonplatonic love with his groundskeeper.

4. *Desert Hearts* **(1986),** Donna Deitch, R. Helen Shaver, Patricia Charbonneau, Audra Lindley, Andra Akers, Dean Butler, Denise Crosby.

Big-city career woman arrives in town for a divorce and settles into an affair with a young lesbian.

> "Years from now, when you talk about this—and you will—please be kind." —Harry Hamlin to Michael Ontkean, *Making Love*, 1982

5. *Making Love* **(1982),** Arthur Hiller, R. Kate Jackson, Harry Hamlin, Michael Ontkean, *Wendy Hiller*, Arthur Hill, Michael Dudikoff.

One sure sign that you're gay: you're married to one of *Charlie's Angels.*

6. *Personal Best* **(1982),** Robert Towne, R. Mariel Hemingway, Scott Glenn, Patrice Donnelly.

Two young women explore lesbianism while training for the Olympics.

7. *Law of Desire* **(1986),** Pedro Almodovar, R. Carmen Maura, Eusebio Poncela, Antonio Banderas, Bibi Andersson.

Gender-bending love stories.

8. *Looking for Langston* **(1988),** Isaac Julien, unrated. Ben Ellison, Matthew Baidoo, Akim Mogaji, John Wilson, Dencil Williams, Guy Burgess, James Dublin, Harry Donaldson, *Jimmy Somerville.*

A stylishdocumentary/dramatization of writer Langston Hughes's life and of gay life in the 20s and 30s.

9. *Another Country* **(1984),** Marek Kanievska, R. Rupert Everett, Colin Firth, Michael Jenn, Robert Addie, Anna Massey, Betsy Brantley, *Cary Elwes.*

British schoolboys who become Russian spies.

Another Country—another gay classic.

10. *Cruising* **(1980),** William Friedkin, R. Al Pacino, Paul Sorvino, Karen Allen, *Powers Boothe.*

With its depiction of all gay men as demonic S/M freaks and potential murderers, this most controversial of gay movies drew the first ever national picketing by gay activists.

A Cut Above: Ten Art House Sensations of the 80s

1. *Wings of Desire* **(1988),** Wim Wenders, PG-13. Bruno Ganz, Peter Falk, Solveig Dommartin, Otto Sander, Curt Bois.

"There are angels on the streets of Berlin" and "Columbo," too. An angel longs to be flesh again in this German oddity, directed by Wim Wenders. Made all the tastier by the presence of American Peter Falk and an incongruous performance by Nick Cave and the Bad Seeds. Some call it a masterpiece, and that seems fair.

2. *House of Games* **(1987),** David Mamet, R. Joseph Mantegna, Lindsay Crouse, Lilia Skala, J. T. Walsh, Meshach Taylor.

Not since *The Sting* has a con movie possessed so many twists and turns, and this one throws in Freud for good measure.

3. *Anna* **(1987),** Yurek Bogayevicz, PG-13. Sally Kirkland, Paulina Porizkova, Robert Fields.

A Czech *All About Eve.*

4. *Insignificance* **(1985),** Nicolas Roeg, R. Theresa Russell, Gary Busey, Tony Curtis, Michael Emil, Will Sampson.

Marilyn Monroe, Albert Einstein, Senator McCarthy, and Joe DiMaggio meet in a hotel and chat.

Marilyn's explanation of Einstein's theory of relativity is priceless.

5. *Apartment Zero* (1988), Martin Donovan, R. Hart Bochner, Colin Firth, Fabrizio Bentivoglio, Liz Smith.

A prissy film buff takes in a mysterious stud/killer as his roomie, falls discreetly in love with him, and then uses him as apartment statuary.

6. *A Zed and Two Noughts* (1988), Peter Greenaway, R. Eric Deacon, Brian Deacon, Joss Ackland, Andrea Ferreol.

Twins and the amputee they love, next on *Oprah.*

7. *Blood Simple* (1985), Joel Coen, R. John Getz, M. Emmet Walsh, Dan Hedaya, Frances McDormand.

A morbid thriller that gives new meaning to the word "comeback."

8. *The Dead* (1987), John Huston, PG. Anjelica Huston, Donal McCann, Marie Kean, Donal Donnelly, Dan O'Herlihy.

John Huston's last movie is a beautiful adaptation of the James Joyce story.

9. *Stranger Than Paradise* (1984), Jim Jarmusch, R. Richard Edson, Eszter Balint, John Lurie.

A road movie for the cappuccino set.

10. *Au Revoir, Les Enfants* (1987), Louis Malle, PG. Gaspard Manesse, Raphael Fejto, Francine Racette, Irène Jacob.

Louis Malle's childhood.

Square Pegs: Ten Unique Masterpieces of the 80s

1. *Brazil* (1985), Terry Gilliam, R. Jonathan Pryce, Robert De Niro, Michael Palin, Katherine Helmond, Kim Greist, Bob Hoskins.

Terrorists are so rampant, their bombs are hardly noticed by urbanites in this not-so-farfetched future tale.

2. *Heathers* (1989), Michael Lehmann, R. Winona Ryder, Christian Slater, Kim Walker, *Shannen Doherty*, Patrick Laborteaux.

A nutty boy begins executing the class bullies and fluff chicks, all to impress a cute girl.

3. *Working Girls* (1987), Lizzie Borden, R. Amanda Goodwin, Louise Smith, Ellen McElduff.

A nitty-gritty look at the unglamorous life of a call girl ring.

4. *Pennies from Heaven* (1981), Herbert Ross, R. Steve Martin, Bernadette Peters, Christopher Walken, Jessica Harper.

A knock-your-socks-off musical that absolutely nobody cared to see.

5. *Liquid Sky* (1983), Slava Tsukerman, R. Anne Carlisle, Paula Sheppard, Bob Brady.

Androgyny, hallucinations, and UFOs.

6. *Hollywood Shuffle* (1987), Robert Townsend, R. Robert Townsend, Anne-Marie Johnson, Starletta Dupois, Helen Martin, Keenen Ivory Wayans, Damon Wayans.

A funny attack on the un(African)-American hiring practices of Hollywood (which in turn slams gays).

7. *My Dinner with André* (1981), Louis Malle, R. André Gregory, Wallace Shawn.

A nonstop conversation, so boring it's fascinating.

8. *I'm Gonna Git You Sucka* (1988), Keenen Ivory Wayans, R. Keenen Ivory Wayans, Bernie Casey, Steve James, Isaac Hayes, Jim Brown, Ja'net DuBois, Anne-Marie Johnson, Antonio Fargas, *Eve Plumb.*

Blaxploitation never had it this good.

9. *Dead Men Don't Wear Plaid* (1982), Carl Reiner, PG. Steve Martin, Rachel Ward, George Gaynes, Carl Reiner.

Made in black and white, this movie spliced Martin into classic Hollywood scenes, featuring footage of Cary Grant, Lauren Bacall, and countless other stars of the golden age of Hollywood.

10. *Pee-wee's Big Adventure* **(1985),** Tim Burton, PG. Pee-wee Herman (Paul Reubens), Elizabeth Daily, Mark Holton, Judd Omen.

Saturday morning's freakiest host gets a movie.

The Ten Most Overrated Movies of the 80s

1. *Out of Africa* **(1985).**

It won an Oscar, but do you know anybody who liked it?

2. *Rain Man* **(1988),** Barry Levinson, R. Dustin Hoffman, Tom Cruise, Valeria Golino.

It's not that hard to play dumb. Cruise did it well, so why did Hoffman get all the kudos?

3. *Blue Velvet* **(1986),** David Lynch, R. Kyle MacLachlan, Isabella Rossellini, Dennis Hopper, Laura Dern, Hope Lange, Jack Nance, Dean Stockwell, Brad Dourif.

A messterpiece. The perfect example of an outrageous film you can't take your eyes off of, which is mistaken for Great Cinema. Responsible for bringing 60s cult actor Dennis Hopper back as a poor man's Jack Nicholson.

4. *Cocoon* **(1985),** Ron Howard, PG-13. Wilford Brimley, Brian Dennehy, Steve Guttenberg, Don Ameche, Hume Cronyn, Jessica Tandy, Tahnee Welch, Jack Gilford, Gwen Verdon, Maureen Stapleton, *Tyrone Power, Jr.*

Any episodes from the first three seasons of *The Golden Girls* are funnier.

5. *The Color of Money* **(1986),** Martin Scorsese, R. Paul Newman, Tom Cruise, Mary Elizabeth Mastrantonio, Helen Shaver, John Turturro, *Forest Whitaker.*

A sequel to *The Hustler* that racked up the awards despite being as interesting as cue powder.

6. *Lethal Weapon* **(1987),** Richard Donner, R. Mel Gibson, Danny Glover, Gary Busey, Darlene Love.

Lame buddy movie in which Gibson literally put his ass on the line.

7. *Tender Mercies* **(1983),** Bruce Beresford, PG. Robert Duvall, Tess Harper, *Betty Buckley*, *Ellen Barkin*, Wilford Brimley.

Just because a movie is quiet and slow doesn't mean it's any good.

8. *Hope and Glory* **(1987),** John Boorman, PG-13. Sebastian Rice Edwards, Sarah Miles, Geraldine Muir, Sammi Davis.

The director earned his last name.

9. *The Mighty Quinn* **(1989),** Carl Schenkel, R. Denzel Washington, Mimi Rogers, Robert Townsend, James Fox, M. Emmet Walsh, Sheryl Lee Ralph, Esther Rolle.

Mighty bad.

10. *Eleni* **(1985),** Peter Yates, PG. John Malkovich, Kate Nelligan, Linda Hunt, Oliver Cotton.

Ronald Reagan's favorite movie. Need I say more?

The Ten Most Underrated Movies of the 80s

1. *Dune* **(1984),** David Lynch, PG-13. Kyle MacLachlan, Francesca Annis, Sting, José Ferrer, Max von Sydow, Juergen Prochnow, Linda Hunt, Freddie Jones, Dean Stockwell, Virginia Madsen, Brad Dourif, Kenneth McMillan, Silvana Mangano, Sian Phillips, Jack Nance, Paul Smith, *Sean Young.*

The ultimate beach movie: it takes place on a desert planet. Thrilling, beautifully photographed, borderline nonsensical, and brilliant.

2. *The Mirror Crack'd* **(1980),** Guy Hamilton, PG. Elizabeth Taylor, Rock Hudson, Tony Curtis, Angela Lansbury, Kim Novak, Edward Fox, Geraldine Chaplin, *Pierce Brosnan.*

A great Agatha Christie yarn with camp scenes galore.

3. *Looker* **(1981),** Michael Crichton, PG. Albert Finney, James Coburn, Susan Dey, Leigh Taylor-Young, *Vanna White.*

Perfect models get offed all over the place—in other words, it's a fantasy film.

4. ***American Gigolo* (1980),** Paul Schrader, R. Richard Gere, Lauren Hutton, *Hector Elizondo.*

Lots to hate here, but this was the role Gere was born to play.

5. ***The Lair of the White Worm* (1988),** Ken Russell, R. Amanda Donohoe, Sammi Davis, Catherine Oxenberg, *Hugh Grant.*

How can you resist a woman with the power to *literally* eat Hugh Grant for lunch?

6. ***Gothic* (1987),** Ken Russell, R. Julian Sands, Gabriel Byrne, Timothy Spall, Natasha Richardson.

The sexually charged story of several literati, as seen through the eyes of a perverse filmmaker.

7. ***Clue* (1985),** Jonathan Lynn, PG. Lesley Ann Warren, Tim Curry, Martin Mull, Madeline Kahn, Michael McKean, Christopher Lloyd, Eileen Brennan, *Howard Hesseman,* Lee Ving, *Jane Wiedlin.*

It had four different endings, so it couldn't be all bad.

8. ***The Coca-Cola Kid* (1984),** Dusan Makavejev, R. Eric Roberts, Greta Scacchi, Bill Kerr.

A charming romantic comedy that, like its name, could be called "bubbly."

9. ***White Dog* (1982),** Samuel Fuller, R. Kristy McNichol, Paul Winfield, Burl Ives, Jameson Parker, Lynn Moody, Marshall Thompson, Paul Bartel, Dick Miller, Parley Baer.

A dog trained to attack black people on sight. A sequel could have included a cat trained to hiss at Aleutian Islanders.

10. ***Vibes* (1988),** Ken Kwapis, PG. Cyndi Lauper, Jeff Goldblum, Julian Sands, Googy Gress, *Peter Falk, Elizabeth Pena.*

The first half of this movie is breezy and clever. It's the second half that's so unusual.

Twenty Movie Moments of the 80s You'll Never Forget

1. Ally Sheedy uses dandruff to simulate snow in a drawing she's doing, *The Breakfast Club* (1985).

2. William Hurt goes right through a door to nail Kathleen Turner, *Body Heat* (1981).

3. Daryl Hannah's mermaid name shatters a bank of television sets, *Splash* (1984), Ron Howard, PG. Tom Hanks, Daryl Hannah, Eugene Levy, John Candy, Dody Goodman, Shecky Greene, Richard Shull.

4. Bare-naked boys run around a pond in *A Room with a View* (1987), James Ivory, R. Helena Bonham Carter, Julian Sands, Denholm Elliott, Maggie Smith, Daniel Day-Lewis, Rupert Graves.

Or, if bare-naked boys aren't your thing, how about the bare-breasted horseback-riding scene in the Phoebe Cates vehicle *Private School*? (1983), Noel Black, R. Phoebe Cates, Betsy Russell, Kathleen Wilhoite, Sylvia Kristel, Ray Walston, Matthew Modine.

If neither of these possibilities is remotely arousing, how about Pee-wee Herman's bar-top "Tequila" routine in *Pee-wee's Big Adventure* (1985)? Yes? Seek help.

5. Whoopi Goldberg brandishes a knife on "Mister," *The Color Purple* (1984).

6. Melanie Griffith wins the gold for topless vacuuming, *Working Girl* (1989). If not for the thrill factor, definitely for the "Huh?" factor.

7. Jodie Foster, full-tilt, *The Accused* (1988).

8. Catherine O'Hara lip-synchs "Day-O," *Beetlejuice* (1988).

9. Rabbit stew, *Fatal Attraction* (1987).

10. Tom Hanks and Robert Loggia piano dancing, *Big* (1988).

11. Michelle Pfeiffer slithers on a piano, *The Fabulous Baker Boys* (1989).

12. The one-hundred-yard dash, *Broadcast News* (1987).

13. Meryl Streep glances into her rearview mirror, *Silkwood* (1983).

"Can't they read my **NO TAILGATING** bumper sticker?"

14. Michael Douglas lands face first in Kathleen Turner's crotch, *Romancing the Stone* (1984).

15. Charles Durning swats a bug and a nervous Dustin Hoffman in drag clutches his chest defensively, *Tootsie* (1982).

Charles Durning puts the moves on Dustin Hoffman in *Tootsie*.

16. Drew Barrymore and E.T. meet face-to-face, *E.T. The Extra-Terrestrial* (1982).

17. A man anxiously tears off his own face, *Poltergeist* (1982).

18. Poodle slaughter, *A Fish Called Wanda* (1988).

19. An obscenely fat man explodes, *Monty Python's The Meaning of Life* (1983).

20. Spiders stream from a tumor on a woman's face, *The Believers* (1987), John Schlesinger, R. Martin Sheen, Helen Shaver, Robert Loggia, Malick Bowens, Harris Yulin, Jimmy Smits, Richard Masur.

Titles from Hell: The Twenty Worst Movie Titles of the Decade (or, Depending on Your Taste, the Best)

1. *C.H.U.D.* (1984), Douglas Cheek, R. John Heard, Daniel Stern, Chris Curry, Kim Greist, *John Goodman.*

2. *My Stepmother Is an Alien* (1988), Richard Benjamin, PG-13. Kim Basinger, Dan Aykroyd, Jon Lovitz, Alyson Hannigan, Joseph Maher, *Juliette Lewis.*

3. *Fatso* (1980), Anne Bancroft, R. Dom DeLuise, Anne Bancroft, Ron Carey, Candice Azzara.

4. *Turk 182!* (1985), Bob Clark, PG-13. Timothy Hutton, Robert Culp, Robert Urich, Kim Cattrall, Peter Boyle, Darren McGavin, Paul Sorvino.

5. *How to Beat the High Cost of Living* (1980), Robert Scheerer, PG. Jessica Lange, Susan St. James, Jane Curtin, Richard Benjamin, Eddie Albert.

6. *Saturn 3* (1980), Stanley Donen, R. Farrah Fawcett, Kirk Douglas, *Harvey Keitel*, Ed Bishop.

7. *The Dorm That Dripped Blood* (1982), Stephen Carpenter and Jeffrey Obrow, R. Laura Lopinski, Pamela Holland, Stephen Sachs.

8. *Tucker: A Man and His Dream* (1988), Francis Ford Coppola, PG. Jeff Bridges, Martin Landau, Dean Stockwell, Frederic Forrest, Mako, Joan Allen, Christian Slater, Lloyd Bridges.

9. *Krull* (1983), Peter Yates, PG. Ken Marshall, Lysette Anthony, Freddie Jones, Francesca Annis, Liam Neeson.

10. ***The Adventures of Buckaroo Banzai Across the Eighth Dimension* (1984),** W. D. Richter, PG. Jeff Goldblum, Peter Weller, Ellen Barkin, Christopher Lloyd, John Lithgow, *Yakov Smirnoff, Jamie Lee Curtis.*

11. ***Cannibal Women in the Avocado Jungle of Death* (1989),** J. D. Athens, PG-13. Shannon Tweed, Adrienne Barbeau, Karen Mistal, *Bill Maher.*

12. ***Tuff Turf* (1985),** Fritz Kiersch, R. James Spader, Kim Richards, Paul Mones, Matt Clark, Olivia Barash, *Robert Downey, Jr.,* Catya Sassoon.

13. ***Big Trouble in Little China* (1986),** John Carpenter, PG-13. Kurt Russell, Suzze Pai, Dennis Dun, Kim Cattrall.

14. ***Vision Quest* (1985).**

15. ***Revenge of the Teenage Vixens from Outer Space* (1986),** Jeff Ferrell, R. Lisa Schwedop, Howard Scott.

16. ***Amazon Women on the Moon* (1987),** John Landis, Robert Weiss, Joe Dante, Carl Gottlieb, and Peter Horton, R. Rosanna Arquette, Steve Guttenberg, Steve Allen, B. B. King, Michelle Pfeiffer, Arsenio Hall, Andrew Dice Clay, Howard Hesseman, Lou Jacobi, Carrie Fisher, Griffin Dunne, Sybil Danning, *Henny Youngman,* Kelly Preston, Paul Bartel.

17. ***Purple People Eater* (1988),** Linda Shayne, PG. Ned Beatty, Shelley Winters, Peggy Lipton, Patrick Harris, Kareem Abdul-Jabbar, Little Richard, Chubby Checker.

The Twenty Coolest Movie Titles of the 80s

1. *Earth Girls Are Easy* (1989), Julien Temple, **PG.** Geena Davis, Jeff Goldblum, Julie Brown, Charles Rocket, Jim Carrey, Damon Wayons, Michael McKean, Angelyne, Larry Linville.

2. *A Zed and Two Noughts* (1988).

3. *Desperately Seeking Susan* (1985).

4. *Raiders of the Lost Ark* (1981).

5. *An Officer and a Gentleman* (1982).

6. *Stop Making Sense* (1984), Jonathan Demme, unrated. David Byrne, Tina Weymouth, Chris Franz, Jerry Harrison.

7. *Eating Raoul* (1982).

8. *The Terminator* (1984).

9. *Action Jackson* (1988).

10. *The Gods Must Be Crazy* (1984), Jamie Uys, **PG.** N!xau, Marius Weyers, Louw Verwey, Sandra Prinsloo, Jamie Uys, Michael Thys, Nic de Jager.

11. *Fast Times at Ridgemont High* (1982).

12. *Hairspray* (1988).

13. *A Fish Called Wanda* (1988).

14. *sex, lies, and videotape* (1989).

15. *Women on the Verge of a Nervous Breakdown* (1988).

16. *She's Gotta Have It* (1986), Spike Lee, **R.** Spike Lee, Tommy Redmond Hicks, Raye Dowell.

17. *Little Darlings* (1980), Ronald F. Maxwell, **R.** Kristy McNichol, Tatum O'Neal, Matt Dillon, Armand Assante, Margaret Blye.

18. *Do the Right Thing* (1989).

19. *Throw Momma from the Train* (1987), Danny DeVito, **PG-13.** Danny DeVito, Billy Crystal, Anne Ramsey, Kate Mulgrew.

20. *Alien Nation* (1988), Graham Baker, **R.** James Caan, Mandy Patinkin, Terence Stamp, Kevyn Major Howard, Peter Jason, Jeff Kober.

18. ***Killer Klowns from Outer Space*** (1988), Stephen Chiodo, PG-13. Grant Cramer, Suzanne Snyder, John Allen Nelson, Royal Dano, John Vernon.

19. ***Assault of the Killer Bimbos*** (1987), Gorman Bechard, R. Karen Nielsen, Debi Thibeault, Lisa Schmidt, Simone (no, really: just Simone).

20. ***Oh, Heavenly Dog!*** (1980), Joe Camp, PG. Chevy Chase, Jane Seymour, Omar Sharif, Robert Morley, Benji.

You Don't Say! Ten Movie Titles That Said It All

1. ***Nuts*** (1987), Martin Ritt, R. Barbra Streisand, Richard Dreyfuss, Maureen Stapleton, Karl Malden, James Whitmore, Robert Webber, Eli Wallach, *Leslie Nielsen*.

Which is what Barbra Streisand was if she thought she could effectively portray a high-class call girl.

2. ***Less Than Zero*** (1987). The critics couldn't resist.

3. ***They All Laughed*** (1981), Peter Bogdanovich, PG. Ben Gazzara, John Ritter, Dorothy Stratten, Audrey Hepburn, Colleen Camp, Patti Hansen, Elizabeth Pena.

They all have good taste.

4. ***8 Million Ways to Die*** (1985), Hal Ashby, R. Jeff Bridges, Rosanna Arquette, Andy Garcia, Alexandra Paul.

Dead on arrival.

5. ***Short Circuit*** (1986), John Badham, PG. Steve Guttenberg, Ally Sheedy, Fisher Stevens, Brian McNamara.

The humor didn't quite compute.

6. ***Tank*** (1983), Marvin J. Chomsky, PG. James Garner, Shirley Jones, C. Thomas Howell, Jenilee Harrison, Dorian Harewood.

It did.

7. ***Jinxed*** (1982), Don Siegel, R. Bette Midler, Ken Wahl, Rip Torn.

After this, Bette Midler was . . . until she went Disney.

8. ***The Nude Bomb*** (1980), Clive Donner, PG. Don Adams, Dana Elcar, Pamela Hensley, Sylvia Kristel, Norman Lloyd, *Rhonda Fleming*.

We're talking atomic here.

9. ***Child's Play*** (1988). Juvenile.

10. ***Heartburn*** (1986), Mike Nichols, R. Meryl Streep, Jack Nicholson, Steven Hill, Richard Masur, Stockard Channing, Jeff Daniels, *Milos Forman*, Catherine O'Hara, Maureen Stapleton, Mercedes Ruehl, *Yakov Smirnoff*, Wilfrid Hyde-White.

It wasn't something you ate.

The Worst Movie of the 80s

Caligula (1980), Tinto Brass, unrated. Malcolm McDowell, Sir John Gielgud, Peter O'Toole, Helen Mirren.

A two-hour sex-ed lesson bound to drive teens to abstinence.

Ten More Quintessentially 80s Movies That Suck

1. ***Heaven's Gate*** (1980), Michael Cimino, R. Kris Kristofferson, Christopher Walken, Isabelle Huppert, John Hurt, Richard Masur, Mickey Rourke, Brad Dourif, Joseph Cotten, Jeff Bridges, Sam Waterston.

Go to hell.

2. ***Tron*** (1982), Steven Lisberger, PG. Jeff Bridges, Bruce Boxleitner, David Warner, Cindy Morgan, Barnard Hughes.

Pac-Man was more fun.

3. ***The Sting II*** (1983), Jeremy Paul Kagan, PG. Jackie Gleason, Mac Davis, Teri Garr, Karl Malden, Oliver Reed.

Jackie Gleason and Mac Davis vs. Paul Newman and Robert Redford. Hmmm. Decisions, decisions. . .

4. *Jaws 3-D* (1983), Joe Alves, PG. Dennis Quaid, Bess Armstrong, Louis Gossett Jr., Simon MacCorkindale, *Lea Thompson*.

Shaddup already.

5. *Where the Boys Are '84* (1984), Hy Averback, R. Lisa Hartman, Wendy Schaal, Lorna Luft, Lynn-Holly Johnson.

They're twenty years older and weren't all that cute to begin with.

6. *Crimes of Passion* (1984), Ken Russell, R. Kathleen Turner, Anthony Perkins, Annie Potts, Bruce Davison.

This is when the government should have intervened and taken control of Kathleen Turner's career.

7. *The Razor's Edge* (1984), Jack Nitzsche, PG-13. Bill Murray, Catherine Hicks, Theresa Russell, Denholm Elliott, James Keach, Saeed Jaffrey, Brian Doyle-Murray.

Deadly dull.

8. *Rhinestone* (1984), Bob Clark, PG. Dolly Parton, Sylvester Stallone, Ron Leibman, Richard Farnsworth, Tim Thomerson.

Fake and gaudy.

9. *Red Dawn* (1984). Commies take the heartland in this, the first PG-13–rated movie ever. And we were worried about Grenada!

> "Tell me: What's the difference between us and them?"
> —Charlie Sheen in *Red Dawn*, 1984

10. *Supergirl* (1984), Jeannot Szwarc, PG. Faye Dunaway, Helen Slater, Peter O'Toole, Mia Farrow, Brenda Vaccaro, Marc McClure, Simon Ward, Hart Bochner.

Superhurl.

Ten Really, Really Bad Movies Featuring Tom Hanks

1. *Bachelor Party* (1984), Neal Israel, R. Also Tawny Kitaen, Adrian Zmed, George Grizzard, Robert Prescott, Wendie Jo Sperber, Michael Dudikoff.

2. *The Man with One Red Shoe* (1985), Stan Dragoti, PG. Also Dabney Coleman, Lori Singer, Carrie Fisher, James Belushi, Edward Herrmann, Charles Durning, Tommy Noonan, *David Ogden Stiers*.

3. *Volunteers* (1985), Nicholas Meyer, R. Also John Candy, *Rita Wilson*, Tim Thomerson, Gedde Watanabe.

4. *Every Time We Say Goodbye* (1986), Moshe Mizrahi, PG-13. Also Christina Marsillach, Benedict Taylor.

5. *The Money Pit* (1986), Richard Benjamin, PG. Also Shelley Long, *Alexander Gudonov, Maureen Stapleton*, Philip Bosco, Joseph Mantegna.

6. *Nothing in Common* (1986), Garry Marshall, PG. Also Jackie Gleason, Eva Marie Saint, Bess Armstrong, Hector Elizondo.

7. *Dragnet* (1987), Tom Mankiewicz, PG-13. Also Dan Aykroyd, Christopher Plummer, Harry Morgan, Elizabeth Ashley, Dabney Coleman.

8. *Punchline* (1988), David Seltzer, R. Also Sally Field, John Goodman, Mark Rydell, Kim Greist, Barry Sobel, Damon Wayans, Paul Mazursky, Pam Matteson.

9. *The 'Burbs* (1989), Joe Dante, PG. Also Carrie Fisher, Rick Ducommun, Corey Feldman, Brother Theodore, Gale Gordon, Bruce Dern.

10. *Turner and Hooch* (1989), Roger Spottiswoode, PG. Also Mare Winningham, Craig T. Nelson, Scott Paulin.

10 Really, Really Bad Movies Featuring Michelle Pfeiffer

1. *Falling in Love Again* (1980), Steven Paul, PG. Also Elliott Gould, Susannah York.

2. *B.A.D. Cats* (TV pilot) (1980), Bernard L. Kowalski, PG. Also Asher Brauner, Vic Morrow, Jimmie Walker, LaWanda Page.

3. *Charlie Chan and the Curse of the Dragon Queen* **(1981),** Clive Donner, PG. Also Peter Ustinov, Angie Dickinson, Lee Grant, Richard Hatch, Brian Keith, Roddy McDowall, Rachel Roberts.

4. *The Solitary Man* **(TV) (1979),** John Llewellyn Moxey. Also Earl Holliman, Carrie Snodgress, Lara Parker, Lane Smith, Nicholas Coster.

5. *Grease 2* **(1982),** Patricia Birch, PG. Also Maxwell Caulfield, Adrian Zmed, Lorna Luft, Didi Conn, Eve Arden, Tab Hunter, Sid Caesar.

6. *Power, Passion and Murder* **(TV) (1983),** Paul Bogart and Leon Ichaso. Also Darren McGavin, Stella Stevens.

7. *Ladyhawke* **(1985),** Richard Donner, PG-13. Also Matthew Broderick, Rutger Hauer, John Wood, Leo McKern.

8. *Into the Night* **(1985),** John Landis, R. Also Jeff Goldblum, David Bowie, Carl Perkins, Richard Farnsworth, Irene Papas, Dan Aykroyd, Paul Mazursky, Roger Vadim, Bruce McGill, Vera Miles, Clu Galager, Don Steel, Kathryn Harrold, Jim Henson, Paul Bartel, Amy Heckerling, Lawrence Kasdan, Jonathan Demme, David Cronenberg.

9. *Sweet Liberty* **(1986),** Alan Alda, PG. Also Alan Alda, Michael Caine, Bob Hoskins, *Lillian Gish.*

10. *Amazon Women on the Moon* **(1987).**

Star 80s: A Decade in the Life of Elizabeth Taylor

In the 70s, it seemed that the most glamorous and tempestuous movie star of the 50s and 60s was all washed up.

La Liz got divorced, remarried, and divorced from sparring partner/hubby Richard Burton, became a pill popper and alcoholic, failed to make even one mildly redeeming film, and was skewered mercilessly time and again by feral hyena Joan Rivers for her hefty weight gain.

She was married to and campaigned for Republican senator John Warner of Virginia—easily

her least cool marriage—and was photographed in a lavender caftan at her fattest, exiting a cab looking like Godzilla.

What a difference a decade can make, especially one as hip as the 80s. Overnight Liz got her shit together.

First, she made one of the most underappreciated minimasterpiece movies of the 80s, the aggressively campy *The Mirror Crack'd*, in which she was hysterical as a fading movie queen who gets into catfights with Kim Novak, stares wildly (flashbacks of *Marnie*) when reminded of past unpleasantries, commits the perfect murder, and dies glamorously. All that and she got to play Rock Hudson's wife.

She woke up and smelled Washington, D.C., and divorced John Warner, making Liz—as *Us*, one of the most popular magazines of the 80s, would say—"suddenly single."

She starred in a tremendously successful restaging of *Little Foxes* (1981), then in a wild and crazy touring company of Noel Coward's *Private Lives*, in which a slimmer Liz starred with ex-ex-hubby Richard Burton, playing off their natural combative/loving vibe. It sold out its entire run, regardless of all the loose ends that made it a logistical nightmare.

Liz had entered the age of the turban.

She then had a well-publicized relationship (whether fling or friendship we may never know) with daytime TV's hottest actor, Anthony "Luke" Geary, after making a memorable guest appearance on his show, *General Hospital*. Her role called for her to play a megalomaniac in a turban. It was too good to be true.

By the mid-80s, Liz was a lean, mean machine, having lost her way down to 110 pounds after kicking pills and booze at the Betty Ford Clinic (1983). That earned her the right to pen a book on weight loss and self-image, *Elizabeth Takes Off* (1987). Her first facelift also helped her look better than ever.

To celebrate her sveltitude, she went blonde and breezed through a triumphant and highly rated "comeback" appearance on TV's *Hotel* (1984), sharing scenes with that other 40s and 50s starlet Anne Baxter.

The blondeness didn't last, nor did Liz's aloneness. She had lots of gentleman friends, including Victor Luna (she even got engaged to him), George Hamilton, and Malcolm Forbes (or so we were led to believe at the time).

But Liz's acting and romancing were actually taking backseats for the first decade of her life. More seminal to her personal evolution was her involvement in AIDS awareness, a cause that absolutely no other celebrities were interested in embracing when she did it in the early 80s. Liz became heavily involved with AIDS Project Los Angeles (APLA) and AmFAR (American Foundation for AIDS Research). She also became a rabid safe sex educator and AIDS funding advocate, appearing at thousand-dollar-a-plate fund-raisers and helping to infect Hollywood with a much needed sense of responsibility that ultimately raised tens of millions of dollars for AIDS. Maybe being married to politico John Warner actually had its purpose.

With her name becoming synonymous with Hollywood's response to the AIDS crisis, Liz did something that other stars had done and that many more would do after her—she launched a perfume. The difference was that Cher's "Uninhibited" stank. Debbie Gibson's "Electric Youth" got old fast. But E.T.'s "Passion" became a multimillion-dollar phenomenon, ensuring that Liz would be able to live in the manner to which she'd grown accustomed (since age ten). Ah, the sweet smell of success!

Passion was such a hit that she launched Passion for Men, a condition to which she could definitely relate.

Plenty of bad things happened to Elizabeth Taylor in the 80s. Aside from losing many friends to AIDS

In order to market her huge-selling Passion perfume and cologne, Liz slimmed down and underwent a major image overhaul. Her classy gift bags portrayed her as anything *but* a bag—chic hairdos, contemporary makeup, and a little nip-and-tuck returned Liz to her rightful position as an icon of passion.

(including Rock Hudson), she also lost Richard Burton, whose boozing caught up with him in 1984. She had the misfortune of playing an opera singer—and doing blackface in a horrifying *Aida* scene—in Franco Zeffirelli's unreleaseable *Young Toscanini* (1988). And even though her appearance in the highly rated, highly 80s Civil War miniseries *North and South* (1985) was just as ravishing as her *Hotel* stint, she wrenched her back in her heavy antebellum gown, an injury bound to flare up sporadically for the rest of her life. She returned to rehab in 1988.

But even though she wasn't living a charmed existence during the 80s, Liz was having a ball, accomplishing more than she had in fifteen years, and was living life inside a slim, busty, suitably goddesslike body.

It didn't last. There were more addictions, pounds, and another husband and divorce to deal with in the 90s, not to mention having both hips replaced, publicly humiliating herself by going to bat for the single least deserving dude on earth (pal Michael Jackson), and taking a role in—gulp—*The Flintstones*.

But the 80s represented Elizabeth Taylor's second wind, and the celeb- and tabloid-mad 80s were panting right along with her.

Baby, It's You: Transcendant Performances of the 80s

The Oscars are notoriously out of touch, and the Golden Globes sometimes seem to be based solely on ticket sales, so here's a list of the film performances of the 80s that didn't receive the acclaim and awards they should have.

1. Sandra Bernhard as an obsessed fan, *The King of Comedy* (1983).

2. Bronson Pinchot as "Serge," *Beverly Hills Cop* (1984).

Bronson Pinchot as "Serge"—good luck placing the accent.

3. Grace Jones as the vamp, *Vamp* (1986).

Interview with the vamp.

4. Alan Ruck as the archetypal schmuck, *Ferris Bueller's Day Off* (1986).

5. Terry Kiser as the very dead "Bernie," *Weekend at Bernie's* (1989).

6. Faye Dunaway as you-know-who, *Mommie Dearest* (1981).

7. Betsy Palmer as "Jason"'s not-all-there mommy, *Friday the 13th* (1980).

8. M. Emmet Walsh as a sleazeball, *Blood Simple* (1985).

9. Sean Penn as a Valley Boy, *Fast Times at Ridgemont High* (1982).

10. Debra Winger as the vaguely demonic voice of E.T., *E.T. The Extra-Terrestrial* (1982).

11. Barbara Billingsley as the helpful passenger who speaks "jive," *Airplane!* (1980).

12. Beverly D'Angelo as Patsy Cline, *Coal Miner's Daughter* (1980).

13. Annie Potts as the gum-snapping receptionist, *Ghostbusters* (1984).

14. Peter Billingsley as "Charlie Brown" personified, *A Christmas Story* (1983).

15. Sally Kirkland as a forgotten Czech film star, *Anna* (1987).

Sean Penn displays his "Assassinate Lincoln" buttons in *Fast Times at Ridgemont High.*

16. Hugh Grant as a charming, self-loathing, gay aristocrat, *Maurice* (1987).

17. Kim Basinger as a sexy blonde who can't hold her liquor, *Blind Date* (1987).

18. Karen Black as a cross-eyed transsexual, *Come Back to the 5 and Dime, Jimmy Dean, Jimmy Dean* (1982).

19. Robert Sean Leonard as a high-strung thespian, *Dead Poets Society* (1989).

20. Imogene Coca as a hood ornament, *National Lampoon's Vacation* (1983).

TV, or You Take the Good, You Take the Bad

TV in the 80s became more than a leisure-time activity; it became a soundtrack for our lives. People frequently left the TV on just for the reassurance that it was playing, the way infants appreciate the hum of a clock placed in their bassinets. During the 80s Americans went from watching TV daily for six hours, thirty-six minutes (1980) to watching seven hours, two minutes (1989), every day . . . *on average.* Part of this was due to the development of powerhouse TV nights, like NBC's killer Thursdays, featuring *The Cosby Show, Family Ties, Cheers,* and *Night Court.* All four of these shows were major hits in 1986, when America spent an average of seven hours, ten minutes (the record) watching the boob tube.

Along with the advent of cable TV (and with it, program-length infomercials, multiple airings of bad movies like *Sunburn,* and the concept of "fifty-seven channels with nothing on"), network TV was thriving, having produced the single most popular TV show of all time (*Cosby*) and presenting a record number of new programs each season.

TV was (and is) an excellent tool not only for learning such useful things as the Heimlich maneuver (*Three's Company*) or how to count to ten in Spanish (*Sesame Street*), but also for becoming phenomenally well versed in social etiquette and American pop culture. As just one example, *The Facts of Life* taught girls they could be virgins almost indefinitely (if they felt like it) and warned us all against the evils of materialism and snobbery ("Blair").

At the start of the 80s, the major trend in prime-time TV was glitz, glamour, and ultraviolence. *Dallas* and *Dynasty* set the trend for potboilers involving the rich and torrid, and action shows like *The A Team* chugged along through body after body before activists complained about the (imagined?) effect all the aggression might be having on kids. By the mid-to late 80s, however, the focus had shifted decisively. The thrust became clever sitcoms (*Cheers, Night Court*) and family-oriented shows (*The Cosby Show, Family Ties, Growing Pains, Who's the Boss?*), signaling our fading infatuation with yuppie greed and growing affection for the family unit, in whatever form, and for a little romance.

TV was influenced by the same fads that affected movies, except on a more immediate basis. New trends—female-driven talk shows, "reality" shows like *Real People,* and the popularization of the ensemble cast—were immediately pounced on by TV producers, so that the medium was in an almost weekly state of evolution.

Following are some of the fittest shows, the ones that actually survive in our memory as being either eye-opening, funny, touching, goofy, or just plain mesmerizing.

The Ultimate 80s TV Show

Dynasty (1981–1989). Harder than music or movies, it is almost impossible to narrow down the field to one archetypal 80s TV show, but *Dynasty* wins out, if not for sheer balls, then for its mirroring of all the most obvious elements of the 80s: glitz (thanks to Nolan Miller's eye-popping gowns), superficiality (thanks to Aaron Spelling's production), greed (thanks to "Blake Carrington"), the concept of the comeback (Joan Collins returns!), and even AIDS (the real-life melodrama that unfolded after one episode in which guest star Rock Hudson passionately kissed Linda Evans without disclosing that he was dying of AIDS—she survived).

Anatomy of a slugfest: Linda Evans and Joan Collins engage in the most undignified female brawl in TV history (1982). Unless the one where they skirmished in the pond was worse…?

One of the most popular *Playboy* covers of the 80s featured a woman pushing 50—Joan Collins took it all off as a statement against age discrimination.

One reason "Alexis" and "Krystle" hated each other—they showed up in one episode wearing the same dress!

Dynasty was basically a glitzy knock-off of the much more popular *Dallas*, but though it lasted only eight seasons as compared with *Dallas*'s twelve, it burned brightly.

The melodrama followed the lives of richies "the Carringtons," and their kin "the Colbys." "Blake" (John Forsythe) was the patriarch, silver haired and strong, "Krystle" (Linda Evans) his loving, helmet-haired wife, and "Alexis" (Joan Collins) his amoral ex-wife. Other characters of note were "Blake"'s daughter, "Fallon" (Pamela Sue Martin, then Emma Samms) and his

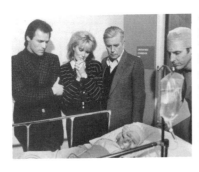

"Dex" (Michael Nader) soothes "Krystle" (Linda Evans) and "Blake" (John Forsythe) during little "Krystina"'s (Jessica Player) heart transplant crisis (1987).

gay/bi/confused son, "Steven" (Al Corley, then Jack Coleman), though the cast shifted countless times in order to keep things fresh. When Diahann Carroll was introduced as "TV's first black bitch," you knew things were getting a little desperate.

Perhaps the highlights of the show were the stagey, outrageous catfights "Krystle" and "Alexis" occasionally engaged in, as in the time they were caught grappling in a pool. Or was it the "Moldavian massacre," where every character on the show was mowed down in a spray of gunfire . . . yet only two of them (the unbearable temp character played by Ali MacGraw and "Steven"'s gay lover) actually bit the bullet? Regardless, every episode was filled to the brim with outrageous back stabbing, and every now and again some well-dressed diva took a faceful of champagne for uttering one bitchy word too many.

> "It was those *trips*, those awful *trips!*" —"Alexis" (in flashback) explaining to "Blake" that she cheated on him only because of his excessive business trips, 1985

Eighty Quintessentially 80s TV Shows

Even "Clair Huxtable" (Phylicia Rashad) seems to think daddy's girl "Rudy" (Keshia Knight Pulliam) is too cute for her own good on *The Cosby Show*.

1. *The Cosby Show* (1984–1992). Not every black family is headed up by an obstetrician and a lawyer, lives in an upper-class home, and exists in a continual state of familial bliss, but surely *some* do. This flashback to classic, wholesome sitcoms such as *Father Knows Best* and *Leave It to Beaver* went a long way toward making up for universally "urban" portrayals of

African-Americans on TV and went on to become the most popular series in history.

A thinly veiled chronicle of star Bill Cosby's own family, *The Cosby Show* capitalized on his wry, authoritarian delivery and the familiar pitfalls of family life. "Heathcliff and Clair Huxtable" (Cosby and Phylicia Rashad, respectively) were still carrying on a mad love affair twenty years after their wedding night, son "Theo" (Malcolm-Jamal Warner) was the lovable dope, and daughter "Denise" (Lisa Bonet) was the fashion-obsessed, snooty Val. "Rudy" (Keshia Knight Pulliam) was the cute baby of the family, "Vanessa" (Tempestt Bledsoe) the cranky middle child ("Jan Brady" city), and college-age daughter "Sondra" (Sabrina LeBeauf) came on board a couple of months after the series debuted. The cast was frequently joined by various grandparents, relatives, and the occasional legend (such as Lena Horne, just passing through).

Fun for the whole family, though any family watching *The Cosby Show* was likely to suffer from a serious inferiority complex. This show was so good (until Raven Symone joined the cast once "Rudy" got too old to be cute), it was hard to blame Cosby for the unwatchable and yet quite successful spin-off, *A Different World* (1987–1993).

2. *Moonlighting* (1985–1989). The most creative TV series of the 80s, with a nonstop array of monologues to the audience, in-jokes, double and triple entendres, and the racy, sexually charged banter of its stars, uptight former model "Maddie Hayes" (Cybill "I always knew I was good" Shepherd) and flip, smug private dick "David Addison" (Bruce Willis).

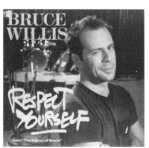

TV star Bruce Willis moonlighted as a singer and movie action hero. His first record was a horrid remake of The Staple Singers' "Respect Yourself." His record company was banking on recognition of Willis as "Addison" from *Moonlighting*, which they accentuated by getting him to do the "Addison" smirk on the record sleeve. It hit the Top 10.

> "We owe [Bill Cosby] our thanks, not only for the laughter and enjoyment, but also for demonstrating the educational potential of prime-time television, for caring about and contributing to our children's moral development, and for showing us how our families can thrive with harmony and love."
> —Coretta Scott King on *The Cosby Show*

"Maddie" owned and operated the Blue Moon Detective Agency, a tax write-off that developed into her *raison d'etre* after she lost her fortune. "Addison" was her cohort and her employee.

Wild theme episodes included a claymation special, an anachronistic restaging of *The Taming of the Shrew* (complete with iambic pentameter), and a black-and-white 40s fantasy sequence inspired by Orson Welles. Goofy, rhyme-crazed receptionist "Agnes Dipesto" (Allyce Beasley) added the manic ditz factor, and the show's hard-boiled mysteries took a backseat to the biggest question since "Who Shot J.R.?": "When will 'Dave' and 'Maddie' do it?"

> "Amnesia cases are our special today/Finding the real you is our forte."
> —"Miss Dipesto," *Moonlighting*

3. *Dallas* (1979–1991). The most watched single episode in television history (until the finale of *M*A*S*H* just over two years later) was the solution to the question on everyone's lips during the summer hiatus of 1981: "Who shot J.R.?" (It was "Kristin," played by Mary Crosby.)

"J. R. Ewing" (Larry Hagman) was the amoral CEO of a Dallas dynasty HQ'ed at the South Fork Ranch, a man with more enemies than this long-running potboiler had revolving characters. The *Dallas* core, aside from "J.R.," were "Sue Ellen Ewing" (Linda Gray), "J.R."'s emotionally distraught wife; "Miss Ellie" (Barbara Bel Geddes), his long-suffering mother; "Jock" (Jim Davis), his gruff daddy; "Bobby" (Patrick Duffy), his competitive brother; "Pamela" (Victoria Principal), "Bobby"'s hussy wife; "Cliff Barnes" (Ken Kercheval), "Pamela"'s brother; "J.R."'s niece "Lucy" (Charlene Tilton), Little Miss Goody Two-shoes; and ranch foreman "Ray Krebbs" (Steve Kanaly).

Other characters were played, over the years, by Christopher Atkins, Priscilla Presley, Priscilla Pointer, Jennilee Harrison, Andrew

> "I don't know what people will remember me for in the end, but I hope one thing is as a good wife."
> —Victoria Principal, good wife to plastic surgeon Dr. Harry Glassman, 1988

Stevens, Barbara Eden (Larry Hagman's old *I Dream of Jeannie* costar), and Audrey Landers, making this a veritable Texan *Love Boat.*

The show constantly pitted the "Ewing" and "Barnes" clans against one another and followed the disintegration of "J.R." and "Sue Ellen"'s marriage. Every episode was full of sparks, affairs, and threats issued in a Texan twang.

In its heyday *Dallas* roped in more viewers than any other show on TV. But then, everything's bigger in Texas.

Spin-off: *Knots Landing* (see #43).

4. *Cheers* (1982–1993). Where everybody knows your name.

We spent aeons waiting for dumb-jock/bartender "Sam Malone" (Ted Danson) and intellectual/reluctant barmaid "Diane Chambers" (Shelley Long) to admit their attraction to each other, but we had a swell time doing it. With regulars like waitress "Carla" (Rhea Perlman), bartenders "Coach" (Nicholas Colasanto) and "Woody" (Woody Harrelson), barflies "Cliff Clavin" (John Ratzenberger) and "Norm" (George Wendt), "Diane"'s ex, "Frasier" (Kelsey Grammer), and "Frasier"'s ice maiden galpal, "Lilith" (Bebe Neuwirth), you laughed like a drunk.

> "Norm!"
> —entire bar to George Wendt/"Norm" any time he made an entrance, *Cheers*

As usual, once the stars "did it," the show lost its punch. It might have lost its bored viewers, too, if Long hadn't taken off (1987) for (debatable) silver screen stardom. Her departure enabled "Rebecca" (Kirstie Alley) to join the crew as the new manager of the bar and as yet another love/hate interest for "Sam."

5. *Miami Vice* (1984–1989). The ultimate "cool" show of the 80s, which was passé before it wound down its five-year run. Miami drug cops "Crockett" (Don Johnson) and "Tubbs" (Philip Michael Thomas) spent more time on their sleek, pastel, Italian outfits and designer stubble than on catching the bad guys.

> "My fans are very, very intelligent. I hear a good deal from bright teenagers as well as the eleven- and twelve-year-olds."
> —Don Johnson, 1985

Designed to be as MTV as possible, the show was drenched in pop songs, and its instrumental theme by Jan Hammer was a number-one hit in its

"Sonny Crockett" (Don Johnson) knee-deep in Miami's vice.

own right. Sheena Easton joined the cast in 1987 as a rock singer who married "Crockett," only to get eighty-sixed soon after, but the hottest guest star was Melanie Griffith (the once and future Mrs. Don Johnson), who added yet another prostitute role to her résumé.

6. *Hill Street Blues* (1981–1987). The most widely acclaimed dramatic series of the 80s and the first cop show to portray the very human private lives of the men and women in blue.

Daniel J. Travanti played "Capt. Frank Furillo" and Veronica Hamel was public defender "Joyce Davenport," his love interest and eventually his wife. The show worked thanks to its enormous, impressive ensemble cast, made up of regulars Betty Thomas, Michael Conrad, Bruce Weitz, James B. Sikking, Joe Spano, Kiel Martin, Taurean Blacque, Rene Enriquez, Ed Marinaro, Barbara Bosson, Robert Hirschfeld, and Barbara Babcock, among others.

> "Let's be careful out there."
> —Michael Conrad, *Hill Street Blues*

The show won an enthusiastic following for its heartfelt dramatics and became a model for similar ensemble dramas to follow (*L.A. Law*, see #36; *St. Elsewhere*, see #62; *E.R.*).

7. *Family Ties* (1982–1989). A Valley Girl, a wise-cracking runt, and a Young Republican were the three

unlikely children of aging hippies "Steven and Elyse Keaton" (Michael Gross and Meredith Baxter Birney, respectively). Michael J. Fox stole the show as comically conservative "Alex P. Keaton," who argued with dumb-bunny sis "Mallory" (Justine Bateman) even more than "J.J." and "Thelma" fought on *Good Times* way back in the 70s. Tina Yothers played "Jennifer," best described as Courtney Love as a child.

Highlights would have to include the show's elaborate Christmas specials, though in retrospect it's fun to watch "Alex" and girlfriend "Ellen" (Tracy Pollan) interact, knowing that they'd later get married in real life.

8. *Wheel of Fortune* (1975–). Though it was around for years before the 80s, it wasn't until host Pat Sajak and hostess Vanna White joined in 1982 that this daytime game show went pre–prime time and became the hottest show in syndication. Vanna was that scraggly *Dynasty* reject who barely spoke and barely managed to flip letters competently and yet became a major celebrity overnight. The public became so enamored of her that she won a starring role as "Aphrodite" in the TV movie *The Goddess of Love* (1987), which was a major B-_-M-B. Would you like to buy a vowel, or solve the puzzle?

9. *The Golden Girls* (1985–1992). Four feisty older women (Bea Arthur, Rue McClanahan, Betty White, and Estelle Getty) shared a Miami condo, all the troubles of dating past fifty, and countless pans of brownies. A ribald and sometimes heartwarming (even purple) show that played up "Blanche"'s (McClanahan's) sluttiness, "Dorothy"'s (Arthur's) bitchiness, "Rose"'s (White's) stupidity, and "Sophia"'s (Getty's) dotty malevolence, all to perfection.

"No, Charo—you can't *live* on *The Love Boat*."

10. *The Love Boat* (1977–1986). Old stars don't die—they just sail away.

The setting was a glamorous Princess cruise ship, where a new cast of guest stars vacationed each week while interacting with the crew of regulars. "Captain Merrill Stubing" (Gavin MacLeod) ran a not-so-tight ship, one full of star-

"Vicki Stubing" (Jill Whelan) has delusions of grandeur.

"Julie" (Lauren Tewes) and "Gopher" (Fred Grandy) never got it on, but they faked it to make one of "Gopher"'s old frat buddies jealous.

crossed rolls in the hay. "Gopher" (Fred Grandy) was the nerdy steward (who in real life later won a seat in Congress), "Julie McCoy" (Lauren Tewes) the perky cruise director, "Doc" (Bernie Kopell) the ship's doctor (and the homeliest Lothario in history), "Isaac" (Ted Lange) the groovy bartender, and little "Vicky" (Jill Whelan) "Captain Stubing"'s misfit daughter.

The show welcomed absolutely *every* living star, scoring such coups as having Loni Anderson ride *The Love Boat* to *Fantasy Island* (a very special four-hour event) and getting Ethel Merman to play "Gopher"'s mom. When Lauren Tewes left the show to take care of her cocaine addiction (1984), it was like an unforeseen iceberg, and the show's campy fun sank without a trace.

11. *The A Team* (1983–1987). A band of Vietnam vets now acting as mercenaries ran around the world assisting those with the most money (and the best intentions— these were the *good* guys, remember). The A Team comprised the motliest crew imaginable, featuring borderline-nutcase "Murdock" (Dwight Schultz), wall of muscle "B. A. Baracus" (Mr. T), silver-haired genius "Hannibal Smith" (George Peppard), and smoothie "Face" (Dirk Benedict). Melinda Culea played "Amy," who was "the girl" on the first season, but thereafter The A Team became strictly "no girls allowed."

The most violent show on TV during the 80s, like having a new *Rambo* on every week.

"I pity the fool."
—Mr. T, *The A Team*

By 1981, the cast had slimmed down—well, at least the number of regulars had. "Tootie" (Kim Fields) is absent, but the mainstays are here: "Mrs. Garrett" (Charlotte Rae), "Jo" (Nancy McKeon), "Natalie" (Mindy Cohn), and "Blair" (Lisa Whelchel).

12. *The Facts of Life* **(1979–1988).** With one of the most singable theme songs of the 80s (just *try* to forget the words—and keep in mind they were written by *Alan Thicke*) and an energetic cast of schoolgirls, this became the longest-running comedy of the decade—even longer than the inferior show it was spun off from, *Diff'rent Strokes* (see #34).

"Mrs. Garrett" (Charlotte Rae) was the wise eccentric who kept a band of young Eastland girls in line. She later started a business (Edna's Edibles) with her favorites. They were "Blair" (Lisa Whelchel), the bitchy, rich show-off; "Jo" (Nancy McKeon), the rebel; "Natalie" (Mindy Cohn), the chubby wiseacre; and "Tootie" (Kim Fields), the roller-skating innocent. Together they formed a group of the world's oldest virgins, until "Natalie" became the first to give in (1988).

It was never explained why a slew of regulars from the first season (including Molly Ringwald) failed to appear in ensuing episodes. Surely we would sooner have seen "Sue Ann Weaver" (Julie Piekarski) return than be subjected to those final episodes with Cloris Leachman, MacKenzie Astin, and a youthful George Clooney. . . .

Dumb and fun and probably the subject of a major motion picture before the year 2000.

13. *The People's Court* **(1981–1993).** The one that started the "real TV" trend, with its surly Judge Wapner, intrepid reporter Doug Llewelyn, trusty bailiff Rusty, and all manner of real-life ignoramuses (ignorami?) suing each other for all of $200 (the ceiling was $1,500). The gimmick was that Wapner's mean-spirited judgments were legally binding. The plaintiffs and defendants were generally too low class for *Geraldo*, which should remind you why it was so much guilty fun watching them duke it out.

14. *Smurfs* **(1981–1990).** The Smurfiest cartoon ever! These blue, elflike creatures debuted in a marketing explosion in the early 80s. Each Smurf was named for his vocation ("Painter Smurf"), except for their patriarchal ruler "Papa Smurf" and the lone female, "Smurfette," who had a thing for "Minnie Mouse" pumps and false eyelashes. Their carefully constructed fables were the smartest things on kid TV, and their narrow escapes from the wicked warlock "Gargamel" and his mangy cat "Azrael" were more thrilling than *The A-Team*. Also, after a couple of episodes, you found yourself substituting the word "Smurf" for every other word in your vocabulary.

15. *Fantasy Island* **(1978–1984).** A mystical island paradise where—if you had enough bucks or if

On a special episode, "Mr. Roarke" welcomed Loni Anderson to the island (1980).

mysterious island puba "Mr. Roarke" (Ricardo Montalban) sympathized with your plight—you could indulge yourself in any fantasy you wished, along the lines of living as Marie Antoinette in eighteenth-century France (as Adrienne Barbeau did). Basically this was a good gig for B actors and has-beens in between filming episodes of *The Love Boat* and *Hotel*, which is exactly why it was immensely entertaining. Of course, the real star of the show was "Tattoo" (the late Herve Villechaize), the politically incorrect midget with an almost unintelligible French accent.

"De plane...de plane!" —Herve Villechaize, *Fantasy Island*

16. *Roseanne* **(1988–).** Coming at the tail end of the decade was this raucous family show created by and starring a woman best described as Lucille Ball, Carol Burnett, and Mary Tyler Moore all rolled into one. In fact, all three of those great comediennes could have stood in the shadow of the roly-poly Roseanne Barr, and it's unlikely that any of them would challenge her to a war of words.

Roseanne turned family life on its ear with her warts-and-all sitcom, which dethroned *The Cosby Show* as the most popular show on TV Though she was legendary for having fired all of her writers regularly and for a personal life that threatened to eclipse the notoriety of Elizabeth Taylor's, Roseanne's comic brilliance and that of her crew (John Goodman, Sara Gilbert, Lecy Goranson/Sarah Chalke, Michael Fishman, and especially Laurie Metcalf) made Roseanne Barr/Roseanne Arnold/Roseanne the queen of TV from 1988 on.

> "There's a lot of '[Sgt.] Bilko' in 'ALF' and he finds a way to manipulate the situation, get what he wants, and make a little mischief."
> —Tom Patchett, producer of *ALF*

17. *ALF* (1986–1990). One always worries over the fate of a TV show whose star is a hand puppet, but this one pulled it off. "ALF" (standing for "alien life form") crash-landed in the garage of the "Tanner" family. The human actors were incidental; the only reason to watch this whimsical show was for its star's wry observations of American ways and habits and to see if he would at long last devour the family cat.

Morgan Fairchild bawls her eyes out as a guest on *Hotel*.

18. *Hotel* (1983–1988). A landlubbing *Love Boat*.

San Francisco hotel the St. Gregory was run by the scrupulous yet imposing "Victoria Cabot" (Anne Baxter) and her staff, including stone-faced "Peter" (James Brolin), heavily kohled "Christine" (Connie Sellecca), front desk girl "Megan" (Heidi Bohay), director of guest relations "Mark Danning" (Shea Farrell), security manager "Billy Griffin" (Nathan Cook), and manager "Julie" (Shari Belafonte-Harper).

The parade of guest stars on this show was frequently identical to that on *The Love Boat*, though *Hotel* did score a major coup by bagging suddenly blonde Elizabeth Taylor after she'd lost all her baby fat. One of several major 80s shows to lose one of its stars to sudden death (Anne Baxter had a stroke and was declared brain dead in 1985).

19. *Square Pegs* (1982–1983). You bonded with the two nerdettes "Lauren" (Amy Linker) and "Patty" (Sarah Jessica Parker), laughed at the dumb Valley Girl "Jennifer" (Tracy Nelson) and her even dumber beau "Vinnie" (Jon Caliri), hated class prude "Muffy" (Jami Gertz), and rolled your eyes at the antics of Groucho Marx impersonator "Marshall" (John Femia) and New Waver "Johnny Slash" (Merrit Butrick), but the coolest thing about this show was its theme song, as served up by The Waitresses. The whole cast attended Weemawee High School and dealt with all the usual teen problems—dating, appearance, grades—in most unusual ways.

> "It behooves me to say..."
> —Jami Gertz, *Square Pegs*

Easily the most uncomfortably realistic (aside from token black character "LaDonna") and hilarious teen show ever, even if its reliance on Valspeak made it limited even before the Nielsens did it in.

20. *General Hospital* (1963–). One of about a trillion soaps that have been on the air since the dawn of time, this one was the most-watched in the 80s, especially during the "Luke" (Tony Geary) and "Laura" (Genie Francis) period. When those crazy kids (he'd raped her, then they'd fallen in love) finally got married in 1981, it became the highest-rated soap event in history and the biggest wedding of the 80s (not counting the 1982 mass marriage of 2,075 "Moonie" couples). Not to mention the fact that Rick Springfield got his start here as "Dr. Noah Drake." As soon as you learned how to work your new VCR, you taped this show religiously—on Beta or VHS.

21. *TV's Bloopers and Practical Jokes* (1984–1986; 1988). With this show Dick Clark launched an annoying fad of showcases for silly, stagey celebrity practical jokes (the joke's on you, Joan Van Ark!) and line-flubbing outtakes from TV shows and commercials. But while the novelty lasted, this show was required viewing.

22. *The Oprah Winfrey Show* (1986–). Her first promo spots featured Oprah teaching us that her name is "OH-prah," not "OH-krah" or "OAF-rah," and

Oprah ponders her many bad hair moves with one of her worst, in *The Color Purple.*

that training session worked wonders. In 1985, she was hosting the locally popular chat show *A.M. Chicago*, one year later she was helming the biggest hit talk show since *Donahue*, and before the 90s rolled around Oprah Winfrey was the richest female entertainer in the world. Her show, relying on outrageous guests and on Oprah's calculated normalcy and wit, made Oprah a superstar for housewives and one of our most respected and beloved celebrities. All that and she damn near won an Oscar for *The Color Purple* (1985).

23. *Gimme a Break!* (1981–1987). Nell Carter played "Nell," a sassy, black Weeble Wobble raising the three daughters left behind by her best friend's death. She lived with the "Kanisky" family, headed by a grouchy police commander (usually just called "Chief"). The daughters were sexually adventurous "Katie" (Kari Michaelsen), brainiac "Julie" (Lauri Hendler), and naive "Sam" (Lara Jill Miller), and they eventually welcomed miniature con artist/orphan "Joey" (Joey Lawrence) into the fold.

"Nell" was unique as a big woman with an even bigger sex drive (to match her heart), and her chemistry with fussy sidekick "Addy" (Telma Hopkins) was tops. Too bad the real-life Nell bottomed out before the show did.

Singing sensation Andy Gibb had already sunk to *Gimme a Break!* cameos (1983) years before dying of a heart condition aggravated by drug abuse in 1988.

24. *thirtysomething* (1987–1991). Little did this show's creators realize that in developing this title, they would be inventing a new catchphrase for youngish baby boomers. This highly praised dramatic series—with memorably heart-tugging stories such as "Nancy"'s (Patricia Wettig's) cancer battle—was really just a highly polished, well-acted *The Young and the Restless* . . . but who's complaining?

25. *Kate & Allie* (1984–1989). A female *The Odd Couple*, with divorced moms Jane Curtin as the tight-lipped "Allie" and Susan Saint James as free-wheeling "Kate." They lived together with their mirror-image daughters (Ari Meyers and Allison Smith) and "Allie"'s son, "Chip" (Frederick Koehler), in order to make ends meet, typifying (or at least entertaining) the single moms who peopled the 80s with greater frequency.

26. *Magnum, P.I.* (1980–1988). Tom Selleck was "Magnum," the hirsute, Hawaii-based private investigator and John Hillerman played "Jonathan Quayle Higgins III," his mannered sidekick, on this stalwart action-adventure series that had everyone guessing if Selleck would ever shave off that cheesy mustache.

"Magnum" commiserates with guest star Carol Burnett.

27. *Late Night With David Letterman* (1982–) The midwestern smart aleck helmed this late night goof-fest entailing stupid pet tricks, the musical stylings of drippy Paul Shaffer, the infamous "monkey cam," and the screechingly John Waters–ian Larry "Bud" Melman. The ultimate college show of the 80s, whose host would become one of America's favorite—and richest—TV personalities by the early 90s.

28. *Who's the Boss?* (1984–1992). So he wouldn't forget his character's name, Tony Danza played "Tony," a very Italian-American guy who worked as housekeeper and nanny to

"Tony" (Tony Danza) shows proof of his beefy appeal—a "Tony Micelli" calendar.

WASPy career woman "Angela"'s (Judith Light's) prissy son "Jonathan." "Tony"'s own teenage daughter, "Sam" (Alyssa Milano), proved to be his biggest handful and one of the hottest teen idols of the decade, but the show's real laughs came from "Angela"'s outrageous mom, "Mona" (Katherine Helmond).

29. *The Dukes of Hazzard* (1979–1985). "Bo and Luke Duke" (John Schneider and Tom Wopat, respectively)—two country studs—and "Daisy" (Catherine Bach)—their buxom cuz—bent the law and had a ton of fun in the Deep South in Hazzard County at the expense of cartoonish "Boss Hogg" (Sorrell Booke) and his idiotic henchmen, "Sheriff Rosco P. Coltrane" (James Best) and "Deputy Enos Strate" (Sonny Shroyer). Wise "Uncle Jesse" (Denver Pyle) gave the kids sound advice, and narrator Waylon Jennings gave the story just the right amount of down-home grit. We tuned in each week to see—if for no other reason—the Dukes' car get trashed.

Their car and girl chasing lost its edge when the competitive, big-headed stars were axed for a half-season after a salary dispute, but we'll always have Hazzard.

30. *21 Jump Street* (1987–1990). One of the fledgling Fox Network's first hit shows, starring

Johnny Depp as "Officer Hanson" (sounds like "handsome," get it?).

Johnny Depp as "Tommy Hanson," Holly Robinson as "Judy Hoffs," Peter DeLuise as "Doug Penhall," and Dustin Nguyen as "H. T. Loki," as a troupe of youthful undercover cops cracking cases and looking their best. A campy series well worth reviewing for when Johnny Depp wins his Oscar.

31. *Growing Pains* (1985–1992). After bombing miserably with his late night talk show *Thicke of the Night* (1983–1984), Alan Thicke rebounded with this enormously successful family sitcom modeled closely after *Family Ties*, except without the bite. The spunky "Seaver" kids were headed up by elder brother/con artist "Mike" (squeaky clean Kirk Cameron), who always seemed to get the whole brood into harmless messes. Future anorexic Tracey

"Some kids have a job at McDonald's. I have a job at Warner Brothers." —Kirk Cameron, 1986

Gold played daughter "Carol," Jeremy Miller was tot "Ben," and Joanna Kerns played "Carol Brady"–like "Maggie," the mom who always knew best.

32. *Benson* (1979–1986). A spin-off from the extremely risqué nighttime soap send-up *Soap* (1977–1981), on which "Benson" (Robert Guillaume) had been an unapologetically attitudinous butler. This time around, "Benson" was more restrained as he attempted to whip "Governor Gatling"'s (James Noble's) mansion into shape while duking it out with ice maiden housekeeper "Kraus" (Inga Swenson) and helping to raise Olsen twins precursor "Katie" (Missy Gold). By the time "Benson" was running for governor against "Gatling," (1986) the show had run its course, but the idea was ripe for the picking: check out the similarities between *Benson* and *The Nanny* (1993–).

33. *Cagney & Lacey* (1982–1988). The first female cop show was also revered for the high-powered acting of its stars and the gutsy storylines that helped make it a multiple Emmy winner. "Chris Cagney" (Sharon Gless) was the single blonde with the drinking problem, roller-coaster love life, and demanding father, and "Mary Beth Lacey" (Tyne Daly) was the beleaguered mother and wife. Really moving if you could sit through an episode, and a constant source of "Would You Be Caught Dead in This Outfit?" Emmy Awards appearances by Daly. Also, this was one of the only TV shows ever to be brought back from certain cancellation by an outpouring of viewer protest (1984).

34. *Diff'rent Strokes* (1978–1986). In this comedy, two poor black orphans named "Arnold" (pint-size Gary Coleman) and "Willis" (lanky Todd Bridges) were raised by a rich white business tycoon, "Mr. Drummond" (Conrad Bain) and alongside his princess daughter, "Kimberly" (Dana Plato). The kids were kept in line by a succession of housekeepers, "Mrs. Garrett" (Charlotte Rae), "Adelaide" (Nedra Volz), and "Pearl" (Mary Jo Catlett), the latter of whom could have been *The Brady Bunch* "Alice"'s long-lost daughter.

Even though Gary Coleman was a scream with his one-liners, his black goldfish "Abraham," and his precocious shenanigans (especially those high-rise water balloons), this show starred three of the most troubled kids on TV. Coleman's chubbiness of cheek was thanks to kidney problems, which required operation after operation, and he was later involved in legal wrangling with his own parents

> "Whatchootalkinabout, Mr. Drummond?"
> —Gary Coleman,
> *Diff'rent Strokes*

over his business choices. Plato robbed a video store but got caught when the clerk told police, "I was robbed by 'Kimberly' from *Diff'rent Strokes*." Bridges was charged with attempted murder but was acquitted. "Mrs. Garrett" (Charlotte Rae) must have been horrified—had to be "Pearl"'s influence.

Still, this show also scored big with its appearance by First Lady Nancy Reagan, who filmed a "Just Say No" episode, and its delicate handling of child sexual abuse when "Arnold" and his friend "Dudley" (Shavar Ross) were assaulted by harmless-seeming Gordon Jump.

35. Silver Spoons (1982–1987). Like "Richie Rich," "Ricky" (Ricky Schroder) was a child of leisure, raised by his toy-inventing genius dad, "Edward Stratton III" (Joel Higgins), in a mansion that sported a near life-size toy train system. Ricky spent most of his time trying to get his dad and his dad's lovely secretary, "Kate Summers" (Erin Gray), together, and he eventually succeeded—they got married in 1985. Even with deliciously devious "Derek" (Jason Bateman) and John Houseman playing "Edward Stratton II," it's hard to believe little kids actually *liked* the spoiled-brat star. How can you like someone whose nickname is "the Rickster"?

36. L.A. Law (1986–1994). Lawyers in love, starring Susan Dey as assistant D.A. "Grace Van Owen," her first role of note since her hippie days as "Laurie Partridge." Her main love interest was law partner "Michael Kuzak" (Harry Hamlin), and there was never any doubt that their rocky relationship was the main reason to tune in. The show benefited from a host of colorful legal eagles—played by Richard Dysart, Alan Rachins, Blair Underwood, Larry Drake, Corbin Bernsen, Jill Eikenberry and real-life husband Michael Tucker, Jimmy Smits, and Susan Ruttan—who helped make this a drama with more than its share of laughs. We were guaranteed at least one courtroom showdown per episode, but there was no telling which cases would be won and which would be lost.

37. Designing Women (1986–1993). Created by politically well-connected Harry and Linda Bloodworth-Thomason, this series was an impressive showcase for the comic barbs tossed by "Mary Jo" (Annie Potts) and "Charlene" (Jean Smart), the selfish prognosticating of former beauty queen (and future heifer) "Suzanne Sugarbaker" (Delta Burke), and long-winded tirades/tell-offs of southern-fried "Julia Sugarbaker" (Dixie Carter). With these chatty, catty interior designers, it was bitch, bitch, bitch. Wide-eyed "Anthony" (Meshach Taylor) was their guy Friday, and *Bewitched* alum Alice Ghostley materialized as dotty designer "Bernice." Ultimately Delta Burke made this show work with her sweeping gestures and her character's un-PC beliefs. A real-life feud between Dixie and Delta and the producers led to a major rift, which only served to make the show's banter even juicier.

38. Saturday Night Live (1975–). Never as cutting edge as it was in the 70s, this Saturday comedy fixture nevertheless became big business in the 80s with cast members Eddie Murphy ("Gumby," "Mister Robinson," Stevie Wonder), Joe Piscopo (every celebrity under the sun, notably Frank Sinatra), Billy Crystal (Sammy Davis Jr., Fernando Lamas), Dana Carvey ("the Church Lady"), and Martin Short ("Ed Grimley") helping to keep the uneven series more funny than not for most of the 80s. The most memorable—and daring—schtick always belonged to Murphy, and his "Buckwheat" (say, "Buttwheat") became a marketing craze that probably would've been a hit movie . . . if he hadn't been too busy making hit movies already. The women—Mary Gross, Robin Duke, Danitra Vance, Nora Dunn, Julia Louis-Dreyfus—were underused and underappreciated, and the increasingly obnoxious presence of the house band and countless "semiregulars" were mistakes, but the show wouldn't get terrifically stale until the 90s.

39. Webster (1983–1988). A blatant *Diff'rent Strokes* knock-off starring yet another ridiculously cute, preternaturally short, funny, black kid. "Webster" (Emmanuel Lewis) gave his adoptive white parents "the Papadapolises" (Alex Karras and real-life wife Susan Clark) a hard time, but usually by accident—he wasn't as pushy or as smart as "Arnold

Jackson." But his antics never failed to incite a rousing laugh track. The show's biggest fan was Michael Jackson, who counted Lewis among his closest pals.

"Webster" and "Isaac"—two black icons of the 80s share notes. Until the success of *The Cosby Show,* black TV stars were rare in the 80s, so it was only logical that "Webster" would meet up with "Isaac" on the racially imbalanced *Love Boat. The Love Boat* almost never showed interracial romance—"Isaac" always fell for visiting black actresses and always bonded with visiting black actors. *Webster,* on the other hand, was an attempt to remake *Diff'rent Strokes* while the show was still on the air, but dealt much more honestly with racial issues.

40. *Pee-wee's Playhouse* (1986–1991). One of the most surreal TV shows ever put on TV, much less sold to kids, was this frenetic romp hosted by "Pee-wee Herman" (Paul Reubens), a veritable Pinky Lee– on-crack. With campy "Miss Yvonne" (Lynne Stewart), mysterious genie head "Jambi" (John Paragon), chatty

furniture, and eye-popping visits by guests like Sandra Bernhard, this show was an instant cult classic and a hit with kids of all ages (even kids with kids of their own). "Pee-wee" had two hit movies, a doll, trading cards—the works, but he blew it all in the early 90s when he got caught doing what any red-blooded TV icon would do while watching *Naughty Nurses* in a porn theater.

The Pee-wee Herman doll now changes hands for over two hundred bucks.

41. *Scarecrow and Mrs. King* (1983–1987). Kate Jackson played "Mrs. King," the Will Rogers–y suburban mom ballsy enough to engage in international espionage with the big boys (the biggest being her cohort and romantic interest, "Scarecrow"/Bruce Boxleitner). Most of the time Kate Jackson just looked relieved to be rid of her "Sabrina Duncan" role on *Charlie's Angels* (1976–1981).

42. *Solid Gold* (1980–1988). Whether hosted by Dionne Warwick, Andy Gibb, Marilyn McCoo, Rex Smith, or Rick Dees, this was TV's flashiest hour of music and dance, with the spandex-sprayed Solid

Gold Dancers interpreting the hottest hits of the day.

43. *Knots Landing* (1979–1993) This long-lasting *Dallas* offshoot followed the family affairs of "J.R."'s alcoholic brother "Gary Ewing" (Ted Shackelford) and his platinum blond wife, "Valene" (Joan Van Ark), and also of the "Fairgates," headed up by Michele Lee as "Karen." Much more fun were lesser characters "Ciji," a trashy singer (Lisa Hartman), and frosted bitch queen "Abby Cunningham" (Donna Mills), the only characters who ever seemed to go over the top; the rest were more down-to-earth thirty- and fortysomethings and laid-back Californians in the quietest, least outrageous of all the popular nighttime soaps of the 80s.

44. *Night Court* (1984–1992). This show, set in a wacky night court presided over by a childlike, Mel Tormé–obsessed judge ("Harry T. Stone"/Harry Anderson), became known for its daringly raunchy one-liners. Eventually a sexual stand-off was established between "Harry" and public defender "Christine" (Markie Post), but only after the first two public defenders (Paula Kelly and Ellen Foley) had been axed. The most hilarious bits were generated by the supporting players, hulking Richard Moll as bailiff "Bull," Charles Robinson as court clerk "Mac," and by Selma Diamond (who died of cancer in the early years of the show), Florence Halop (ditto), and Marsha Warfield, all of whom played wisecracking co-bailiffs. John Larroquette played "Dan Fielding," the most uncompromising male slut on TV. Imagine the storyline if "Dan" had met "Blanche Devereaux" of *The Golden Girls*—definitely cable-access material.

45. *Perfect Strangers* (1986–1993). Like *Mork from Mypos,* shepherd "Balki" (Bronson Pinchot) moved in with his American cousin "Larry" (Mark Linn-Baker) as a convenient excuse for Pinchot to provide pithy, Myposian-accented commentary on those crazy Americans. Like *Growing Pains,* this popular show lasted for years with a very low profile and virtually no major celeb guest stars, a feat rarely accomplished by shows after their fourth season.

46. *The Fall Guy* (1981–1986). Lee Majors starred as "Colt Seavers," a professional stunt man who brags that he's been seen with Farrah (as in Fawcett, Majors's real-life ex). Doug Barr, Heather Thomas

(Heather Locklear's doppelgänger), Nedra Volz, Markie Post, and Jo Ann Pflug rounded out the cast and generally assisted "Colt" as he moonlighted as a bounty hunter, a profession that just about everyone on 80s TV seemed to dabble in (*The A Team*, *Hunter*, and others).

47. *A Current Affair* (1987–1996). The first of a tidal wave of tabloid TV shows with "hard-hitting" stories made up of celebrity gossip and undercover investigations. Future talk show host and Connie Chung hubby Maury Povich was the first host, replaced by Joan Crawford impersonator Maureen O'Boyle when he left.

48. *Hart to Hart* (1979–1984). Robert Wagner and Stefanie Powers played "Jonathan and Jennifer Hart," a couple almost as much in love with each other as they were rich. Along with the help of their creaky manservant "Max" (Lionel Stander) and their lovable dog "Freeway," the sophisticated couple waltzed through a string of simple mysteries dressed to the nines. Coincidentally both suffered the untimely deaths of their more famous, real-life partners (Wagner's wife, Natalie Wood, drowned and Powers's lover William Holden died in a drunken fall) within a few months of each other (1981). Every episode seemed to end in a husband-and-wife clinch, though their mutual adoration was about as warm as two Gabors hugging and air kissing.

49. *Remington Steele* (1982–1987). Stephanie Zimbalist played "Laura Holt," a dedicated private investigator who had to resort to renaming her agency after a made-up (impressive-sounding) figurehead, "Remington Steele," in order to drum up business. Pierce Brosnan arrived on the scene, claiming to *be* "Remington Steele," and the two joined forces to solve mysteries with the help of "Mildred Krebs" (Doris Roberts), their assistant. Ths show was so bad, it's hard to believe that *Moonlighting* (see #2) borrowed much from its premise, though Bruce Willis didn't look as good in a tux as Pierce Brosnan did.

50. *Trapper John, M.D.* (1979–1986). Pernell Roberts played the title role, a tireless San Francisco doctor based on the character played by Wayne Rogers in *M*A*S*H*. His foil was for-ladies-only "Gonzo Gates" (Gregory Harrison). In an obvious ode to "Hot Lips Houlihan" from *M*A*S*H*, 80s TV screen queen Christopher Norris had the misfortune to be branded "Nurse Ripples." An array of dead, dying, or comedic patients was paraded through San Francisco Memorial's portals. Why Americans are so taken by medical dramas set in the most depressing place on earth—the hospital—defies logic.

51. *Highway to Heaven* (1984–1988). Michael Landon helped solidify his image as one of the most beloved figures on TV by playing an angel, no less, in this saccharine tearjerker made all the more poignant in reruns by Landon's untimely cancer death. Angel "Jonathan Smith"'s right-hand man was played by Victor French, and together the pair helped teach foolish mortals the error of their ways. A great big four-year-long warm fuzzy.

52. *Newhart* (1982–1990). Yet another hit for Bob Newhart, this time set in the quaint New England–based Stratford Inn, which his character "Dick" managed with his lovely wife "Joanna" (Mary Frann). The couple had a formerly rich, eternally spoiled maid named "Stephanie" (Julia Duffy), her preppy beau "Michael" (Peter Scolari), and bumbling handyman "George" (Tom Poston) to contend with. Later in the series, backwoods Larry, Darryl, and their other brother Darryl (William Sanderson, Tony Papenfuss, and John Volstad) helped take the show to new heights. The show may have seemed an extended advertisement for scenic Vermont, but not for the fictional Stratford Inn—there was little or no evidence that the inn was cleaned, cared for, or even particularly well managed during all the years the "Loudons" worked at it.

53. *Star Search* (1983–). Ed McMahon (a bright, shimmering star in his own right) hosted this outrageously cheesy *Gong Show* without the gong. Contestants competed for the top prize in the categories of comedian, singer, actor, dancer, and even—most hilariously—"spokesmodel." As bad as most of the "talent" was, this show had its success stories, from Sam "Sugar Don't Bite" Harris (his first album went gold after he was named "Best New Star") to 90s superstar Rosie O'Donnell and even Jenny Jones.

54. *Knight Rider* (1982–1986). The world has the unlikely success of this show to thank for the existence of David Hasselhoff, star of the 90s. Hasselhoff played "Michael Long," a cop who was killed and then resuscitated as "Michael Knight" (shades of *The Six Million Dollar Man*) so he could rid the world of pain, suffering, and bad guys. He did so with a super-intelligent computer called "KITT," mounted in his slick Trans-Am.

55. Real People (1979–1984). Influential and popular reality show hosted by a zany band of pseudoreporters—Sarah Purcell, Skip Stephenson, Byron Allen, Fred Willard, John Barbour, and Bill Rafferty—who roved the country in search of bizarre, unique, and/or downright insane folks they branded "real." You never knew if their next visit would be to a drag ball, an obsessed fan, or an idiot savant. No, wait—that's just Skip.

56. Head of the Class (1986–1991). After *WKRP in Cincinnati* (1978-1982) stopped broadcasting, it was only a couple of years before "Johnny Fever" (Howard Hesseman) settled into a new sitcom, this time playing "Charlie Moore," the unconventional teacher of a class of gifted kids. Sort of a *Welcome Back, Kotter* in reverse, or a *Smart Pegs*. Star pupil Robin Givens ("Darlene Merriman") wound up married to—and divorced from—heavyweight champ Mike Tyson.

57. Mr. Belvedere (1985–1990). Fussy butler "Mr. Belvedere" (Christopher Hewett) ruled the roost and a brood of generic sitcom brats while in the employ of the "Owens" family. Bob Uecker starred as "George Owens," and Ilene Graff as wife "Marsha." Why the smug bastard wasn't fired the first time he mouthed off is lost to TV history, and why former baseball washout (and future beer commercial sensation) Uecker was permitted to work as a comic actor is equally mysterious.

58. Murder, She Wrote (1984–1996). Stage and screen vet Angela Lansbury conquered TV in a big way playing New England mystery novelist "Jessica Fletcher," who stumbled into—and solved—mystery after mystery. "Jessica"'s Cabot Cove, Maine, accent lessened as the years flew by, as did Lansbury's odds of ever winning an Emmy (she went down in TV history as the actress nominated the most times for a single role without ever winning).

59. Mork & Mindy (1978–1982). Robin Williams made his first big impression as "Mork from Ork," a zany space alien shacking up with "Mindy McConnell" (Pam Dawber) as he tried to assimilate Earth culture. His regular reports to "Orson" (a disembodied voice) were great opportunities for Williams to improv, and his exclamation "Shozbot!" and split-fingered greeting "Nanu nanu" leaked into our vocab overnight.

60. That's Incredible! (1980–1984). No it's not, not really.

Cathy Lee Crosby, Frank Tarkenton, and John Davidson hosted this *Real People*–inspired reality show full of Evel Knievel–esque stunts, tricks, and feats of derring-do. Crosby and Davidson had the blank expressions and air of incestuous siblings, or at the very least automatons, while Tarkenton just poured on the down-home charm.

61. The Wonder Years (1988–1993). Fred Savage became an overnight superstar as "Kevin Arnold," the wide-eyed, mischievous central character of this series based in the turbulent late 60s. Daniel Stern narrated the episodes via voice-over as Savage grew from boy to teen, and tackled all the usual problems that went along with it. The primary interest of the show was nostalgia, capitalizing on all the music and memories of 1968 with each episode.

62. St. Elsewhere (1982–1988). Touching ensemble show centered around St. Eligius, a fiscally strapped hospital nicknamed "St. Elsewhere" since it became the destination for all manner of undesirables. Ed Flanders, William Daniels, Ed Begley Jr., Mark Harmon, David Morse, Howie Mandel, Alfre Woodard, Cynthia Sikes, Christina Pickles, Denzel Washington, and Norman Lloyd were the main doctor regulars (in a rapidly changing staff), and Byron Stewart played orderly "Warren Coolidge," and each week brought a new assortment of bizarre patients (most memorably "Mrs. Hofnagel"/Florence Halop) and doctorly strife. After rapes, suicides, sudden departures, and mental illness, *St. Elsewhere* also gave us TV's first character to develop AIDS (Harmon), yet still the show managed to be more funny than it was depressing.

63. Ripley's Believe It or Not (1982–1986). Jack Palance conjured his most malevolent deliveries for this spooky series that chronicled amazingly true stories from history. He did so side by side with his equally creepy daughter Holly Palance (and later, creepiest of all, Marie Osmond). Stories were generally of the "steel tube passes through man's head, leaves him unharmed" variety, and the show's title was repeated after each segment like a mantra.

64. House Calls (1979–1982). This mundane hospital comedy—starring Lynn Redgrave and Wayne Rogers as a hospital administrator and playboy doctor, respectively—is more 80s for its behind-the-scenes dish than its rather 70s look: Redgrave exited the show after producers balked at her breast-feeding her baby on the set (and, coincidentally, after a salary dispute). David Wayne was a hoot as coot "Dr. Amos Wetherby," the last surgeon in the world you'd want operating on your noggin: he was *senile*.

65. Simon & Simon (1981–1988). Antagonistic brothers "Simon" (Jameson Parker) and "Simon" (Gerald McRaney) were—and I know very few series in the 80s featured characters in this profession—pauper private eyes in this light drama that capitalized on its *Magnum, P.I.* lead-in. It paired two classic 80s archetypes—the Vietnam vet and the preppie—forced not only to work together, but to be related as well.

66. At the Movies (1982–1990). Snide Gene Siskel and gelatinous Roger Ebert (scriptwriter of *Beyond the Valley of the Dolls*) hosted this opinionated movie critique show after first launching *Sneak Previews* on PBS and before moving on to *Siskel & Ebert & the Movies*. They spent more time insulting each other than the films at hand, and it seemed obvious to everyone but them that they were kept employed to make the rest of the world laugh at their nerdy self-righteousness. Still, they were better than their successors, Bill Harris and catty wildcard Rex Reed.

67. Mickey Spillane's Mike Hammer (1984–1987). Stacy Keach brought Mickey Spillane's tough-talkin', womanizin' creation to life in this hard-boiled series but got thrown into the slammer in England for cocaine possession early on. This little setback halted the show's momentum somewhat, as Keach served several months for his very 80s transgression.

68. The Tracey Ullman Show (1987–1990). The acclaimed Fox variety show hosted by Carol Burnett's spiritual daughter, British comedienne Tracey Ullman, who employed more accents than Meryl Streep has even *heard of* in a series of comedy sketches. This creative show spawned the classic 90s animated series *The Simpsons* and featured Paula Abdul as its choreographer before she split to be forever our girl. Ullman deserved the acclaim if only as belated kudos for her earlier hit song "They Don't Know."

69. 227 (1985–1990). *The Jeffersons* (1975–1985) was a classic 70s show that lasted well into the 80s (unfortunately, since it really sucked by then), and Marla Gibbs as "Florence" the maid had been its greatest asset. In *227* she returned as "Mary Jenkins," along with her family a resident of a D.C. tenement. Soon enough the tenement seemed downright glitzy, and Marla's outfits went from Sears to Saks. But in this show the real star was again a supporting player—bodacious Jackée Harry (later just Jackée) as bodacious neighbor "Sandra." Kind of like *The Cosby Show* on a budget.

70. Dance Fever (1979–1987). Host Deney Terrio (and, at the end, Adrian Zmed) guided us through a series of couples competing for a $25,000–$50,000 prize. There was no uniformity—couples could perform high-powered disco dances, ballroom twirls, or hard-to-follow modern moves. But if you wanted the prize, the guy better throw the girl around a *lot*; acrobatics were always a plus.

71. Charles in Charge (1984–1985, 1987–1990). After "Chachi" (Scott Baio) bit the dust, "Charles" (also Scott Baio) was born. "Charles" was a young *au pair* boy, helping a busy couple raise their three kids. This was the show that refused to die, reviving itself in syndication after it got axed by CBS. Willie Aames (from *Eight Is Enough*, 1977–1981) played the best buddy "Buddy," a role familiar to him since he'd starred opposite Baio in the 1982 movie *Zapped!* a raunchy teen sex comedy.

Watching this TV show, you never believed for a second that "Charles" was in charge of anything or that the "Pembroke" family would be dumb enough to entrust their kids to this shady character. But it was Scott Baio, so what could you do? At least it wasn't his brother, Jimmy. Now *that* just wouldn't have worked.

72. *Wiseguy* (1987–1990). Ken Wahl was the sultry title character "Vinnie Terranova," an FBI agent with a knack for blending into any sleazy pigpen he needed to in order to expose corruption and nail mobsters and other strangers to the wall. Besides Wahl's looks (heavily promoted) and the show's outstanding roster of guest stars (Kevin Spacey, Joan Severance, Deborah Harry, Glenn Frey, Maximilian Schell), this show was most beloved for its miniserieslike way of stretching storylines over a half dozen episodes, instead of wrapping things up in an hour. Wahl was supposed to be the next big thing after this, but never was. Instead he was replaced by Steven Bauer, one of the most 80s actors alive.

73. *Beauty and the Beast* (1987–1990). A major cult series that revived the classic fairy tale, this show followed the fantastic romance between "Catherine Chandler" (Linda Hamilton) and "Vincent" (Ron Perlman), a strange beast who saved her life after a savage beating. "Vincent" nursed "Catherine" to health in a mazelike city located far beneath Manhattan. These two had a lengthy and nongraphic romance—can you imagine what the response would have been to semi-nude lovemaking scenes featuring that hairy beast? And Ron Perlman's costume was pretty scary, too.

74. *Hunter* (1984–1991). The violent adventures of a career cop, "Sergeant Rick Hunter," played very convincingly by menacing Fred Dryer. His sidekick and love interest was "Sergeant Dee Dee McCall" (Stepfanie Kramer—someone please send her mother a baby name book), and we got to spend years watching their relationship do a slow burn as bullets flew.

75. *The Richard Simmons Show* (1980–1984). The most annoying public figure of the 80s, bar none, was queeny Richard Simmons. Not because he was queeny, but because he was loud, grating, and could crank out crocodile tears when chatting with his obese fans to the tune of hundreds of millions of dollars a year. Blame *General Hospital* for the craze that

was Richard Simmons—he got his start playing himself on that show. In no time flat he was a multimillion-dollar industry. Like Leo Sayer in sweats, he shouted, "Come on, people!" at us all decade long. Even when he lost his regular show, he came at us on video. He was enough to make you turn to Häagen-Dazs.

Richard Simmons prays to the god of fitness.

76. *MacGyver* (1985–1992). Richard Dean Anderson played the title role as a secret agent for the mysterious group calling itself Phoenix. He had a gadget for every occasion, and if he didn't have a gadget handy, he was able to whip something up out of the clear blue sky.

77. *The Hogan Family* (1986–1990). Originally called *Valerie*, this show was a genuinely funny vehicle for Valerie Harper. When she asked for more money and had a dispute with the producers, her character was unceremoniously killed off in a car accident—a bit grisly for a light family comedy. The show was then called *Valerie's Family* for a time. Finally it found its final name, focusing on characters played by Jason Bateman, Josh Taylor, Danny Ponce, and Jeremy Licht, and on Valerie's replacement . . . Sandy Duncan! What a nightmare. One day your mom is Valerie Harper, the next thing you know, Sandy Duncan is moving in.

78. *Falcon Crest* (1981–1990). Another of the great nighttime soaps of the decade, this one headed up by bona fide (former) film star and Oscar winner Jane Wyman, playing "Angela Channing," tough-as-nails matriarch of the wine-rich "Channings." Set at Falcon Crest Vineyard, this was sort of like *Wine-asty*.

Robert Foxworth and Susan Sullivan played "Chase and Maggie Gioberti," her nephew and his wife; Abby Dalton was "Julia Cumson," her daughter; Margaret Ladd was "Emma Channing," her nutty daughter;

> **"I'm not a real big wine drinker."** —Apollonia, on joining the cast of *Falcon Crest*, 1985

Lorenzo Lamas was "Lance Cumson," her scheming son; Billy Moses was "Cole Gioberti"; and Ana Alicia played the resident bitch/slut, "Melissa."

As was usual with night-time soaps, there were about a million other guest stars and smaller, recurring roles, but the biggest blast came when screen legend (and born-again lady) Lana Turner arrived on the scene in 1982 as "Chase"'s mom. Other

Jane Wyman and Abby Dalton didn't have the warmest of relations on *Falcon Crest*.

stars who spent a little time at Falcon Crest were Gina Lollobrigida, Anne Archer, Apollonia, and Ken Olin.

Keep in mind that Wyman started her run on *Falcon Crest* one year after her ex-husband, Ronald Reagan, ascended to the White House. He lasted eight years. She lasted *nine*.

It was TV history when Lana Turner guested on *Falcon Crest*. No, she wasn't playing a 39-year-old model. They wouldn't let her.

79. Tales from the Darkside (1984–1988). The 80s were packed with *Twilight Zone*–like anthology series—*The Twilight Zone* itself was remade, *Alfred Hitchcock Presents* was redone, *Darkroom* had a short run, and so on. But this was the best, because it was not only gross, it was campy, just like *Night of the Living Dead*. Funny coincidence, since that cult classic was a film on the résumé of this show's creator, George Romero.

80. *The Morton Downey, Jr., Show* (1988–1989). Phenomenally popular while it lasted, this talk show laid the groundwork for Howard Stern, Rush Limbaugh, and all the other shock jocks with its in-your-face host hollering pro-America diddly squat and provoking all his guests to the brink—sometimes *past* the brink—of violence.

Too Young to Die: Twenty Greatest 80s TV Shows Canceled in Their Prime

1. *Bosom Buddies* (1980–1982). One of the funniest shows of the decade was this *Some Like It Hot hommage* performed by Tom Hanks and Peter Scolari. In order to find lodging at a women-only hotel, they transformed (thanks to drag) into "Buffy and Hildy," two extraordinarily macho girls. In fact, one early scene had them performing "Macho Man" by The Village People while wearing wigs and undergarments. The supporting cast was among the best on TV at the time: sassy Telma Hopkins, blonde bombshell Donna Dixon, chubby jokester Wendy Jo Sperber, worldly Holland Taylor, and ancient Lucille Benson. After this gem got axed, it wasn't long before Hanks made a big *Splash* (1984) on the silver screen.

"Henry"/"Hildy" and "Kip"/"Buffy" in another fine mess.

2. *Police Squad* (1982). From the makers of *Airplane!* surely the funniest TV show of all time. And don't call me "Shirley."

3. *Angie* (1979–1980). Donna Pescow as lovable Italian girl and Robert Hays as her beau. Worth putting in a time capsule just for Debralee Scott.

4. *Oh, Madeline* (1983–1984). This hilarious Madeline Kahn sitcom should have been the next *I Love Lucy*, not the next *Life with Lucy*.

5. Best of the West (1981–1982). Joel Higgins and raspy-voiced Carlene Watkins as cowboy and cowgirl, in one of the only western spoofs ever aired.

6. Too Close for Comfort (1980–1983, 1984–1986). Ted Knight played cartoonist "Henry Rush," the genius behind "Cosmic Cow." His wife, "Muriel," was perky Nancy Dussault, his daughters, "Jackie" and "Sarah" were played by thin, sensible Deborah Van Valkenburgh and curvy, brain-dead Lydia Cornell. But the main reason to remember this show was "Sarah"'s fruity best friend "Monroe" (JM J. Bullock).

7. It's Your Move (1984–1985). Jason Bateman as a manipulative, conniving, borderline sociopathic monster.

8. Filthy Rich (1982–1983). Delta Burke and Dixie Carter—pre-*Designing Women*—as nouveau riche Texans.

9. Cover Up (1984–1985). Gorgeous Jon-Erik Hexum had the misfortune of landing this plum role as "Rambo"-like agent "Mac Harper" to Jennifer O'Neill's "Dani Reynolds." The misfortune was that while goofing off with a prop gun, he accidentally blew a chunk of his skull into his brain and eventually died from his injury. A Rudolph Valentino–like death cult has sprung up around his memory.

10. Jennifer Slept Here (1983–1984). Ann Jillian as the ghost of Marilyn Monroe, or rather "Jennifer Farrell."

11. Bay City Blues (1983). *Hill Street Blues* on a baseball diamond.

12. Open All Night (1981–1982). A twenty-four-hour convenience store sitcom that could make you laugh until the sun came up.

13. China Beach (1988–1990). A moving Vietnam *M*A*S*H*, with Ricki Lake and Dana Delany making big impressions.

14. The Days and Nights of Molly Dodd (1987–1991). Blair Brown is the ultimate yuppie.

15. Fridays (1980–1982). An even more unconventional alternative to *Saturday Night Live*, with Michael Ritchie's twisted Barbie doll skits.

16. Mary (1985–1986). No, really; this Mary Tyler Moore comeback was *good*.

17. Partners in Crime (1984). Loni Anderson and Lynda Carter together. Why didn't anyone think of this sooner? Why didn't this show last longer?

18. The Tortellis (1987). Funny *Cheers* spin-off starring Jean Kasem and Dan Hedaya as the ultimate white-trash "Tortellis." Even "Carla" was ashamed of them.

19. Frank's Place (1987–1988). Tim Reid helped make this one of the most critically acclaimed comedies ever to be canceled.

20. Berrenger's (1985). *Dallas* in a department store, with Sam Wanamaker and Anita Morris.

Gone Too Soon?: Ten TV Shows That Probably Weren't as Good as You Remember Them, but You Miss Them All the Same

1. We Got It Made (1983–1984, 1987–1988). Teri Copley as the kind of maid who doesn't even *have* to do windows.

2. Flamingo Road (1981–1982). Morgan Fairchild. Just . . . Morgan Fairchild.

3. Harper Valley P.T.A. (1981–1982). Barbara Eden put the T. & A. in P.T.A.

4. Sledge Hammer! (1986–1988). A cop who named his gun "Gun."

5. Paper Dolls (1984). Another Morgan Fairchild starrer, about the cutthroat world of modeling in New York. You just know that little Kate Moss watched every episode.

6. Jack and Mike (1986–1987). Shelley Hack's *Moonlighting*.

7. Max Headroom (1987). An icon of the 80s and a thoroughly inventive show. "Max" was a disembodied head and voice on a TV screen. What else *is* there?

8. Mr. Merlin (1981–1982). Barnard Hughes played 1600-year-old wizard "Merlin," and they *still* had to use makeup to get him to look younger for the part.

9. Wizards and Warriors (1983). The first TV series about Dungeons and Dragons . . . and the last.

10. Lime Street (1985). This one actually had a good excuse for ending prematurely—its star, Samantha Smith, died in a plane crash.

Never Too Young to Die: Bad 80s TV Shows Canceled Early on That Never Should Have Existed in the *First* Place

1. Dolly (1987–1988). This show had only two things going for it, and I'm not talking about the singing or dancing.

2. New Love, American Style (1985–1986). Hateful.

3. a.k.a. Pablo (1984). a.k.a. Pablum.

4. The Colbys (1985–1987). This brood wasn't even good on *Dynasty*, and Barbara Stanwyck looked more like a mummy than a matriarch.

5. Life with Lucy (1986). Vivian Vance was rolling over in her grave.

6. AfterMASH (1983–1984). *M*E*S*S**.

7. Joanie Loves Chachi (1982–1983). Joanie never *did* have very good taste in men.

"Joanie and Chachi" (Erin Moran and Scott Baio) warble their lives away.

8. The Brady Brides (1981). *Three's Company* starring "Jan and Marcia Brady."

9. The Late Show Starring Joan Rivers (1986–1987). That back-stabbing tramp! Oh, please! Oh!

10. Here's Boomer (1980–1982). And there's the pound.

11. Manimal (1983). Way over everyone's heads.

12. Three's a Crowd (1984–1985). And a drag.

13. Hooperman (1987–1989). Can't someone ban John Ritter from working as an actor?

14. Bring 'Em Back Alive (1982–1983). Better off dead.

15. Condo (1983). In foreclosure.

16. Finder of Lost Loves (1984–1985). They were lost for a reason.

17. Double Trouble (1984–1985). Either of the twins on this show was boring enough on her own.

18. Emerald Point N.A.S. (1983–1984). One soap too many.

19. Tales of the Gold Monkey (1982–1983). Raider of *Raiders of the Lost Ark*.

20. Mr. Smith (1983). A chimp star with a higher I.Q. than any other actor on TV. So . . . what's so hard to believe about that?

One example of over-enthusiastic marketing is this *Mr. Smith* lab set, which was licensed while the show was still being developed. Its makers banked on the cute chimp and technical-looking equipment. But the show bombed and nobody wanted to buy an object offering a toy "needle" and a pretend "octoscope."

Disease of the Week: TV Movies

1. _The Burning Bed_ (1985), Robert Greenwald. Farrah Fawcett, Paul LeMat, Penelope Milford, Richard Masur.

Farrah torches her _Charlie's Angels_ image as a woman who sets her white-trash hubby ablaze.

Bad hair day for Farrah—oh, whoops! That's her starring as a battered woman in _The Burning Bed_.

2. _The Day After_ (1983), Nicholas Meyer. Jason Robards, Jr., Steve Guttenberg, JoBeth Williams, John Lithgow.

The aftermath of World War III. Sorry, Sting, but apparently the Russians _don't_ love their children, too.

3. _Something About Amelia_ (1985), Randa Haines. Ted Danson, Glenn Close, Roxana Lal.

Ted Danson uses his lovable "Sam Malone" image to make a story of incest all the more sickening.

It _Cheers_ this creep up to molest his daugher in _Something About Amelia_.

4. _An Early Frost_ (1985), John Erman. Aidan Quinn, Gena Rowlands, Ben Gazzara, Sylvia Sidney, John Glover, D. W. Moffett.

The first AIDS movie, which bizarrely made Aidan Quinn a sex symbol.

5. _Invitation to Hell_ (1984), Wes Craven. Susan Lucci, Robert Urich, Joanna Cassidy, Kevin McCarthy, Patty McCormack, Soleil Moon Frye.

TV's "Erica Kane" literally plays Satan in heels as the owner of a health club for yuppies. Scintillating subtext.

6. _Murder in Texas_ (1981), William Hale. Farrah Fawcett, Andy Griffith, Katharine Ross, Sam Elliott, Craig T. Nelson.

Farrah's first big dramatic break, as a pretty blonde corpse.

7. _The Ann Jillian Story_ (1988), Corey Allen. Ann Jillian, Tony LoBianco, Viveca Lindfors.

The beginning of a horrifying trend: playing yourself in a TV movie about your life.

8. _For Ladies Only_ (1981), Mel Damski. Gregory Harrison, Patricia Davis, Dinah Manoff, Viveca Lindfors, Louise Lasser, Lee Grant, Marc Singer.

I'm not a male stripper, but I play one on TV.

9. _Consenting Adults_ (1985), Gilbert Cates. Marlo Thomas, Martin Sheen, Barry Tubb, Talia Balsam, Ben Piazza.

Coming out of the closet is a breeze when your mom is _That Girl_.

10. _A Very Brady Christmas_ (1988), Peter Baldwin. Florence Henderson, Robert Reed, Ann B. Davis, Maureen McCormick, Eve Plumb, Jennifer Runyon, Barry Williams, Christopher Knight, Mike Lookinland.

The first _Brady_ revival that was a major hit and a harbinger of the very _Brady_ 90s. Not the real Cindy, though.

Queens of the Screen: Women Most Likely to Star in an 80s Made-for-TV Movie or Miniseries

1. Lindsay Wagner, as in _Princess Daisy_ (1983). The undisputed bionic queen of TV.

2. Farrah Fawcett, as in _Poor Little Rich Girl: The Barbara Hutton Story_ (1987). It took an entire decade of sophisticated dramatic roles before some people forgot that she'd played "Jill Munroe" on _Charlie's Angels_ (1976–1981). They still remembered she'd been on the show, they just finally forgot the character's name.

3. Mare Winningham, as in _Single Bars, Single Women_ (1984). Has been on TV more frequently than static.

4. Jaclyn Smith, as in _Rage of Angels_ (1983). The Garbo of bad TV actresses.

5. Elizabeth Montgomery, as in *Amos* (1985). The good witch of the set.

6. Valerie Bertinelli, as in *Shattered Vows* (1984). One role at a time.

7. Lynda Carter, as in *Rita Hayworth: The Love Goddess* (1983). Her turn as Rita Hayworth was not so wonderful.

8. Mariette Hartley, as in *M.A.D.D.: Mothers Against Drunk Driving* (1983). The Kodak pitch-woman starred in this, a telefilm that defined the grass-roots antidrunk driving movement, a major early 80s issue.

9. Ann Jillian, as in *Girls of the White Orchid* (1985). Platinum bland.

10. Loni Anderson, as in *The Jayne Mansfield Story* (1980). Loni Anderson was born to play these parts.

Behind Every Great Woman There Is a Great Man. And on TV, It's Usually. . .

1. Gregory Harrison, as in *For Ladies Only* (1981). I'll strip for you if you'll strip for me.

2. Mickey Rooney, as in *Bill* (1981). Rooney is typecast as an intellectually challenged man whom everyone inexplicably loves.

3. Dennis Weaver, as in *Cocaine: One Man's Seduction* (1983). He just said maybe.

4. Harold Gould, as in *Help Wanted: Male* (1982). He'd later become a staple as "Rose"'s boyfriend "Miles."

5. Bruce Boxleitner, as in *Passion Flower* (1986). Lust in the tropics.

6. Robert Wagner, as in *There Must Be a Pony* (1986). Like a two-hour special episode of *Hart to Hart*, with Elizabeth Taylor as "Jennifer Hart."

7. Jason Robards, Jr., as in *The Day After* (1983). Tomorrow's another day. *Maybe.*

8. Stacy Keach, as in *The Blue and the Grey* (1985). Hammer time.

9. Sam Elliott, as in *Murder in Texas* (1981). *Magnum, P.I.*'s older brother.

10. Kenny Rogers, as in *Kenny Rogers as The Gambler* (1980). Just in case you don't bother to read the credits.

Maxi Minis: Five Miniseries That Ate America

By the early 80s the miniseries was in its heyday. Aired on multiple nights and sometimes comprising ten or more hours of hand-wringing, the miniseries gave TV producers budgets as big as feature film producers and the biggest stars the small screen had to offer. By the late 80s, Americans tired of holing up, tied to the tube, watching stories that might have made good two-hour movies putter along for eight. When *War and Remembrance*, the sequel to the hugely popular *The Winds of War*, bombed (1988-1989), it was the end of the major miniseries as a form.

1. *The Thorn Birds* (1983).
Richard Chamberlain can't decide whether to advance in the priesthood or sleep with Rachel Ward. Which would *you* choose?

If there be thorns: Richard Chamberlain tries to resist Rachel Ward in *The Thorn Birds*.

2. *The Winds of War* (1983).
Seven nights, eighteen hours, $40 million, and a cast of thousands. World War II pales in comparison.

3. *North and South* (1985).
Kind of like the Civil War if it had been fought by the cast of *Dynasty*.

4. *Shogun* (1980).
Richard Chamberlain, turning Japanese.

5. *The Blue and the Grey* (1985).
An earthier *North and South*, minus Elizabeth Taylor.

The Ten Ultimate TV "Events" of the 80s

1. *Night of 100 Stars* (1981). The concept was to present a star-studded gala to benefit the Motion Picture Retirement Fund. The execution was a steady, almost mechanical series of walk-ons by well over a hundred stars, like some obsessive checklist of who is and who *was* who. A glittery spectacle in a decade of glitz, *Night of 100 Stars* paraded everyone from Princess Grace of Monaco to Harrison Ford—everone except for poor Jimmy Cagney, who, wheelchair bound, was forgotten backstage.

> **"She's waited her whole *career* to meet that man."**
> —Lana Turner's *Night of 100 Stars* escort, Eric Root, on Turner's excitement at meeting Sir Laurence Olivier, 1981

2. The final episode of *M*A*S*H* (1983). One of TV's longest-running and most popular dramas—chronicling the lives, loves, and laughs in a mobile army surgical unit during the Korean War—came to a momentous end with the most watched single episode of any TV show, *ever*.

3. Kristin shot J. R. (1980). As a testimonial to the international appeal of the series, note that the Turkish parliament adjourned early so its members could rush home to see the answer to TV's all-time greatest cliff-hanger: "Who shot J.R?"

4. Jim and Tammy Faye Bakker on *Nightline* (1987). Like watching Ted Koppel hosting *The Muppets*.

5. *Brideshead Revisited* (1982). Less a miniseries than a long-term relationship (it was broadcast over a two-month period), this story of two Oxford boys became the most popular show in PBS history.

6. *Capone's Vault* (1986). More people watched this independent, syndicated special than any other syndicated event of the 80s. Unfortunately, when Geraldo Rivera finally opened the room that was alleged to have been one of mobster Al Capone's treasure troves, it turned out there was absolutely *nothing* going on inside (like its host's head).

7. The Baby Jessica rescue (1987). Some kid fell down a well and the whole world's heart skipped a beat. Big whoop—I fell out of bed and broke my collarbone once. Where were *you*?

8. "Diane" exits *Cheers* (1987). The Long goodbye.

9. The wedding of "Luke and Laura" (1981). Boy meets girl, boy rapes girl, boy marries girl.

10. *The Making of a Male Model* (1983). Originally called *The Look*, this supertrashy, supercampy telefilm told the whole tawdry story of how to become the hottest male model in America. It was Joan Collins's first major TV project after her *Dynasty* comeback and Jon-Erik Hexum's last project before his death on the set of *Cover Up*.

Ten Quintessentially 80s TV Commercials

1. The California Raisin Advisory Board (1986). Introducing the marketing fad the California Raisins, Claymation wonders singing their rendition of "I Heard It through the Grapevine." The Raisins were so popular, they wound up generating $500 million in merchandising sales by 1987, or $50 million *more* than the entire California raisin industry.

2. Wendy's (1983). Old-as-the-hills Clara Peller barking, "Where's the beef?" The spot made her a worldwide celebrity and won her a role in the no-brainer movie *Moving Violations* (1985) before she died.

3. Federal Express (1984). Fast-talking John Moschitta droning the FedEx mantra at a mile a minute.

4. Canned Food Information Council (1985). A curvaceous metallic robot from the future, purring, "In the year 3000, food will come in amazing containers that save nutrients, freshness of time. It will be food in cans."

5. Seagram's wine coolers (1986). Bruce Willis putting the moves on an unknown blonde (Sharon Stone) in a bar.

6. Dr Pepper (1980). Made everyone want to be a Pepper, regardless of whether they actually drank the stuff.

7. Coca-Cola (1982). Mean Joe Greene tosses his disgusting, sweaty game jersey to a kid who obviously thinks he's making out like a bandit.

8. Pepsi (1984). Michael Jackson in one of the most hair-raising commercials of all time.

9. Chrysler (1981). Lee Iacocca does the talking, restoring public confidence in the car company that was bailed out by the U.S. government.

10. Nike (1987). When Michael Jackson—owner of the entire Beatles catalog since the mid-80s—allowed the use of "Revolution" for this commercial, the surviving Beatles got royally pissed.

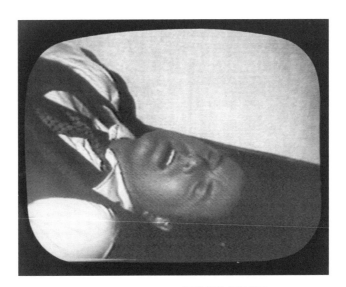

"J. R. Ewing" wonders if this is THE END for him.
(See *The Ten Ultimate TV "Events" of the 80s,* page 143)

Music Appendix

Grammys

Album of the Year

1980: *Christopher Cross,* Christopher Cross

1981: *Double Fantasy,* John Lennon and Yoko Ono

1982: *Toto IV,* Toto

1983: *Thriller,* Michael Jackson

1984: *Can't Slow Down,* Lionel Richie

1985: *No Jacket Required,* Phil Collins

1986: *Graceland,* Paul Simon

1987: *The Joshua Tree,* U2

1988: *Faith,* George Michael

1989: *Nick of Time,* Bonnie Raitt

Record of the Year

1980: **"Sailing,"** Christopher Cross

1981: **"Bette Davis Eyes,"** Kim Carnes

1982: **"Rosanna,"** Toto

1983: **"Beat It,"** Michael Jackson

1984: **"What's Love Got to Do With It?"** Tina Turner

1985: **"We Are the World,"** USA for Africa

1986: **"Higher Love,"** Steve Winwood

1987: **"Graceland,"** Paul Simon

1988: **"Don't Worry, Be Happy,"** Bobby McFerrin

1989: **"Wind Beneath My Wings,"** Bette Midler

Song of the Year

1980: **"Sailing,"** Christopher Cross

1981: **"Bette Davis Eyes,"** Donna Weiss and Jackie DeShannon

1982: **"Always on My Mind,"** Johnny Christopher, Mark James, Wayne Thompson

1983: **"Every Breath You Take,"** Sting

1984: **"What's Love Got to Do with It?"** Graham Lyle, Terry Britten

1985: **"We Are the World,"** Michael Jackson, Lionel Richie

1986: **"That's What Friends Are For,"** Burt Bacharach, Carole Bayer Sager

1987: **"Somewhere Out There,"** James Horner, Barry Mann, Cynthia Weil

1988: **"Don't Worry, Be Happy,"** Bobby McFerrin

1989: **"Wind Beneath My Wings,"** Larry Henley, Jeff Silbar

Pop Vocal: Male

1980: **Kenny Loggins,** "This Is It"

1981: **Al Jarreau,** "Breakin' Away"

1982: **Lionel Richie,** "Truly"

1983: **Michael Jackson,** *Thriller*

1984: **Phil Collins,** "Against All Odds (Take a Look at Me Now)"

1985: **Phil Collins,** *No Jacket Required*

1986: **Steve Winwood,** "Higher Love"

1987: **Sting,** *Bring on the Night*

1988: Bobby McFerrin, "Don't Worry, Be Happy"

1989: Michael Bolton, "How Am I Supposed to Live Without You?"

1988: The Manhattan Transfer, *Brasil*

1989: Linda Ronstadt, Aaron Neville, "Don't Know Much"

Pop Vocal: Female

1980: Bette Midler, "The Rose"

1981: Lena Horne, *Lena Horne: The Lady and Her Music Live on Broadway*

1982: Melissa Manchester, "You Should Hear How He Talks about You"

1983: Irene Cara, "Flashdance . . . What a Feeling"

1984: Tina Turner, "What's Love Got to Do With It?"

1985: Whitney Houston, "Saving All My Love for You"

1986: Barbra Streisand, *The Broadway Album*

1987: Whitney Houston, "I Wanna Dance with Somebody (Who Loves Me)"

1988: Tracy Chapman, "Fast Car"

1989: Bonnie Raitt, "Nick of Time"

Pop Performance: Duo or Group with Vocal

1980: Barbra Streisand, Barry Gibb, "Guilty"

1981: The Manhattan Transfer, "Boy from New York City"

1982: Joe Cocker, Jennifer Warnes, "Up Where We Belong"

1983: The Police, "Every Breath You Take"

1984: The Pointer Sisters, "Jump (for My Love)"

1985: U.S.A. for Africa, "We Are the World"

1986: Dionne and Friends, "That's What Friends Are For"

1987: Bill Medley, Jennifer Warnes, "(I've Had) The Time of My Life"

Rock Vocal: Male

1980: Billy Joel, *Glass Houses*

1981: Rick Springfield, "Jessie's Girl"

1982: John Cougar, "Hurts So Good"

1983: Michael Jackson, "Beat It"

1984: Bruce Springsteen, "Dancing in the Dark"

1985: Don Henley, "The Boys of Summer"

1986: Robert Palmer, "Addicted to Love"

1987: Bruce Springsteen, *Tunnel of Love*

1988: Robert Palmer, "Simply Irresistible"

1989: Don Henley, *The End of Innocence*

Rock Vocal: Female

1980: Pat Benatar, *Crimes of Passion*

1981: Pat Benatar, "Fire and Ice"

1982: Pat Benatar, "Shadows in the Night"

1983: Pat Benatar, "Love Is a Battlefield"

1984: Tina Turner, "Better Be Good to Me"

1985: Tina Turner, "One of the Living"

1986: Tina Turner, "Back Where You Started"

1987: No award given

1988: Tina Turner, *Tina Live in Europe*

1989: Bonnie Raitt, *Nick of Time*

Rock Performance: Duo or Group with Vocal

1980: Bob Seger & the Silver Bullet Band, *Against the Wind*

1981: **The Police,** "Don't Stand So Close to Me"

1982: **Survivor,** "Eye of the Tiger"

1983: **The Police,** *Synchronicity*

1984: **Prince and the Revolution,** *Purple Rain*

1985: **Dire Straits,** "Money for Nothing"

1986: **Eurythmics,** "Missionary Man"

1987: **U2,** *The Joshua Tree*

1988: **U2,** "Desire"

1989: **Traveling Wilburys,** *Traveling Wilburys, Volume One*

New Artist

1980: **Christopher Cross**

1981: **Sheena Easton**

1982: **Men at Work**

1983: **Culture Club**

1984: **Cyndi Lauper**

1985: **Sade**

1986: **Bruce Hornsby and the Range**

1987: **Jody Watley**

1988: **Tracy Chapman**

1989: **Milli Vanilli (revoked)**

MTV Video Music Awards

Best Video of the Year

1984: **"You Might Think,"** The Cars

1985: **"The Boys of Summer,"** Don Henley

1986: **"Money for Nothing,"** Dire Straits

1987: **"Sledgehammer,"** Peter Gabriel

1988: **"Need You Tonight/Mediate,"** INXS

1989: **"This Note's for You,"** Neil Young

Viewers Choice Award

1984: **"Thriller,"** Michael Jackson

1985: **"We Are the World,"** U.S.A. for Africa

1986: **"Take on Me,"** a-ha

1987: **"With Or Without You,"** U2

1988: **"Need You Tonight/Mediate,"** INXS

1989: **"Like a Prayer,"** Madonna

Best Concept Video

1984: **"Rockit,"** Herbie Hancock

1985: **"Smuggler's Blues,"** Glenn Frey

1986: **"Take on Me,"** a-ha

1987: **"Sledgehammer,"** Peter Gabriel

1988: **"Learning to Fly,"** Pink Floyd

1989: **No award given**

Best Male Video

1984: **"China Girl,"** David Bowie

1985: **"I'm on Fire,"** Bruce Springsteen

1986: **"Addicted to Love,"** Robert Palmer

1987: **"Sledgehammer,"** Peter Gabriel

1988: **"U Got the Look,"** Prince

1989: **"Veronica,"** Elvis Costello

Best Female Video

1984: **"Girls Just Want to Have Fun,"** Cyndi Lauper

1985: **"What's Love Got to Do with It?"** Tina Turner

1986: **"How Will I Know?"** Whitney Houston

1987: **"Papa Don't Preach,"** Madonna

1988: **"Luka,"** Suzanne Vega

1989: **"Straight Up,"** Paula Abdul

Best Group Video

1984: **"Legs,"** ZZ Top

1985: **"We Are the World,"** U.S.A. for Africa

1986: **"Money for Nothing,"** Dire Straits

1987: **"Wild, Wild Life,"** Talking Heads

1988: **"Need You Tonight/Mediate,"** INXS

1989: **"Cult of Personality,"** Living Colour

Best New Artist in a Video

1984: **"Sweet Dreams (Are Made of This),"** Eurythmics

1985: **"Voices Carry,"** 'Til Tuesday

1986: **"Take on Me,"** a-ha

1987: **"Don't Dream It's Over,"** Crowded House

1988: **"Welcome to the Jungle,"** Guns n' Roses

1989: **"Cult of Personality,"** Living Colour

Video Vanguard Award

1984: **The Beatles, David Bowie, Richard Lester**

1985: **David Byrne, Godley & Creme, Russell Mulcahy**

1986: **Madonna, Zbigniew Rybeznski**

1987: **Julien Temple, Peter Gabriel**

1988: **Michael Jackson**

1989: **George Michael**

Performers at Live Aid (July 13, 1985) in Order of Appearance

1. **Status Quo** (U.K.)
2. **The Style Council** (U.K.)
3. **The Boomtown Rats** (U.K.)
4. **Adam Ant** (U.K.)
5. **INXS** (Australia)
6. **Ultravox** (U.K.)
7. **Loudness** (U.K.)
8. **Spandau Ballet** (U.K.)
9. **Bernard Watson** (U.S.)
10. **Joan Baez** (U.S.)
11. **Elvis Costello** (U.K.)
12. **The Hooters** (U.S.)
13. **Opus** (Austria)
14. **Nik Kershaw** (U.K.)
15. **The Four Tops** (U.S.)
16. **B. B. King** (Holland)
17. **Billy Ocean** (U.S.)
18. **Ozzy Osbourne** (U.S.)
19. **Run-D.M.C.** (U.S.)
20. **Yu Rock Mission** (Yugoslavia)
21. **Sade** (U.K.)
22. **Sting** (U.K.)
23. **Rick Springfield** (U.S.)
24. **Phil Collins** (U.K.) [see also 62—thanks to the Concorde]
25. **REO Speedwagon** (U.K.)
26. **Howard Jones** (U.K.)
27. **Autograph** (Russia)
28. **Bryan Ferry** (U.K.)
29. **Crosby, Stills and Nash** (U.S.)
30. **Udo Lindenberg** (Germany)
31. **Judas Priest** (U.S.)
32. **Paul Young** (U.S.)
33. **Paul Young/Alison Moyet** (U.S.)
34. **Bob Geldof** (U.K.)
35. **Bryan Adams** (U.S.)
36. **U2** (U.K.)
37. **The Beach Boys** (U.S.)
38. **Dire Straits/Sting** (U.S.)
39. **George Thorogood and the Destroyers/Bo Diddley/Albert Collins** (U.S.)
40. **Queen** (U.S.)
41. **David Bowie/Mick Jagger** (U.S./U.K.)
42. **Simple Minds** (U.S.)
43. **David Bowie** (U.K.)
44. **The Pretenders** (U.S.)
45. **The Who** (U.K.)
46. **Santana/Pat Metheny** (U.S.)
47. **Elton John** (U.K.)
48. **Ashford & Simpson/Teddy Pendergrass** (U.S.)
49. **Elton John/Kiki Dee** (U.K.)

50. **Elton John/Kiki Dee/Wham!** (U.K.)
51. **Madonna** (U.S.)
52. **Mercury and May** (U.K.)
53. **Paul McCartney** (U.K.)
54. **Paul McCartney/David Bowie/Pete Townshend/Alison Moyet/Bob Geldof** (U.K.)
    U.K. FINALE: All sing "Let It Be"
55. **Tom Petty** (U.S.)
56. **Kenny Loggins** (U.S.)
57. **The Cars** (U.S.)
58. **Neil Young** (U.S.)
59. **The Power Station** (U.S.)

60. **The Thompson Twins/Madonna** (U.S.)
61. **Eric Clapton** (U.S.)
62. **Phil Collins** (U.S.) [see also 24]
63. **Robert Plant/Jimmy Page/Mick Jones** (U.S.)
64. **Duran Duran** (U.S.)
65. **Patti LaBelle** (U.S.)
66. **Hall & Oates/Eddie Kendricks/David Ruffin** (U.S.)
67. **Mick Jagger** (U.S.)
68. **Mick Jagger/Tina Turner** (U.S.)
69. **Bob Dylan/Keith Richard/Ron Wood** (U.S.)
    U.S. FINALE: All sing "We Are the World"

HERstory: An Interview with Cyndi Lauper

Speaking in July of 1995, Cyndi was still possessed of the brassy sense of humor and accent that helped make her famous, but she was more sophisticated. Gone were the eye-popping thrift store rags she used to wear to express herself and repulse the easily shockable. She still dressed with distinction, but with a downtown flair. Her face was made up in the image of a 40s film star, a woman in her forties who looked about fifteen years younger. In short, she was unmistakably a star, one of the famous ones who stands out in any crowd and whom you could identify from across the street in the evening.

Cyndi Lauper talked as freely as most people think. She didn't hold anything back. "I don't censor myself," she said, stating the obvious without a trace of irony.

For example, she was up front about why not all of her biggest hits were represented on her "best of," *Twelve Deadly Cyns . . . and Then Some.* With characteristic frankness, she grimaced when speaking of her number-ten movie theme hit, "The Goonies 'R' Good Enough": "I *hated* that. It was *terrible.*"

She also grew disenchanted with "True Colors" after the song, which she did not write, became a commercial theme for Kodak and AT&T. But its enduring popularity, her affection for it, and the chord it strikes for misfits around the world led her to revive it in her concerts.

MR: You've always been an outspoken critic of the Catholic Church—

CL: That's because I'm a recovering Catholic. I went to a few of their organizations and schools. I speak from experience....There's, y'know, the Sisters of Charity, the Sisters of Mercy, and it just so happens that I was with the Sisters of No Charity and No Mercy at All.

MR: Were *all* of the nuns and priests who schooled you rotten?

CL: When you take a group of people and you repress them and they cut themselves off from their feelings as a human—and a human being has sexual feelings, has bodily feelings—what you are handing over to children is a monster. Because if you are not connected to who you are in your heart, and you don't understand and have compassion for yourself, how in the wide world of sports are you gonna have compassion with forty screaming children?

Maybe God's a woman. . . . I'm against all their teaching that women are evil and that their power and their sexuality is evil. Let's kinda like get a little beyond that, get Christ-like, you know what I mean? [The Church] is losing popularity anyway. Let's face it: They don't have the draw anymore. They're not selling the tickets that they used to.

MR: What do you think of having such a passionate gay following?

CL: You always have to remember—no matter what you're told—that God loves all the flowers, even the wild ones that grow on the side of the highway. You know, if you can remember that, it somehow makes [life] more peaceful and easy to deal with.

Ever outspoken, she proclaimed herself a proud liberal who voted Democrat in 1992. This despite the fact that Tipper Gore once spearheaded a campaign that labeled her "She-Bop"—a veiled ode to another favorite Catholic pastime, masturbation—as "filthy." The flap enraged Lauper, though she laughed over it ten years after the fact. She was particularly angered because she'd written the song so cleverly that few listeners—least of all children—could actually identify its controversial subject.

She may have voted for the Clinton–Gore ticket, but Tipper was never completely forgiven.

CL: I voted for *Mrs.* Clinton and *Mr.* Gore! [Giggles mischievously.]

MR: Your message has always been feminist, even during the 80s, when some women seemed to shy away from the term "feminism." Are you a feminist?

CL: It is not a dirty word, "feminism." I just think that women belong in the human population with the same rights as everybody else. And *of course* I'm a feminist. I was born a female, and I would like some of those rights. The problem is, "A feminist looks like this, or is like that." We are *taught* not to like ourselves as women, we are *taught* what we're supposed to look like, what our measurements are supposed to be. I never hear what measurements *men* are supposed to be. Just *women*.

Me and my not-quite-foot-long manhood aren't so sure about that last one, but we get the point and agree that women are subjected to far worse "looks tyranny."

MR: How do you feel when you perform?

CL: For me, singing is magical. You feel hooked in, grounded, and connected above and below. I feel alive. And I go to a different place, that's all. There's something very healing about music. And that's the part of it that I love. Some people will understand, and some people won't.

MR: You lost your voice for a year once. How do you prevent that from happening now?

CL: I studied vocal therapy. It gave me the opportunity to take care of my voice and be with my voice and understand my instrument. It's just like a guitar player. A guitar player changes his strings, makes sure the thread is right, wipes down the guitar, doesn't leave it by the heat. [My voice] is my instrument. I gotta take care of it, and it'll take care of me.

MR: How was it growing up in Queens as such an unusually talented kid?

CL: I felt like an alien. It's so silly, 'cause I'm very grateful, but I'd wanted to go to a music and arts school. This counselor made my mother cry. He told her that—'cause at the time my mom was a waitress—"Do you want your daughter to wind up being a waitress, too, and have no career and no life?" And she'd went up there to try to get me into music and art, 'cause I could sing. I could stand in front of a whole auditorium and entertain them. There would be times when I would be standing there singing in the fourth grade [choir] and teachers would pass, lookin' for the voice. And they'd say, "It's *that* girl," and it was always a big girl. But I was dyslexic and I couldn't read so good. And they didn't put me in music school.

MR: You can answer the question "Are you big in Japan?" with a resounding "Yes!" How does it feel to be more popular in some countries than in others?

CL: It's really great to come back home where it's nice and calm. Whenever I do public stuff, it's not calm. But I'm used to it. It's hard to be famous. 'Cause it's really just me, anyway. Always was.

MR: What makes being famous so hard?

CL: Like, *you* could say somethin'. I'll think about it. And if *I* say somethin' to *you*, and I see it in print . . . it would have a *lot more weight!* (Both laugh.) Or friends will say (affects high-pitched accent), "I saw *you!!* You were havin' a good time, weren't you?" Or, "I read *that!!* What the hell were you *talkin'* about?" It's a surreal existence sometimes. [But I can handle it] as long as I can walk on the streets freely and watch life and be part of it, even if I *am* a bit of an oddball. I can't create in an ivory tower.

MR: What do you think of 80s nostalgia?

CL: (Gently) Oh, it's *silly*. You know that old expression "Bein' here now?" It's the way you should live. *Here.* I mean, I like dressing up. I like the 20s, different parts of the century. But *the 80s?* It's *1995!* C'mon! I can't hold still. I'm *working*.

Movies Appendix

Academy Awards

Movies

1980: *Ordinary People*

1981: *Chariots of Fire*

1982: *Gandhi*

1983: *Terms of Endearment*

1984: *Amadeus*

1985: *Out of Africa*

1986: *Platoon*

1987: *The Last Emperor*

1988: *Rain Man*

1989: *Driving Miss Daisy*

Director

1980: Robert Redford, *Ordinary People*

1981: Warren Beatty, *Reds*

1982: Richard Attenborough, *Gandhi*

1983: James L. Brooks, *Terms of Endearment*

1984: Milos Forman, *Amadeus*

1985: Sydney Pollack, *Out of Africa*

1986: Oliver Stone, *Platoon*

1987: Bernardo Bertolucci, *The Last Emperor*

1988: Barry Levinson, *Rain Man*

1989: Oliver Stone, *Born on the Fourth of July*

Actor

1980: Robert De Niro, *Raging Bull*

1981: Henry Fonda, *On Golden Pond*

1982: Ben Kingsley, *Gandhi*

1983: Robert Duvall, *Tender Mercies*

1984: F. Murray Abraham, *Amadeus*

1985: William Hurt, *Kiss of the Spider Woman*

1986: Paul Newman, *The Color of Money*

1987: Michael Douglas, *Wall Street*

1988: Dustin Hoffman, *Rain Man*

1989: Daniel Day-Lewis, *My Left Foot*

Actress

1980: Sissy Spacek, *Coal Miner's Daughter*

1981: Katharine Hepburn, *On Golden Pond*

1982: Meryl Streep, *Sophie's Choice*

1983: Shirley MacLaine, *Terms of Endearment*

1984: Sally Field, *Places in the Heart*

1985: Geraldine Page, *The Trip to Bountiful*

1986: Marlee Matlin, *Children of a Lesser God*

1987: Cher, *Moonstruck*

1988: Jodie Foster, *The Accused*

1989: Jessica Tandy, *Driving Miss Daisy*

Supporting Actor

1980: Timothy Hutton, *Ordinary People*

1981: Sir John Gielgud, *Arthur*

1982: Louis Gossett, Jr., *An Officer and a Gentleman*

1983: Jack Nicholson, *Terms of Endearment*

1984: Haing S. Ngor, *The Killing Fields*

1985: Don Ameche, *Cocoon*

1986: Michael Caine, *Hannah and Her Sisters*

1987: Sean Connery, *The Untouchables*

1988: Kevin Kline, *A Fish Called Wanda*

1989: Denzel Washington, *Glory*

Supporting Actress

1980: Mary Steenburgen, *Melvin and Howard*

1981: Maureen Stapleton, *Reds*

1982: Jessica Lange, *Tootsie*

1983: Linda Hunt, *The Year of Living Dangerously*

1984: Dame Peggy Ashcroft, *A Passage to India*

1985: Anjelica Huston, *Prizzi's Honor*

1986: Dianne Wiest, *Hannah and Her Sisters*

1987: Olympia Dukakis, *Moonstruck*

1988: Geena Davis, *The Accidental Tourist*

1989: Brenda Fricker, *My Left Foot*

Song

1980: "Fame," *Fame*

1981: "Arthur's Theme," *Arthur*

1982: "Up Where We Belong," *An Officer and a Gentleman*

1983: "Flashdance . . . What a Feeling" *Flashdance*

1984: "I Just Called to Say I Love You," *The Woman in Red*

1985: "Say You, Say Me," *White Nights*

1986: "Take My Breath Away," *Top Gun*

1987: "(I've Had) The Time of My Life," *Dirty Dancing*

1988: "Let the River Run," *Working Girl*

1989: "Under the Sea," *The Little Mermaid*

Golden Globes

Film—Drama

1980: *Kramer vs. Kramer*

1981: *Ordinary People*

1982: *On Golden Pond*

1983: *E.T. The Extra-Terrestrial*

1984: *Terms of Endearment*

1985: *Amadeus*

1986: *Out of Africa*

1987: *Platoon*

1988: *The Last Emperor*

1989: *Rain Man*

Film—Musical/Comedy

1980: *Breaking Away*

1981: *Coal Miner's Daughter*

1982: *Arthur*

1983: *Tootsie*

1984: *Yentl*

1985: *Romancing the Stone*

1986: *Prizzi's Honor*

1987: *Hannah and Her Sisters*

1988: *Hope and Glory*

1989: *Working Girl*

Director

1980: Francis Ford Coppola, *Apocalypse Now*

1981: Robert Redford, *Ordinary People*

1982: Warren Beatty, *Reds*

1983: Richard Attenborough, *Gandhi*

1984: Barbra Streisand, *Yentl*

1985: Milos Forman, *Amadeus*

1986: John Huston, *Prizzi's Honor*

1987: Oliver Stone, *Platoon*

1988: Bernardo Bertolucci, *The Last Emperor*

1989: Clint Eastwood, *Bird*

Actor—Drama

1980: Dustin Hoffman, *Kramer vs. Kramer*

1981: Robert De Niro, *Raging Bull*

1982: Henry Fonda, *On Golden Pond*

1983: Ben Kingsley, *Gandhi*

 Robert Duvall, *Tender Mercies*

1984: Tom Courtenay, *The Dresser*

1985: F. Murray Abraham, *Amadeus*

1986: Jon Voight, *Runaway Train*

1987: Bob Hoskins, *Mona Lisa*

1988: Michael Douglas, *Wall Street*

1989: Dustin Hoffman, *Rain Man*

Actor—Musical/Comedy

1980: Peter Sellers, *Being There*

1981: Ray Sharkey, *Idolmaker*

1982: Dudley Moore, *Arthur*

1983: Dustin Hoffman, *Tootsie*

1984: Michael Caine, *Educating Rita*

1985: Dudley Moore, *Micki & Maude*

1986: Jack Nicholson, *Prizzi's Honor*

1987: Paul Hogan, *"Crocodile" Dundee*

1988: Robin Williams, *Good Morning, Vietnam*

1989: Tom Hanks, *Big*

Actress—Drama

1980: Sally Field, *Norma Rae*

1981: Mary Tyler Moore, *Ordinary People*

1982: Meryl Streep, *The French Lieutenant's Woman*

1983: Meryl Streep, *Sophie's Choice*

1984: Shirley MacLaine, *Terms of Endearment*

1985: Sally Field, *Places in the Heart*

1986: Whoopi Goldberg, *The Color Purple*

1987: Marlee Matlin, *Children of a Lesser God*

1988: Sally Kirkland, *Anna*

 Sigourney Weaver, *Gorillas in the Mist*

1989: Jodie Foster, *The Accused*

 Shirley MacLaine, *Madame Sousatzka*

Actress—Musical/Comedy

1980: Bette Midler, *The Rose*

1981: Sissy Spacek, *Coal Miner's Daughter*

1982: Bernadette Peters, *Pennies from Heaven*

1983: Julie Andrews, *Victor/Victoria*

1984: Julie Walters, *Educating Rita*

1985: Kathleen Turner, *Romancing the Stone*

1986: Kathleen Turner, *Prizzi's Honor*

1987: Sissy Spacek, *Crimes of the Heart*

1988: Cher, *Moonstruck*

1989: Melanie Griffith, *Working Girl*

Supporting Actor

1980: Robert Duvall, *Apocalypse Now*

Melvyn Douglas, *Being There*

1981: Timothy Hutton, *Ordinary People*

1982: John Gielgud, *Arthur*

1983: Louis Gossett, Jr., *An Officer and a Gentleman*

1984: Jack Nicholson, *Terms of Endearment*

1985: Haing S. Ngor, *The Killing Fields*

1986: Klaus Maria Brandauer, *Out of Africa*

1987: Tom Berenger, *Platoon*

1988: Sean Connery, *The Untouchables*

1989: Martin Landau, *Tucker: The Man and His Dream*

Supporting Actress

1980: Meryl Streep, *Kramer vs. Kramer*

1981: Mary Steenburgen, *Melvin and Howard*

1982: Joan Hackett, *Only When I Laugh*

1983: Jessica Lange, *Tootsie*

1984: Cher, *Silkwood*

1985: Dame Peggy Ashcroft, *A Passage to India*

1986: Meg Tilly, *Agnes of God*

1987: Maggie Smith, *A Room with a View*

1988: Olympia Dukakis, *Moonstruck*

1989: Sigourney Weaver, *Working Girl*

The Biggest Box Office Stars of the 80s

1980: 1. Burt Reynolds
2. Robert Redford
3. Clint Eastwood
4. Jane Fonda
5. Dustin Hoffman
6. John Travolta
7. Sally Field
8. Sissy Spacek
9. Barbra Streisand
10. Steve Martin

1981: 1. Burt Reynolds
2. Clint Eastwood
3. Dudley Moore
4. Dolly Parton
5. Jane Fonda
6. Harrison Ford
7. Alan Alda
8. Bo Derek
9. Goldie Hawn
10. Bill Murray

1982: 1. Burt Reynolds
2. Clint Eastwood
3. Sylvester Stallone
4. Dudley Moore
5. Richard Pryor
6. Dolly Parton
7. Jane Fonda
8. Richard Gere
9. Paul Newman
10. Harrison Ford

1983: 1. Clint Eastwood
2. Eddie Murphy
3. Sylvester Stallone
4. Burt Reynolds
5. John Travolta
6. Dustin Hoffman
7. Harrison Ford
8. Richard Gere
9. Chevy Chase
10. Tom Cruise

1984: 1. Clint Eastwood
    2. Bill Murray
    3. Harrison Ford
    4. Eddie Murphy
    5. Sally Field
    6. Burt Reynolds
    7. Robert Redford
    8. Prince
    9. Dan Aykroyd
    10. Meryl Streep

1985: 1. Sylvester Stallone
    2. Eddie Murphy
    3. Clint Eastwood
    4. Michael J. Fox
    5. Chevy Chase
    6. Arnold Schwarzenegger
    7. Chuck Norris
    8. Harrison Ford
    9. Michael Douglas
    10. Meryl Streep

1986: 1. Tom Cruise
    2. Eddie Murphy
    3. Paul Hogan
    4. Rodney Dangerfield
    5. Bette Midler
    6. Sylvester Stallone
    7. Clint Eastwood
    8. Whoopi Goldberg
    9. Kathleen Turner
    10. Paul Newman

1987: 1. Eddie Murphy
    2. Michael Douglas
    3. Michael J. Fox
    4. Arnold Schwarzenegger
    5. Paul Hogan
    6. Tom Cruise
    7. Glenn Close
    8. Sylvester Stallone
    9. Cher
    10. Mel Gibson

1988: 1. Tom Cruise
    2. Eddie Murphy
    3. Tom Hanks
    4. Arnold Schwarzenegger
    5. Paul Hogan
    6. Danny DeVito
    7. Bette Midler
    8. Robin Williams
    9. Tom Selleck
    10. Dustin Hoffman

1989: 1. Jack Nicholson
    2. Tom Cruise
    3. Robin Williams
    4. Michael Douglas
    5. Tom Hanks
    6. Michael J. Fox
    7. Eddie Murphy
    8. Mel Gibson
    9. Sean Connery
    10. Kathleen Turner

The Top Ten Domestic Box Office Champs of the 80s

1. *E.T. The Extra-Terrestrial* (1982): $400 million
2. *Return of the Jedi* (1983): $263 million
3. *Batman* (1989): $252 million
4. *Raiders of the Lost Ark* (1981): $243 million
5. *Beverly Hills Cop* (1984): $235 million
6. *The Empire Strikes Back* (1980): $223 million
7. *Ghostbusters* (1984): $221 million
8. *Back to the Future* (1985): $209 million
9. *Indiana Jones and the Last Crusade* (1989): $198 million
10. *Indiana Jones and the Temple of Doom* (1984): $180 million

TV Appendix

Emmys

Drama Series

1979–80: *Lou Grant*

1980–81: *Hill Street Blues*

1981–82: *Hill Street Blues*

1982–83: *Hill Street Blues*

1983–84: *Hill Street Blues*

1984–85: *Cagney & Lacey*

1985–86: *Cagney & Lacey*

1986–87: *L.A. Law*

1987–88: *thirtysomething*

1988–89: *L.A. Law*

1989–90: *L.A. Law*

Actor: Drama Series

1979–80: Ed Asner, *Lou Grant*

1980–81: Daniel J. Travanti, *Hill Street Blues*

1981–82: Daniel J. Travanti, *Hill Street Blues*

1982–83: Ed Flanders, *St. Elsewhere*

1983–84: Tom Selleck, *Magnum, P.I.*

1984–85: William Daniels, *St. Elsewhere*

1985–86: William Daniels, *St. Elsewhere*

1986–87: Bruce Willis, *Moonlighting*

1987–88: Richard Kiley, *A Year in the Life*

1988–89: Carroll O'Connor, *In the Heat of the Night*

1989–90: Peter Falk, *Columbo*

Actress: Drama Series

1979–80: Barbara Bel Geddes, *Dallas*

1980–81: Barbara Babcock, *Hill Street Blues*

1981–82: Michael Learned, *Nurse*

1982–83: Tyne Daly, *Cagney & Lacey*

1983–84: Tyne Daly, *Cagney & Lacey*

1984–85: Tyne Daly, *Cagney & Lacey*

1985–86: Sharon Gless, *Cagney & Lacey*

1986–87: Sharon Gless, *Cagney & Lacey*

1987–88: Tyne Daly, *Cagney & Lacey*

1988–89: Dana Delany, *China Beach*

1989–90: Patricia Wettig, *thirtysomething*

Supporting Actor: Drama Series

1979–80: Stuart Margolin, *The Rockford Files*

1980–81: Michael Conrad, *Hill Street Blues*

1981–82: Michael Conrad, *Hill Street Blues*

1982–83: James Coco, *St. Elsewhere*

1983–84: Bruce Weitz, *Hill Street Blues*

1984–85: Edward James Olmos, *Miami Vice*

1985–86: John Karlen, *Cagney & Lacey*

1986–87: John Hillerman, *Magnum, P.I.*

1987–88: Larry Drake, *L.A. Law*

1988–89: Larry Drake, *L.A. Law*

1989–90: Jimmy Smits, *L.A. Law*

Supporting Actress: Drama Series

1979–80: Nancy Marchand, *Lou Grant*

1980–81: Nancy Marchand, *Lou Grant*

1981–82: Nancy Marchand, *Lou Grant*

1982–83: Doris Roberts, *St. Elsewhere*

1983–84: Alfre Woodard, *Hill Street Blues*

1984–85: Betty Thomas, *Hill Street Blues*

1985–86: Bonnie Bartlett, *St. Elsewhere*

1986–87: Bonnie Bartlett, *St. Elsewhere*

1987–88: Patricia Wettig, *thirtysomething*

1988–89: Melanie Mayron, *thirtysomething*

1989–90: Marg Helgenberger, *China Beach*

Comedy Series

1979–80: *Taxi*

1980–81: *Taxi*

1981–82: *Barney Miller*

1982–83: *Cheers*

1983–84: *Cheers*

1984–85: *The Cosby Show*

1985–86: *The Golden Girls*

1986–87: *The Golden Girls*

1987–88: *The Wonder Years*

1988–89: *Cheers*

1989–90: *Murphy Brown*

Actor: Comedy Series

1979–80: Richard Mulligan, *Soap*

1980–81: Judd Hirsch, *Taxi*

1981–82: Alan Alda, *M*A*S*H*

1982–83: Judd Hirsch, *Taxi*

1983–84: John Ritter, *Three's Company*

1984–85: Robert Guillaume, *Benson*

1985–86: Michael J. Fox, *Family Ties*

1986–87: Michael J. Fox, *Family Ties*

1987–88: Michael J. Fox, *Family Ties*

1988–89: Richard Mulligan, *Empty Nest*

1989–90: Ted Danson, *Cheers*

Actress: Comedy Series

1979–80: Cathryn Damon, *Soap*

1980–81: Isabel Sanford, *The Jeffersons*

1981–82: Carol Kane, *Taxi*

1982–83: Shelley Long, *Cheers*

1983–84: Jane Curtin, *Kate & Allie*

1984–85: Jane Curtin, *Kate & Allie*

1985–86: Betty White, *The Golden Girls*

1986–87: Rue McClanahan, *The Golden Girls*

1987–88: Beatrice Arthur, *The Golden Girls*

1988–89: Candice Bergen, *Murphy Brown*

1989–90: Candice Bergen, *Murphy Brown*

Supporting Actor: Comedy Series

1979–80: Harry Morgan, *M*A*S*H*

1980–81: Danny DeVito, *Taxi*

1981–82: Christopher Lloyd, *Taxi*

1982–83: Christopher Lloyd, *Taxi*

1983–84: Pat Harrington, Jr., *One Day at a Time*

1984–85: John Larroquette, *Night Court*

1985–86: John Larroquette, *Night Court*

1986–87: John Larroquette, *Night Court*

1987–88: John Larroquette, *Night Court*

1988–89: Woody Harrelson, *Cheers*

1989–90: Alex Rocco, *The Famous Teddy Z*

Supporting Actress: Comedy Series

1979–80: Loretta Swit, *M*A*S*H*

1980–81: Eileen Brennan, *Private Benjamin*

1981–82: Loretta Swit, *M*A*S*H*

1982–83: Carol Kane, *Taxi*

1983–84: Rhea Perlman, *Cheers*

1984–85: Rhea Perlman, *Cheers*

1985–86: Rhea Perlman, *Cheers*

1986–87: Jackée Harry, *227*

1987–88: Estelle Getty, *The Golden Girls*

1988–89: Rhea Perlman, *Cheers*

1989–90: Bebe Neuwirth, *Cheers*

Daytime Drama Series

1979–80: *The Guiding Light*

1980–81: *General Hospital*

1981–82: *The Guiding Light*

1982–83: *The Young and the Restless*

1983–84: *General Hospital*

1984–85: *The Young and the Restless*

1985–86: *The Young and the Restless*

1986–87: *As the World Turns*

1987–88: *Santa Barbara*

1988–89: *Santa Barbara*

1989–90: *Santa Barbara*

Top Ten TV Shows

1979–80:
1. *60 Minutes*
2. *Three's Company*
3. *That's Incredible!*
4. *M*A*S*H*
5. *Alice*
6. *Dallas*
7. *Flo*
8. *The Jeffersons*
9. *The Dukes of Hazzard*
10. *One Day at a Time*

1980–81:
1. *Dallas*
2. *60 Minutes*
3. *The Dukes of Hazzard*
4. *Private Benjamin*
5. *M*A*S*H*
6. *The Love Boat*
7. *The NBC Tuesday Night Movie*
8. *House Calls*
9. *The Jeffersons* (tie)
9. *Little House on the Prairie* (tie)

1981–82:
1. *Dallas* (9 P.M.)
2. *Dallas* (10 P.M.)
3. *60 Minutes*
4. *Three's Company* (tie)
4. *CBS NFL Football* (tie)
6. *The Jeffersons*
7. *Joanie Loves Chachi*
8. *The Dukes of Hazzard* (9 P.M.)
9. *Alice* (tie)
9. *The Dukes of Hazzard* (8 P.M.) (tie)

1982–83:
1. *60 Minutes*
2. *Dallas*
3. *M*A*S*H* (tie)
3. *Magnum, P.I.* (tie)
5. *Dynasty*
6. *Three's Company*
7. *Simon & Simon*
8. *Falcon Crest*
9. *NFL Monday Night Football*
10. *The Love Boat*

1983–84:
1. *Dallas*
2. *Dynasty*

3. *The A Team*
4. *60 Minutes*
5. *Simon & Simon*
6. *Magnum, P.I.*
7. *Falcon Crest*
8. *Kate & Allie*
9. *Hotel*
10. *Cagney & Lacey*

1984–85: 1. *Dynasty*
2. *Dallas*
3. *The Cosby Show*
4. *60 Minutes*
5. *Family Ties*
6. *The A Team* (tie)
6. *Simon & Simon* (tie)
8. *Knots Landing*
9. *Murder, She Wrote*
10. *Falcon Crest* (tie)
10. *Crazy Like a Fox* (tie)

1985–86: 1. *The Cosby Show*
2. *Family Ties*
3. *Murder, She Wrote*
4. *60 Minutes*
5. *Cheers*
6. *Dallas* (tie)
6. *Dynasty* (tie)
6. *The Golden Girls* (tie)
9. *Miami Vice*
10. *Who's the Boss?*

1986–87: 1. *The Cosby Show*
2. *Family Ties*
3. *Cheers*
4. *Murder, She Wrote*
5. *Night Court*
6. *The Golden Girls*

7. *60 Minutes*
8. *Growing Pains*
9. *Moonlighting*
10. *Who's the Boss?*

1987–88: 1. *The Cosby Show*
2. *A Different World*
3. *Cheers*
4. *Growing Pains* (Tuesday)
5. *Night Court*
6. *The Golden Girls*
7. *Who's the Boss?*
8. *60 Minutes*
9. *Murder, She Wrote*
10. *The Wonder Years*

1988–89: 1. *Roseanne* (9 P.M.) (tie)
1. *The Cosby Show* (tie)
3. *Roseanne* (8:30 P.M.) (tie)
3. *A Different World*
5. *Cheers*
6. *60 Minutes*
7. *The Golden Girls*
8. *Who's the Boss?*
9. *The Wonder Years*
10. *Murder, She Wrote*

1989–90: 1. *Roseanne*
2. *The Cosby Show*
3. *Cheers*
4. *A Different World*
5. *America's Funniest Home Videos*
6. *The Golden Girls*
7. *60 Minutes*
8. *The Wonder Years*
9. *Empty Nest*
10. *Chicken Soup*